"*Star Trek* may or may not have been 'Christian,' but it was highly spiritual. Star Trek and religion ask many of the same questions. Doing good, being honest, helping others, understanding, friendship, self-sacrifice, loyalty—these are all *Star Trek* themes. They are also the main tenets of Christianity. *The Gospel According to Star Trek: The Original Crew* is a smart and engaging book and Kevin C. Neece's passion for the subject matter and excellent research make for a fascinating read!"

—BarBara Luna, Actress, *Star Trek* episode "Mirror, Mirror"
(role of Marlena Moreau)

"Stories do more than entertain. They subtly shape our loves, beliefs, and what we think is possible. Stories are written by someone from somewhere, so the better we understand that person and his worldview, the better we can appreciate how his stories work on us. This is why Trekkies need to read Kevin C. Neece's penetrating and winsome study on Gene Roddenberry and his *Star Trek* series. They will be challenged and pleasantly encouraged."

—Mike Wittmer, Professor of Systematic Theology,
Grand Rapids Theological Seminary

"Kevin C. Neece reveals the innumerable ways *Star Trek* parallels the Christian story of love, sacrifice, peace, and justice, while demonstrating how this gospel connection is why *Star Trek* resonates with so many people on such a deep level. In a Christian subculture that often focuses on how pop culture is 'anti-Christian,' *The Gospel According to Star Trek: The Original Crew* is a refreshing reminder that God is everywhere—that if we seek him, we will find him."

—Renea McKenzie, Editor in Chief, ThinkingThroughChristianity.com

THE GOSPEL ACCORDING TO STAR TREK: THE ORIGINAL CREW

THE GOSPEL ACCORDING TO

STAR TREK

The Original Crew

Kevin C. Neece

FOREWORD BY
John Tenuto

 CASCADE *Books* • Eugene, Oregon

THE GOSPEL ACCORDING TO STAR TREK: THE ORIGINAL CREW

Cascade Books
An Imprint of Wipf and Stock Publishers
199 W. 8th Ave., Suite 3
Eugene, OR 97401

www.wipfandstock.com

PAPERBACK ISBN: 978-1-62564-059-8
HARDCOVER ISBN: 978-1-4982-8740-1
EBOOK ISBN: 978-1-5326-0113-2

Cataloguing-in-Publication data:

Names: Neece, Kevin C.

Title: The gospel according to Star Trek : the original crew / Kevin C. Neece.

Description: Eugene, OR: Cascade Books, 2016 | Includes bibliographical references.

Identifiers: ISBN 978-1-62564-059-8 (paperback) | ISBN 978-1-4982-8740-1 (hardcover) | ISBN 978-1-5326-0113-2 (ebook)

Subjects: LSCH: 1. Star Trek television programs. | 2. Star Trek films—History and criticism. | 3. Theology.

Classification: PN1992.8 S74 N40 2016 (print) | PN1992.8 (ebook)

Manufactured in the USA.   09/20/16

For Melissa and Aidan,
The brightest stars in my galaxy.

"The primary philosophy in Star Trek, stripped of everything else, was 'Love one another.' I think Jesus might have said something like that once too."

—DAVID GERROLD

Contents

Section 3: The Gospel According to the Animated Series

Section 4: The Gospel According to the Original Series Films

Section 5: The Gospel According to the Kelvin Timeline

Foreword

If there is a great conundrum in *Star Trek*, it may be the question as to why Khan Noonien Singh wears a single glove on his right hand during the events of *Star Trek II: The Wrath of Khan*. Is it a reference to Adam Smith's invisible hand—the idea that individual actions have latent consequences? Or, does the glove represent Khan losing his "grip" on reality or propriety? Or, is the glove a symbol—like the rest of Khan's tattered clothes—of a leader whose kingdom has sundered? Was his hand injured during his years on Ceti Alpha V? Is it foreshadowing of what would happen to his other hand at the end of the movie, injured so badly in a glove of pain and wounds? Or, could it simply be because it looks cool?

When asked about the meaning of the glove, instead of providing easy answers, writer and director Nicholas Meyer chooses another tack: for him, the audience's interpretation is as valid as that of the creator-artist. "Why do you think he doesn't take off the other glove?" Meyer says in the film's audio commentary, "It's not my job to supply answers. It's your job as the audience to supply answers." And, according to Meyer, whatever you think (or feel), *that* is the answer. Of course, the resultant conclusion that could be drawn from this statement is either that there are as many "correct" answers to the Khan-glove question as there are interpretations or, conversely, there isn't any such thing as a "correct" answer. It depends on whether the glass is half full or half empty.

This must be at least one of the many reasons that *Star Trek* continues to inspire, fifty years after the premiere of "The Man Trap" on NBC, Thursday, September 8, 1966: the elusive quality of its meanings and narrative morals. *Star Trek* is polysemic. Diverse people, or the same person at different stages of his or her life, view the adventures of Captain James

Tiberius Kirk and crew with contrasting, or evolving, or reevaluating eyes. That *Star Trek* is the result of many hands adds to its polysemic nature: creator Gene Roddenberry especially, but also producer Robert Justman, art director Walter "Matt" Jefferies, writer Gene Coon, story editor D. C. Fontana—and many others—all added to the recipe that baked *Star Trek*. Simply put, there is no wrong way to think about *Star Trek*. Once in the hands of the audience, all interpretations become valid.

This is the journey taken by Kevin C. Neece in *The Gospel According to Star Trek: The Original Crew*. His love of *Star Trek* as an adventure show during his youth reformulates into a spiritual appreciation for the symbolism and meanings behind those special effects and science fiction narratives. Neece avoids the trope (or trap) of using a single line of dialogue (Uhura's "Don't you understand? It's not the sun up in the sky. It's the Son of God," from "*Bread and Circuses*," or Kirk's "We find the one quite adequate," from "Who Mourns for Adonais?") to argue for his interpretation. Instead, there is a more thoughtful and detailed discussion that blends together the ideas of the gospel, added to the dialogue of the scripts, added to interviews and commentary from the creators, added to historical and cultural events. An example is the discussion of whether Spock's sacrifice in *The Wrath of Khan* is at all a biblical metaphor of Jesus' sacrifice. If nothing else, the discussion of the date on which the film begins will provide an appreciation for the blending of creative interpretation with historical research.

Most especially, *The Gospel According to Star Trek: The Original Crew* recognizes that both a Christian interpretation of *Star Trek* in general, and specifically which Christian themes should be applied to which episodes, are actually matters of hearts and minds. Jewish, Muslim, Buddhist, agnostic, and other spiritual interpretations are equally valid. There is no one way to see *Star Trek*. *The Gospel According to Star Trek* is one way, but a way that uses biblical, scholarly research as its starting point.

What does the Khan glove mean? Maybe it's none of the explanations previously provided. Maybe it's something else entirely. Or, maybe it is all of these. The important thing is what we think. Sharing, and perhaps debating, our interpretations is an important aspect of Star Trek fandom. Kevin C. Neece tells us what he thinks in this book and in doing so, gives us something new to think about.

—John Tenuto
  Professor of Sociology, College of Lake County
  Star Trek Fan

Acknowledgments

G ratitude doesn't begin to cover it. In the past eight years since the idea for this book began to grow in my mind, I have owed my thanks to so many friends who have offered encouragement, support, enthusiasm, and advice, along with so many other essential resources and connections, without which this project could not have been completed. I am overwhelmingly blessed. It's impossible to say enough, so I have chosen to keep it brief. I offer my deepest thanks, appreciation, and love to all those below. Dr. David Naugle: For the eyes with which I was able to see Star Trek—and everything else—in a new way.

My parents, Richard and Jill Neece: For a bedroom to write in away from the world and constant faith and love for my whole life.

My sister, Dr. Kasey Neece-Fielder: For not killing me before I reached my teen years and for always believing in me. And for marrying Brian, whom I thank for being my sister's best friend and constant support.

My grandparents, Phyllis Smith; Lillian, Vernie, and Ann Neece; and great aunt Gethrol Barnes: for constant faith and love.

My parents-in-law, Malcolm and Melba McDow: For long patience and faithful support.

My grandfather-in-law, William H. Justice Sr.: For making my education possible and blessing me with kindness and love in the last years of his life.

My Undiscovered Country Project (UCP) First Officer Tim Van Orden: For constant faithfulness, believing in me when I didn't, and teaching me the true meaning of the word "Shiny!"

Beth Van Orden: For making Tim a better man and being a marvelous audio commentary guest.

Rev. Dr. Scott Youngblood: For inspiring Tim.

Jeff Sellars: For friendship, advice, and beginning my relationship with Wipf and Stock.

Dr. Mark J. Boone: For years of friendship, an editing partnership, guest blog posts, and introducing me to Jeff.

Adam Jones: For kind encouragement and wise counsel, without which this book might not have found itself.

Mike Poteet: For guest blog posts, reading chapters, and faithful advice and aid.

Eugene Chu: For twenty-five–plus years of friendship, and the computer on which most of this book was written.

Jenay Hale: For transcribing notes and a lot of this book, and for loyal friendship.

My former UCP Communications Officer, Hannah Vestal: For faithful service, a sweet spirit, and nerdy friendship.

Rich Frohlich and Texas Radio Theatre: For making higher quality UCP audio commentaries possible.

John Humphreys: For getting me through school and becoming my friend for life.

Carol Riggan and the Riverside Area Community Club, Riverside, Iowa: For welcoming me to Trekfest when I was unbelievably young and green and sitting me down with Walter Koenig and BarBara Luna.

Walter Koenig: For honesty.

BarBara Luna: For enthusiasm for my fledging work and introducing me to Curtis Webster.

Curtis Webster: For Spirit of Star Trek, a helping hand, and for introducing me to Larry Nemecek.

Larry Nemecek: For kind support and valuable advice.

Steve Neill: For Spock ears, encouragement, and so much more.

All the "Spockologists" and all the friends and fans of UCP: For keeping my warp engine humming with your enthusiasm and investment.

Alyssa and the owners and staff of Roots Coffeehouse: For giving me a place to feel at home—a place where many, many hours of research were done and a big chunk of this book was written—and for countless cups of wonderful coffee, tea, and kindness.

Memory Alpha contributors and editors: For maintaining the finest source of in-universe Star Trek knowledge on Earth, without which my work would have been nearly impossible.

Christina Luckings of Chrissie's Transcripts Site: For dedication and generosity in creating a vital resource I simply could not do without.

Matt Wimer, Rodney Clapp, and everyone at Cascade Books: For enthusiasm, flexibility, support, and faith. I couldn't have asked for a better publisher or publishing experience.

Leigh Hickman: For true friendship. Every semicolon in this book is dedicated to you.

Finally, and most importantly, I am grateful to and for my wife Melissa and son Aidan, who are why I get up in the morning, why I have hope for my life, and the reason I want to be a better version of myself. I love you both so very much.

_____

The Undiscovered Country

M y first step toward discovering *The Gospel According to Star Trek* was walking away from Star Trek.

Growing up, I was a huge Trekkie. That probably had a lot to do with when I became aware of Star Trek. I'd seen the Original Series on late-night television and thought it was pretty hokey. Was I really supposed to believe that those brightly colored wooden blocks that people loosely stuck into slots on the *Enterprise* were data tapes? That a twenty-third–century computer would make mechanical noises? I thought it looked pretty laughable. But I hadn't seen much of it and, despite my inability to forgive what seemed like outdated visual effects, I thought the concept was great.

So, when *Star Trek: The Next Generation* was announced, I was very excited. Finally! A Star Trek series that would actually look good! (At the time, I clearly had no appreciation for the artistry and skill demonstrated on the original *Star Trek*. Forgive me. I was eight.) Eagerly anticipating the quality and credibility of 1980s sets, costumes, and visual effects, I was counting the days until the series premiered. I honestly don't remember watching "Encounter at Farpoint" for the first time. But I stayed with *Next Generation* into my teens and around Trek's twenty-fifth anniversary, I got into the original crew movies, which I loved. I even got the first Star Trek Christmas ornament, the Original Series *Enterprise*, released in celebration of the anniversary. I got a new ship each year and strung up Christmas lights in my bedroom's box window so I could leave them up year-round.

But, somewhere around the fifth season of *TNG*, I started watching less. *Deep Space Nine* was beginning and I was trying to learn to like it. But I was getting busy with school and other obligations and started missing episodes. As I fell behind in my viewing, it became harder and harder to catch up through reruns. By the time *Voyager* premiered, I had mostly stopped watching new episodes and once *TNG* was off the air, I didn't keep up with *Deep Space Nine* and maybe saw part of one episode of *Voyager*. This was the beginning of, essentially, a fourteen-year Star Trek hiatus, during which I watched none of the series and only got out to see the movies. After I saw *Star Trek: Insurrection*, however, I wondered if seeing the movies would continue to be worthwhile. Finally, *Nemesis* looked like it might be better than its predecessor and I wanted to see it, but somehow never got around to it.

I still loved the series and the films, but I just wasn't that (ahem) *engaged*. The reasons for this are hard to pin down, but I felt that Star Trek had grown too fast and in too many directions for me to keep up with it. Someday, I expected I would return, but I didn't know when. I'm ashamed to admit this, but during this period, I even stopped collecting the Star Trek Christmas ornaments. (Insert years of painful regret here.) I wasn't against Star Trek; I just wasn't as close to it as I had been.

My flagging faithfulness aside, remnants of my fandom lurked beneath the surface and even emerged from time to time, mostly when there was a Trek film in theatres. That is, with the exception of *Nemesis* in 2002, which I neglected to see, though I did purchase the first season of *TNG* on DVD when it was released that same year. While it didn't herald the return to full Trekkie status I'd hoped for, watching it certainly spurred some renewed Trek interest. So, I started collecting the movies in that format as well, though I didn't watch them. I gathered them slowly because I was only buying used and was very stingy on the price. Ultimately, my collection lacked two films—*Generations* and *Nemesis*. This remained the case for quite some time.

Then in 2008, while I was serving as a live-in caregiver for my grandfather-in-law, I finally found the two remaining films cheaply enough and bought them. A few nights later at Granddad's house, having not seen a minute of Star Trek in six years, I suddenly had the strongest urge to return. I missed the characters, the universe, the stories. I wanted to experience everything I'd not seen before. I wanted to be a Trekkie again.

The only Star Trek DVDs I had with me that night were *Generations* and *Nemesis*, because I had neglected to take them back to my house. I hadn't liked *Generations*, but wanted some lead-in to the final screen voyage of Picard and crew, so it would have to do. It was still not the strongest film in the franchise, but *it was Star Trek*! Despite the film's weaknesses, it was like a grand reunion with old friends. I was in love with Star Trek all over again. The next night, I would finally get to see *Nemesis*. I could barely stand the anticipation. The day couldn't be over fast enough. I got my grandfather-in-law to bed and went straight for the den. It was Star Trek time!

I had so much fun seeing a brand-new adventure with all my old *Next Generation* friends that I was totally blind to the film's shortcomings. All I saw were my favorite Trek actors, more seasoned and adept than ever at bringing life to my favorite Trek characters. I saw cool new uniforms, beautiful sets, and sleek visual effects, underscored by awesome Jerry Goldsmith music. I was loving every second. It was funny, adventurous, high stakes, and exciting! Who could ask for more? I couldn't have been happier or, ultimately, more emotionally responsive. Something about that film—as flawed as I would later see that it is—affected me very deeply.

And then it occurred to me: Data was a Christ figure.

Here I must explain that, in the intervening years between my gradual exit from the Star Trek universe and my triumphant, tearful return, I had undergone what I have since referred to as a worldview conversion. In particular, this conversion had to do with the broadening, deepening, and strengthening of my understanding of a Christian worldview. I had grown up in an Assemblies of God church at which my great aunt, who had founded the church with her late husband, was pastor, my grandmother led the singing, and my mother played the piano. So I was no stranger to the gospel. I had decided to follow Christ not a year before I got into Star Trek and had been very involved with youth ministry at the Baptist church my family was later a part of.

After high school, I started working at the largest Christian bookstore in America and attending an upstart college ministry/church plant based on engaging postmodern culture and philosophy and rethinking our ideas of what the Church truly is. (This would later be called an "emergent" church, but there was no such terminology at that time and present-day emergent churches are much different from what we did.) These experiences combined to interest me further in reading and writing, in philosophy, theology and, in particular, Christology. But all that crystallized when I went to Dallas Baptist University.

I was attending on a scholarship my grandfather-in-law provided for all his grandchildren, as well as for many other students. I was a Communications major and went simply to get a degree to hang on the wall so I could get a better job in video production or film. But, when I had the opportunity to take Intro. to Philosophy, I thought it would be a good extension of what I was already exploring at my church and at the store. On the first day of class, Dr. David Naugle gave a lecture, of which I do not remember a word. What I do remember, though, is that he opened my eyes to the real value of education, not just for furthering my career, but for becoming a better human being and a better Christian. He revealed to me that, at their best, intellectual pursuits are spiritual pursuits. After class, I went directly to my advisor to ask how I could change my major. In short order, I was earning an interdisciplinary degree in Communication and Philosophy.

I took every course taught by Dr. Naugle I could from that time forward, all the way through my graduate degree. I became a member of his Paideia College Society and presented papers at every annual Paideia conference. The process was endlessly exciting, enriching, and life-changing. It was this experience that finally pushed me to realize that I wanted to be a career author and speaker and led me to teach at DBU after I graduated. It was also this experience that caused all the interests, talents, and ideas that had been in my head for so long to lock together into a vision of who I was and who I was becoming. In this reality, I saw all things as under the dominion of Christ and shot through with God's story. It was with these new eyes, this new understanding, that I came back to Star Trek.

I'd been writing on media and pop culture almost exclusively throughout my time at DBU, even becoming a film critic for a Baptist newspaper. So I had become quite adept at putting my Christian worldview into conversation with films, television, and music. But, for whatever reason, it had never occurred to me to look at Star Trek in this way. So, after seeing *Nemesis* and realizing that Data was reflecting Jesus, I wanted to explore further. I decided to go through the entirety of *Next Generation* and watch Data develop as a character. Would I see any glimmers of what was to come? Would I find other parallels between Data and Christ? I expected I would, and therefore intended to write my next Paideia paper on the subject.

Before I could finish *Next Generation*, the first J.J. Abrams Star Trek film was on its way to theatres, so I decided to take a break from *TNG* to get up to speed on the Original Series before seeing the reboot. As I went through both series and the new film, I began looking at all of Star Trek—not just Data—with my Christian worldview lenses on. My paper was soon no longer about Data, but about what I was seeing in Star Trek and how it was deepening and informing my faith. Everywhere I looked, I saw the philosophy, theology, and critical thinking I had done over the previous several years reflected. I saw parallel after parallel with Scripture and with a Christian worldview. In fact, I saw things in Star Trek that I felt the Church had lost and needed to hear, holes in our understanding and practice of the gospel that Star Trek's spiritual humanism directly and cogently addressed.

When I wrote that first paper, "The Undiscovered Country: Star Trek and the Christian's Human Journey," I knew it was the beginning of a book. So, to help me further my research and writing and to build a platform from which to share that book, I started The Undiscovered Country Project, which I termed my "ongoing voyage through Star Trek from a Christian worldview perspective." With the help of my good friend and UCP First Officer, Tim Van Orden, I launched a blog and a series of audio commentaries on the Original Series, *TNG*, and the Star Trek films. With the help of my other good friend and colleague Jeff Sellars, that original paper was expanded and published in Jeff's book, *Light Shining in a Dark Place: Discovering Theology Through Film.*

From its inception, *The Undiscovered Country* was the intended title of the book you are now reading. That plan changed while I was doing research on competing titles for my book proposal. At some point I realized that, while I was familiar with many of the titles and authors in the field of Star Trek and religion, I had no idea who had written *The Gospel According to Star Trek*. For those who may be unfamiliar, books whose titles begin with *The Gospel According to . . .* are practically their own sub-genre, perhaps comprising the cornerstone of books discussing media and pop culture from a Christian perspective. There are *Gospel According to . . .* titles from various publishers on everything from Harry Potter and the Beatles to Superman and Dr. Seuss. I knew the names of many of these books' authors: Connie Neal, Mark I. Pinsky, and the man who, it could be argued, started it all with *The Gospel According to Peanuts*, Robert L. Short. Somehow, though, the name of the author of *The Gospel According to Star Trek* had eluded me.

So, I looked it up. And, to my surprise, I didn't find it. I had been certain there was such a book. There was a *Gospel According to Science Fiction* and a *Gospel According to Star Wars*, but no *Gospel According to Star Trek*? This was just wrong. To that point, I had considered *The Gospel According to . . .* an overused title trope. I respected the genre, but thought the title was a bit of an easy grab. Now, however, *The Gospel According to Star Trek* was not a corny title. It was my mission. There was no *Gospel According to Star Trek* because I hadn't written it yet!

So, here we are. Eight years after I began this journey, I'm writing the book I've envisioned for so long. And it's only the first one. In these pages, you'll find my examination of the stories of the original crew—Kirk, Spock, McCoy, and their compatriots. It is the beginning of a journey that will include a book for every Star Trek series. I'll be employing a number of interpretive and analytical methods, from applying Star Trek's humanism to a Christian worldview and vice versa, to discussing the influence of Scripture on Star Trek's stories, to clarifying and exploring the spiritual beliefs of the series' creator, to finding surprisingly deep—if wholly unintentional—metaphors within its narratives. The varieties of approaches reflected in this book are a natural result of the variety of ways in which I have been able to engage my Christian worldview with the Star Trek universe. And it's just the beginning.

This book is an introduction, a survey. It represents the broadest possible glimpse of the richness available in a Christian engagement with the original crew stories of Star Trek—including the latest versions of those stories in the "Kelvin Timeline" films. Granted, Star Trek itself is a vast topic and one that I am still exploring. I am writing this book and all the subsequent books in this series, not from the place of having arrived, but from a place of still being very much on the journey. I feel comfortable doing this because, in many ways, I expect to always be in the process of discovery. Conventional wisdom tells us that one would need to have "arrived" as an "expert" to be able to write a book of such broad scope as this one. Experience tells us, however—as does Star Trek—that none of us ever arrive. We are always on a continuing voyage of learning and growth.

After fifty years, six (soon to be seven) television series and thirteen films, the Trek universe is a wide and varied place to explore. So, in a sense, *The Gospel According to Star Trek* series is itself a trek. It is a journey through a complex network of stories and characters, and a continuing series of philosophical discussions, big questions, and even bigger answers. It is, ultimately, a human journey and one that, for me, has been incredibly encouraging and enriching for my faith—not in the confines of church and religion, but in the whole of life. That's really what we're here to discover: a whole-life gospel that is for everyone, that doesn't hide from or shun humanity, but embraces it as God's very good work. As Star Trek seeks to understand what it means to be human, it provides us with some essential elements of what it means to be human to the glory of God.

If you're a Christian, I hope this book series deepens and encourages your faith in Christ and your appreciation of Star Trek and its values. If you're not, I hope it helps you see that the things we love about Star Trek are deep within us as human beings and that there may in fact be a reason for that. If nothing else, I hope my story, my journey as reflected in this series, will in some way help you as you explore the undiscovered country at the heart of the gospel and at the heart of Star Trek: the human soul.

SECTION 1

Creator and Questor
The Restless Heart of Gene Roddenberry

1

Creator

In discussing Star Trek from a Christian worldview perspective, it seems best to begin at the source. As vast as its universe is, as varied as its collective of contributors may be, Star Trek is, essentially, a very personal project and reflects above all else the worldview, vision, and beliefs of one man— Gene Roddenberry. It is important, however, to note that Roddenberry is Star Trek's creator, but he is not its author. He certainly invented the Star Trek universe and guided its creation, but he did more rewriting than writing in the three Trek television series with which he was directly involved, ultimately being more responsible for character than content. Nonetheless, the central themes and structures upon which Star Trek is built begin with him and the resulting series and films—even when they deviate from his original vision—seem to always echo with something of his ideas.

Just as his influence is felt throughout the Trek universe, so we will be frequently returning, throughout this book, to the essential ideals and aspirations upon which he based his vision of the future. In this chapter, then, it is my goal to clarify as best I can what Gene Roddenberry's beliefs were. Certainly, much of his philosophy is well known, but my intention here is to examine the spirituality inherent in that philosophy and, in particular, to reflect as accurately as possible his beliefs about religion and about the existence and nature of God.

Honestly, this is not entirely necessary. As it is, Star Trek carries a great deal of resonance with a Christian worldview, regardless of its origins. However, I want to avoid the trap of recasting Star Trek in a way that ignores its roots or tries to claim some secretly pro-Christian agenda behind the scenes. I'm interested in critical analysis, not just appropriation. In my view, then, it is essential to a Christian engagement of Star Trek to understand the franchise for what it is, as accurately as possible. For me, that quest begins with Gene Roddenberry.

The religious background of Star Trek's creator has been recounted often. Born in El Paso, Texas, on November 3, 1920, to Southern Baptist parents, Eugene Wesley Roddenberry grew up in a house where his mother insisted on weekly attendance of Sunday services for Gene and his siblings, but his father rarely joined them. While his exposure to Christianity and the Southern Baptist church was undoubtedly formative for him, it was ultimately his father's feelings toward religion that shaped young Gene's views. "He did not think the church was particularly the guidance that he would have pushed me to have," Roddenberry recounted. "He felt that it was good for me to go to church but that I should be damn careful of what the ministers said."[1]

As he often looked to his father as an example of good character (with a few notable caveats), the idea imparted to Gene was that the moral instruction he received in church was often good, but that Christian doctrine was largely to be ignored as nonsense. He never paid much attention to sermons as a child, he said, because he was "more interested in the deacon's daughter and what we might be doing between services." As he tells it, he started listening to the pastor's words at around the age of fourteen. "I listened to the sermon, and I remember complete astonishment because what they were talking about were things that were just crazy." Communion was particularly puzzling to him, with talk of eating flesh and drinking blood quickly putting him off. "My first impression was, 'Jesus Christ! This is a bunch of cannibals they've put me down among!'" Whether or not it is entirely likely that he had been totally oblivious to the Baptist church's observance of the Lord's Supper for the first fourteen years of his life, his account serves to illustrate his profound sense of disconnection from Christian faith and practice, as well as his general lack of understanding regarding Christian doctrine. Whatever the case, it is clear that Roddenberry's early religious experiences led him to the conclusion that religion primarily consisted of what he called "largely magical, superstitious things."[2]

Based on these and many other statements regarding religion and Christianity in particular, Roddenberry has gained a widely accepted reputation as an atheist. The arguments for this idea appear strong. In addition to speaking of religion and the Bible in terms of magic and myth,

1. Alexander, *Star Trek Creator*, 39.
2. Ibid.

he often derided traditional Western conceptions of God. At one point, he expressed concern to his assistant, Susan Sackett, about then-President Jimmy Carter's claim of having a "personal relationship with God," calling such ideas "petty superstitions."[3] He was well known as a humanist and his signature creation, Star Trek, is widely regarded as one of the great bastions of humanism in popular culture. Of course, as author Joel Engel notes in his biography of Roddenberry, "Not all humanists are necessarily devout atheists." He adds, however, "But Roddenberry was, and in his atheism he exhibited the same certainty that religious fundamentalists do."[4]

While Engel's biography of Roddenberry is unauthorized, his is far from the only voice of certainty regarding Roddenberry's atheism. Long-time Star Trek producer and writer Brannon Braga—himself an avowed and vocal atheist—has referred to the world of Star Trek as one in which, "religion is completely gone. Not a single human being on Earth believes in any of the nonsense that has plagued our civilization for thousands of years." Citing Roddenberry as a "secular humanist" who "made it well-known to writers of *Star Trek* and *Star Trek: The Next Generation* that religion and superstition and mystical thinking were not to be part of his universe," Braga says that "On Roddenberry's future Earth, everyone is an atheist. And that world is the better for it."[5]

As mentioned above, my analysis of Star Trek does not hinge on Roddenberry's beliefs. Were he as committed an atheist as Engel, Braga, and others claim, my interpretation of his work and its positive impact on my Christian faith would remain almost entirely unchanged. That is, assuming Star Trek itself would be the same. In reality, without Roddenberry's religious background and theological views, it is likely that many important aspects of Star Trek would be very different. My goal, then, is to understand and represent Roddenberry's beliefs as accurately as a I can and the preponderance of evidence leads me to a clear conclusion: For all his talk of religion as foolishness and the Bible as a collection of fairy stories, it is, to my findings, the atheism of Gene Roddenberry that is a myth.

3. Engel, *Gene Roddenberry*, 156.
4. Ibid.
5. Braga, "Every Religion Has a Mythology."

2

Roddenberry, Religion, and a Malfunctioning Brain

As I dive into this exploration of Roddenberry's beliefs, I will use as my springboard one of the most pervasive quotations of an allegedly atheistic nature attributed to Gene Roddenberry—what I'll call the Malfunctioning Brain quote. This quotation has circulated around the Internet for years, appearing alongside Roddenberry's photograph in a number of "celebrity atheist" lists and even in magazine articles and published books. In fact, it is so regularly repeated as to seem to be the default quotation for anyone wishing to quickly and definitively describe Roddenberry as an atheist. It is also an incorrectly cited and partially fabricated misquote. Once and for all, I'd like to set the record straight on where this quotation came from, what Roddenberry actually said, and what his real words mean, with respect to his beliefs about religion, religious people, and God. Here is the Malfunctioning Brain quote as it normally appears:

> I condemn false prophets. I condemn the effort to take away the power of rational decision, to drain people of their free will—and a hell of a lot of money in the bargain. Religions vary in their degree of idiocy, but I reject them all. For most people, religion is nothing more than a substitute for a malfunctioning brain.

It is important to note that this quotation is not atheistic. It is certainly disparaging of religion, or at least certain types of religion, but says nothing whatsoever about the existence of God. Even on its surface, then, whether accurate or inaccurate, it is by no means "proof" that Gene Roddenberry was an atheist.

It also happens to be inaccurate, though consistently so. On rare occasions, the line, "I condemn charlatans" appears before "I condemn false
prophets," but the quotation rarely changes otherwise. When I originally
encountered these words during my research, I immediately wondered
whether they were accurate. Certainly, I knew of Roddenberry's general
disdain for religion, but what gave me pause was the closing sentence, "For
most people, religion is nothing more than a substitute for a malfunctioning brain." Knowing what I did about Roddenberry at the time—which was
not nearly as much as I know now—this bit seemed inconsistent with his
personality. Roddenberry's ideals of tolerance, acceptance, and respect for
his fellow humans did not seem well-served by, nor reflected in, the sentiment that most religious people are basically idiots who cannot think on
their own. I could easily imagine Roddenberry disparaging religion and
religious institutions. I could imagine him hurling insults at someone in
the heat of anger (his temper was almost as well-known as his kindness),
but I could not imagine him calling an entire group of humans—the vast
majority of them, in fact—brainless fools. It seemed far too insulting and
mean-spirited for Roddenberry. I therefore began searching for the original
source of these words.

According to multiple online attributions of this quote, Gene Roddenberry was supposedly interviewed by either *The Humanist* or the magazine *Free Inquiry* in 1991 or 1992. (A 1992 interview would have been a
neat trick, since he died in 1991.) He was indeed interviewed extensively
by David Alexander for *The Humanist* in 1991,[1] [2] but this passage does not
appear in that conversation. Roddenberry was, to the best of my findings,
never interviewed by *Free Inquiry*, though he was written about and quoted
by that publication with some frequency for a time.[3] Again, these words do
not appear in that publication. While these oft-repeated citations are easily
discredited, the true original source for this quote remained elusive to me
for some time.

The Malfunctioning Brain quote has come under some scrutiny in
recent years, as others have apparently discovered the quotation's lack of
reliable documentation. It had been listed amongst others for some time

1. Alexander, "Interview of Gene Roddenberry."

2. Alexander would later include portions of this lengthy interview in *Star Trek Creator*, his authorized biography of Roddenberry.

3. This conclusion is based on emails and phone calls between the author and *Free
Inquiry*'s editorial staff.

in the Gene Roddenberry entry on PositiveAtheism.org's Celebrity Atheist List, but as of the writing of this book, it appears this way:

> Roddenberry Did Not Say This:
>
> "I condemn false prophets, I condemn the effort to take away the power of rational decision, to drain people of their free will—and a hell of a lot of money in the bargain. Religions vary in their degree of idiocy, but I reject them all. For most people, religion is nothing more than a substitute for a malfunctioning brain."
>
> —Phony Quote (as far as we can tell), not found in "Interview of Gene Roddenberry: Writer, Producer, Philosopher, Humanist," in *The Humanist* (March–April, 1991), as cited here for several years, thanks to Jeff for alerting us of this fact. If anybody can find this quote in a legitimate primary source, we would want either a scan or a photocopy of the original source in order to restore the quote; we will not accept secondary sources, but only the primary source (magazine that contained the interview, etc.).[4]

This is one of only two times I have encountered any question of the quotation's veracity outside my own research.[5] It may seem a small thing to have an inaccurate quote floating about the Internet, but if the words misrepresent what someone said or believed, they should be corrected, if nothing else, out of respect for the person to whom the words are attributed. This quotation has become so popular that it has adorned fan-created posters, coffee mugs, and T-shirts, and has been referenced in several legitimate news articles and blog posts as an accurate reflection of Gene Roddenberry's feelings about religion and religious people. It even appears on the reputable Star Trek reference website *Ex Astris Scientia* as a justification for its assertion that "Gene Roddenberry was an active atheist who struggled against any form of religion."[6] [7] The Malfunctioning Brain quote is not, however, an accurate representation, either of Roddenberry's

---

4. Positive Atheism Website, "Positive Atheism's Big List of Quotations."

5. Incidentally, I contacted PositiveAtheism.org about my findings but, as of the time of this writing, I have received no response and the quotation remains unchanged.

6. "Religion in Star Trek," Ex Astris Scientia.

7. Notice, once again, that criticism or rejection of religion is instantly equated with atheism. As I will discuss further in this chapter, irreligiousness, even antireligiousness, is not the same thing as atheism.

words or of his intent, as I discovered when I found the real source of this quotation—*Gene Roddenberry: The Last Conversation* by Yvonne Fern.[8]

A document of an ongoing dialogue between Fern and Roddenberry in the final months of his life, *The Last Conversation* is perhaps the single most insightful and revealing work I have read on Gene Roddenberry. Certainly it is a more intimate portrait of Roddenberry's internal life than most books, articles, and interviews have been, simply because Roddenberry allowed Fern—an incredibly sensitive and perceptive writer—extraordinary access to himself, his home, and his private world. The book is written as a narrative, recording pieces of countless conversations between Fern and Roddenberry and stringing them together so that they read almost like a Platonic dialogue. This allows for an enormous amount of context, leaving little room for misinterpretation, as Fern frequently refuses to allow Roddenberry to leave a topic of conversation before pinning him down on exactly what he means to say. She also, as will be seen, has no problem objecting when she feels the Great Bird of the Galaxy is wrong.

The words that became the Malfunctioning Brain quote are part of a somewhat protracted exchange in the book, regarding Roddenberry's thoughts on religion. The first part of the quotation begins on page 119,[9] where Roddenberry says, "I condemn charlatans. I condemn false prophets. I condemn the effort to take away the power of rational decision, to drain people of their free will—and a hell of a lot of money in the bargain."[10] This is the only portion of the Malfunctioning Brain quote that is an accurate reproduction of Roddenberry's words. However, the words are taken quite out of context when they are presented as Roddenberry's condemnation of all religions as false, manipulative, and greedy and, in particular, of all religious people as addled-brained fools.

The original conversation stretches back several pages, but the relevant part begins on page 117, when Roddenberry is talking about accepting people and treating them fairly, even if he disagrees with them. "We don't look down on others, as inferior, in the Star Trek world, in either Star Trek world,"[11] Roddenberry says. "We've evolved beyond that—" Here, Fern cuts

8. Fern later married *Star Trek* producer Herb Solow and changed her first name to Harrison. She now writes and speaks as Harrison Solow. I will, however, refer to her as Yvonne Fern throughout this book, both in the interest of clarity and because I am speaking of her written work, for which she was credited by that name.

9. Page numbers are from the revised and expanded edition.

10. Fern, *Last Conversation*, 117–120.

11. Here, Roddenberry is speaking of the world of Star Trek television and films and

him off. "Wait. Wait," she says. "You're going to have to explain that. This view of tolerance needs to be explored a little more. You're liberal and tolerant—about racial equality, abortion, homosexuality, women's rights, sex, all the popular issues—but when you meet up with, say, a Baptist, for example, you will unhesitatingly condemn him to oblivion. You choose your points of tolerance very carefully."

This incites an exchange about the freedom of individuals and groups—with the particular example of the Ku Klux Klan—to express their views, no matter how "ignorant" they may be. Roddenberry says he hopes such individuals would change their beliefs on their own and Fern challenges him on whether such deeply seated beliefs can be changed. He responds that *Star Trek* had received thousands of letters "from people who say that they have unlearned some of the prejudices they learned in childhood—they have discovered tolerance or the value of peaceful coexistence or the meaning of friendship or this or that from *Star Trek* . . .". Roddenberry then directly addresses Fern's accusation that he would "unhesitatingly condemn" a Baptist. "And as for Baptists," he says, "my family was Southern Baptist. I don't condemn them. I don't encourage people to condemn them."

"Well, religion in general, then," Fern replies, "I've heard what you had to say about religion, about born-agains and evangelicals in particular. It doesn't sound very tolerant to me." "Doesn't it?" Roddenberry asks, "I'm sorry. I never meant to give that impression. If I did, then I will correct it. I condemn charlatans. I condemn false prophets, I condemn the effort to take away the power of rational decision, to drain people of their free will—and a hell of a lot of money in the bargain." Ironically, then, these words, so frequently quoted as Roddenberry's condemnation of all religions and religious people, are actually taken from his explanation of the fact that he did not hold such beliefs. It is especially important to note that Roddenberry's criticisms are consistently leveled, not at religious people, but at religion—specifically of the kind promoted by "false prophets" and "charlatans."

Most versions of the Malfunctioning Brain quote do not include the line, "I condemn charlatans," but instead begin with "I condemn false prophets." In context, however, the reference to charlatans helps to reinforce the fact that Roddenberry is not referring to all religions or all religious people, but to those he saw as hucksters and manipulators. On page

---

what he refers to in *Last Conversation* as his "Star Trek dreamworld," a purer vision of the future as he imagined it, without all the conflict and content limitations necessitated by making a television program or major motion picture.

119, he says he is speaking of "all religions which use the notion of God as a weapon against humanity." This is followed immediately in the book by a quote from Star Trek producer Robert Justman, who says, "The kind of organized religion that infuriated Gene was exploitive. Human beings exploit. Human beings are the only species on earth that I know of who kill their own kind. Constantly."[12] The clear message here is that Roddenberry is objecting not to all religions, but to a particular use of religion that exploits human beings. In this context, Christians should wholeheartedly agree with Roddenberry's sentiments, just as Jesus condemned religious leaders of his day who would "tie up heavy loads, hard to carry, and put them on men's shoulders"[13] and make a new convert "twice as much a child of hell"[14] as themselves.

Granted, Roddenberry probably viewed the vast majority of religion as exploitative—especially in the era of the televangelist—and therefore had a strong distrust of religious institutions and certainly rejected them all in his own life. However, while he dismissed most religious beliefs as superstition, he acknowledged the strong moral instruction that can come from religion. In fact, he credited his family's involvement in the Southern Baptist church as an influential part of his moral development. In a 1989 interview, veteran broadcaster Tom Snyder asked Roddenberry, "You know, you may live in a big house and have a big show, but I know you care very deeply for people. Where does that come from?" Roddenberry replied, "I think it comes from, again, from family. I was raised in a church, which I don't believe in today, but those lessons of caring for people and lessons about the poor should be taken care of and the lessons about justice should be done and so on, you do get in a church."[15] In this context, then, the accurate portion of the Malfunctioning Brain quote takes on new shades of meaning which, while not entirely different from the meaning implied in the popular misquote, nonetheless convey a greater tolerance for religion than Roddenberry is typically known for.

The rest of the Malfunctioning Brain quote is pieced together from an exchange that takes place on page 119 of *Last Conversation*, when Roddenberry states that, while the Catholic religion "very well may be" a part of the truth, " . . . it's not The Truth." Fern asks, "So if religion engenders even

12. Ibid., 119.
13. Matt 23:4.
14. Matt 23:15.
15. Snyder, "Interview with Gene Roddenberry."

a truth, how can you dismiss it?"[16] Roddenberry's answer to that question comprises a short paragraph, from which select words have been extracted and reassembled to create the remaining portion of the Malfunctioning Brain quote. As a reminder, the quoted text is, "Religions vary in their degree of idiocy, but I reject them all. For most people, religion is nothing more than a substitute for a malfunctioning brain." Here is the text as it appears in the book, with the relevant words in italics.

> Well, first of all, there's a *very great difference* among those *religions* you mentioned. There are *degrees of idiocy.* Some are less culpable than others. *But I reject them all,* because *for most people*—not for you, perhaps not for other intelligent people—but for most of these poor devils, it's *a substitute brain.* And a very *malfunctioning* one. I don't dismiss the people who believe in this or that. I dismiss the structure and, more than that, the very idea of the system of the organized church.[17]

Clearly, there is quite a bit more here than the popular misquote implies. In fact, it is hard to imagine how this quotation came to be so distorted. While it is reasonable that someone could have been repeating what they had read from an inaccurate memory, it seems strange that the first part of the quotation is perfectly accurate, while the second part is comprised of scrambled bits of text, taken from a segment two pages later in the book. Either someone purposely composed this quote or there is a story behind the quote that involves both complete accuracy and a foggy memory. Rather than speculate,[18] I'll return to the quote itself.

16. Fern, *Last Conversation*, 119.

17. Ibid., 119–120.

18. The most accurate quotation of this section of *Last Conversation* I have found is from the blog "Only a Game," in the fifth entry in a series on science fiction and religion. In it, blogger Chris Bateman refers to Fern's interview with Roddenberry, though he fails to mention that it is a book. He then quotes Fern accurately, from page 108, asking Roddenberry to explain his view of tolerance and accusing him of having a superior attitude. Bateman then skips ahead to Roddenberry's words on page 111, beginning with "I never meant to give that impression," and accurately quotes the book up until the line "a hell of a lot of money in the bargain." He then, perplexingly, recalls the rest of the quote as it appears popularly, not as it appears in the book, though he does include the line, "I condemn charlatans." When I contacted Bateman about the discrepancy, he could not recall why he had misquoted the book the way he had. It is possible that this is the original source of the widely circulated misquote, though somewhat unlikely, since the blog post appeared in 2009 and Positive Atheism reports having the quote on their site for "several years" before posting their correction, which was added no later than 2012. Additionally, if the misquote had originated on "Only a Game," it is unlikely it would

The last line of the false quote that refers to religion in general is "Religions vary in their degree of idiocy, but I reject them all." In the original book, Roddenberry's words are not drastically different in their tone and again reflect his general disdain for organized religion, though he does not necessarily attribute "degrees of idiocy" to all religions. However, it is the effect of religion on people, as he sees it, and a philosophical disagreement with the idea of an organized church that Roddenberry cites as his reasons for rejecting religion in his own life, though he acknowledges that there are many "intelligent people" who are religious.

By contrast, in the false quotation, Roddenberry is quoted as saying that "For most people, religion is nothing more than a substitute for a malfunctioning brain," implying that most religious people are mentally impaired, incapable of thinking on their own and needing religion to think for them. As I have mentioned, it was this depiction of Roddenberry's thoughts on religious people that originally raised a red flag for me. Whatever his feelings toward the Bible, churches, or religion in general, it seemed out of character for Roddenberry to disparage a whole group of people—indeed, the majority of people in the world—in such a dismissive way. And the truth is, he didn't.

He rejected religion, he said, because "for most people—not for you, perhaps not for other intelligent people—but for most of these poor devils, it's a substitute brain. And a very malfunctioning one." In other words, Roddenberry felt that religion often encourages people who would otherwise think for themselves to let religion do their thinking for them. In this, he was right in line with many Christian thinkers, including Mark Noll, who famously wrote that "The scandal of the evangelical mind is that there is not much of an evangelical mind."[19] It is not religious people Roddenberry said have malfunctioning brains. It is instead religion that he says functions poorly as a substitute for rational thinking. In this, Roddenberry was absolutely right. When people let religion do their thinking for them, they are really submitting to the whims of religious leaders, without questioning, discerning, and thinking for themselves to determine if what they are hear-

---

have had time to circulate enough to have been given the incorrect *Humanist* citation, which Positive Atheism used for those "several years," much less the *Free Inquiry* attribution seen elsewhere. It is, however, the best available lead and the only "transitional form" I have found between *Last Conversation* and the Malfunctioning Brain quote. Bateman's post can be viewed at http://onlyagame.typepad.com/only_a_game/2009/05/religion-in-science-fiction-5-star-trek.html.

19. Noll, *Scandal of the Evangelical Mind*, 3.

ing is right. This is exactly the opposite if what Scripture teaches, as Paul encourages his readers to "be transformed by the renewing of your mind so that you may test and approve what is the will of God."[20] Or as John the Evangelist writes, "Do not believe every spirit, but test the spirits."[21] And again, Paul says, "We are no longer to be children, tossed back and forth by the waves and carried about by every wind of teaching by the trickery of people who craftily carry out their deceitful schemes."[22] Blind faith is dangerous and is discouraged in Scripture, which rails just as hard as Roddenberry against "false prophets"[23] and "the effort to take away the power of rational decision."[24]

Finally, Roddenberry further clarifies his views regarding religious people by saying, "I don't dismiss the people who believe in this or that. I dismiss the structure and, more than that, the very idea of the system of the organized church."[25] Today, Roddenberry might be surprised at the number of faithful followers of Christ who would agree with him in that regard. Many people in recent years—young adults and postmodern Christian thinkers, forerunners of Emergent Christianity and even high-profile figures like author Anne Rice—have embraced faith in Christ, while rejecting or radically rethinking institutional Christianity. Their reasons for doing so vary but, on the whole, they share with Roddenberry a sense of the troubled nature of the institutional church and a profound disconnect between the teachings of Christ and the trappings of contemporary religion, which include the kind of manipulation, greed, and corruption Roddenberry was so disgusted by.

While holding this view of organized religion, however, he refrained from disparaging religious people and many of their moral and ethical beliefs, even if their theological beliefs seemed superstitious to him. Later in *Last Conversation*, he says, "Yvonne, I must personally condemn a system I see as deserving of condemnation." Fern asks, "But you don't necessarily condemn the beliefs contained therein?" "No. Not at all," Roddenberry replies.

---

20. Rom 12:2.
21. 1 John 4:1.
22. Eph 4:14.
23. Matt 7:15, 2 Pet 2:1.
24. Fern, *Last Conversation*, 117.
25. Ibid., 120.

"In *Star Trek*, there is room for many beliefs, and there are many beautiful, helpful values contained in those beliefs. How could I condemn them?"[26]

This statement, like many others by Roddenberry and within Star Trek itself, refutes the popular idea that there was no room in Roddenberry's worldview or in Star Trek for people of religious conviction or for spiritual beliefs. While choosing not to embrace religion in his own life, Roddenberry tried to maintain an attitude of respect for the religious beliefs of others, however limiting he may have believed them to be. As he told biographer David Alexander, he and his second wife, Majel Barrett-Roddenberry, had both left Protestant churches earlier in their lives, "in favor of non-sectarian beliefs which included respect for all other religions . . ."[27]

It was, however, not always this way for Roddenberry. His strong disagreement with religion had, in his younger years, led him to judgmental attitudes toward certain religious practices. In an interview with former Jesuit priest Terrance Sweeney in 1985, Roddenberry recalled, "I remember as a young man being in Mexico City, at the Lady of Guadalupe Cathedral, I think it was. I watched people crawl from ten miles away, from the city, with bleeding knees. I felt and understood that—at least to me—this was as foolish as the things I'd always laughed at on television when I saw the African tribesmen do the same thing."[28] The foolishness of these actions, to Roddenberry, had to do with what he saw as an approach to the Divine that was too simple. It seemed to him that such actions could not possibly have any efficacy toward reaching God. "I wish I could simply bleed or flagellate myself to get closer to him," he continues, "But unfortunately it's not that easy. In fact, for many years, I was bitterly angry about people hurting themselves, and I categorized anyone who believed this way as stupid."[29]

But Roddenberry grew beyond this way of thinking to ultimately become less hostile toward people who held to these practices, even as he continued to disagree with them. "I think that those who find pleasure and relief in being at that—I was going to say level, putting myself above them, but I don't mean to do that—if this is the way they want to believe, and it gives them some understanding of themselves, then fine. God—whatever you are—bless them, make them happy. For me it's not that simple."[30]

26. Ibid., 114.
27. Alexander, *Star Trek Creator*, 422.
28. Sweeney, *God &*, 14.
29. Ibid., 15.
30. Ibid.

In an interview with journalist Ellen Adelstein, Gene Roddenberry's son, Eugene "Rod" Roddenberry Jr., summarized his father's views on religion this way:

> I have my own beliefs and I've read a number of his. I know his thoughts on religion evolved throughout his life. You know, one of the things I'm learning on my own projects is he wrestled with the concept of God, religion and traditional, structured religions, versus just the belief in something greater. And, towards the end of his life, I believe he considered himself a humanist—which wasn't atheist. It didn't necessarily leave God out. But it was, I believe, to believe in yourself and humanity first, for us to all work together for the greater good. You don't have to not believe in God. Whatever your religion is, you keep it, but focus on humanity first. Let's put all our differences aside and work together. You know, God will be there, regardless.[31]

Here, Roddenberry Jr., echoes the sentiment of tolerance toward religion and religious people expressed by his father, while also addressing the issue of whether or not his father believed in God, making a point to remark that the elder Roddenberry's worldview "wasn't atheist." While this statement might be surprising to some, Roddenberry Jr., is not the only one to directly refute the idea that his father was an atheist. In *The Last Conversation*, Fern describes Dr. Charles Musès as Roddenberry's "old, dear friend," and mentor. In Roddenberry's words, she says, Musès was "a *most* intimate friend" who "understood Star Trek long before I or anyone else . . .".[32] Of particular note are Musès' words regarding Roddenberry's fondness for the poem *A Sleep of Prisoners* by Christopher Fry. "It was a favorite of his," Musès says. "It expresses his true religion—a far cry from atheism."[33] Similarly, when Roddenberry Jr., interviewed Ernie Over, the elder Roddenberry's personal assistant for many years, for his documentary film, *Trek Nation*, Over said to him, "Your father was not anti-God. He was anti-religion . . . I don't think he did not believe in a Supreme Being, but [believed] that it was manifested through individual works."[34] While it seems unlikely that Roddenberry's son, his mentor, and his personal assistant would all say he was not an

---

31. Adelstein, "Interview with Rod Roddenberry."
32. Fern, *Last Conversation*, 37.
33. Ibid.
34. Colthorp, *Trek Nation*, supplemental disc.

atheist if he really was one, this is hardly the only evidence for the idea that Roddenberry should not be properly understood as an atheist.

Roddenberry was indeed dissatisfied with the biblical image of what he felt was an unloving, unjust, tyrannical God. As Joel Engel describes it, the view of God Roddenberry retained from his childhood was "the God who, in the words of the 'Battle Hymn of the Republic,' wielded a 'terrible, swift sword'; a God whose wrath was to be feared, and for whom love was less important than respect."[35] Engel notes that this vision of God was reflected by Roddenberry's own father, Eugene Edward Roddenberry, "the product of a strict southern upbringing, and a man holding bigoted and racist views."[36] Certainly, this is a view of God that most modern Christians also reject and it says more about the religious environment of Roddenberry's childhood than about God or the Bible itself.

Though he incorrectly labels Roddenberry an atheist, Engel accurately represents Roddenberry's often unwavering commitment to an idea once he'd made up his mind. "By definition," he says, "such absolute certitude precludes the ability to examine or accept the validity of opposing viewpoints."[37] Indeed, Roddenberry said of his rejection of Christianity in his teenage years, "[M]y thinking about religion sort of stultified at that time and I just decided not to pay any attention to it."[38] For the most part, then, Roddenberry's views on religion—and Christianity in particular—did not grow, for many years, beyond the perceptions of a fourteen-year-old. In many ways, the same is too often true for Christians, a fact which frequently results in the kinds of portrayals of God that helped drive Roddenberry away from Christian faith.

Roddenberry was irreligious, hedonistic, and by no measure a believer in traditional Western conceptions of God. He rejected Christianity and was opposed to organized religion. He saw the Bible largely as myth. He regarded the idea of a God with whom one can have a relationship and to whom worship is owed as superstitious. None of these facts qualify him as an atheist. The truth is, Gene Roddenberry was a theist—just not the most common kind.

35. Engel, *Gene Roddenberry*, 46.
36. Ibid., 48.
37. Ibid., 156.
38. Alexander, *Star Trek Creator*, 40.

3

The Theology of
Gene Roddenberry

While nuances certainly exist, the essential definition of atheism is simple. The word is comprised of the Greek root *theos*, meaning "God," and the prefix *a*, meaning "not."[1] Atheism, then, is the belief that God is "not," or, that God does not exist. While earlier applications of the term can were used with reference to disbelief in a particular god or gods,[2] in modern times, the word "atheism" has generally referred to, as William L. Rowe puts it, disbelief in "the existence of any sort of divine reality."[3]

In very brief, the only thing an atheist believes about God is that he, she, or it does not exist. Therefore, if one attributes any characteristic or quality to God other than nonexistence, that person is categorically not an atheist. Gene Roddenberry had many ideas about the nature of God, not one of which was God's nonexistence. With this in mind, I'd like to give some attention to the various statements Roddenberry made about God and to construct at least a working understanding of his theology.

"I believe in a kind of god."

It's one thing to say, based on a critical analysis, that Roddenberry's irreligious and antireligious statements are not atheistic, but more than that, Roddenberry himself even rejected the atheist label at least once and

1. McKim, *Westminster Dictionary of Theological Terms*, 20.

2. "The cry of the heathen populace in the Roman empire against the Christians was 'Away with the atheists! To the lions with the Christians!'" 1911 *Encyclopædia Britannica*.

3. Rowe, "Atheism," *Shorter Routledge Encyclopedia of Philosophy*, 73.

specifically described his form of theism on multiple occasions. In *Last Conversation*, Roddenberry proposes the idea that perhaps the human imagination is not simply a function of the mind, but also something that exists, independent of human consciousness. When asked to define what that something might be, he calls it "A mystery. A flashlight in the dark. God." Fern seems somewhat incredulous.

> "You're pretty well known for not believing in God. Do you claim him now?"

> "Oh, well, people are often pretty well known for things which are not true."

> "Well, is it?"

> "No, it's not. I believe in a kind of god. It's just not other people's god. I reject religion. I accept the notion of God."[4]

Fern then points out that "the notion of God" is not the same thing as God and presses Roddenberry for further clarification. After initially attempting to dodge the question, Roddenberry finally relents.

> Alright. God, to me, is intrinsic to humanity. To the whole cause of humanity. To the imaginative principle. To what we create, and think. He—or I should say "it"—is a source, yes, but more an involvement with the unknown. God is like the leap outside one-self—something that has no discernable source, but is a source.

"Inspiration?" Fern offers. "That's as good a word as any," replies Roddenberry. "Better than most." Fern notes that the word "inspiration" is derived from the Latin *inspiro*, which means, in her words, "to breathe into." Within Roddenberry's definition, she says, this suggests, "a breath of life from an unknown source." Roddenberry appears satisfied with this description. "A breath of life," he says. "I like that. It is a breath of life, this god thing. It's not a thing you pray to, it's a thing you use to answer your own prayers. Humanity needs God in order to be humanity—it is part of them."[5]

This breath, to Roddenberry, was more than a "notion," and more than just a part of humanity. Roddenberry saw God as a reality intrinsic to the universe, perhaps even a scientifically provable one. "I think God is as much a basic ingredient of the universe as neutrons and positrons," he told Terrance Sweeney. "I suspect there is a scientific equation in matter and

4. Fern, *Last Conversation*, 67.
5. Ibid.

time and energy, and that we'll ultimately discover the missing ingredient. God is, for lack of a better term, clout. This is the prime force, when we look around the universe."[6]

"God is not a person."

As his above exchanges with Sweeney and Fern allude, it wasn't just the idea of God as a warlike, vengeful being that Roddenberry rejected; it was the idea of a personal God—that is, a God who is a person—in which he also disbelieved. It is this disbelief that many Roddenberry observers have characterized as atheism. As we have seen, however, the conclusion that Roddenberry was an atheist is one that his consistent statements on the matter of his view of God do not support. However, his statements about God—even his use of the term "God" to describe what he believed in—can easily lead to the equally false assumption that he was a traditional monotheist, believing in a single, separate, and external God.

Roddenberry remarked to Sweeney that, "God is not a person, not a simple thing like that," calling such an idea "a petty, superstitious approach to the All, the Infinite."[7] His belief in the nonexistence of a personal God—biblical or otherwise—was based on his belief in the existence of a God that is "too great and too encompassing to be explained and appreciated by any single system of belief."[8] He likely intended this statement with particular emphasis on organized religion and on the belief in God as a separate, personal being. As he told Ellen Adelstein,

> I think the more that you delve into science, the incredible mystery of the universe, the incredible precision and all of this, you begin to realize that God—creative force or whatever it is—is so far beyond what we can even imagine that you kind of move out of your belief that there's someone up there with a long, white beard, and so on.[9]

While a "long, white beard" is hardly a tenant of Christian theology, Roddenberry's point is well taken: traditional concepts of God, for him, simply won't do; he sees them as far too limiting of the Divine. So, if, in

6. Sweeney, *God &*, 12.

7. Ibid., 14.

8. Alexander, *Star Trek Creator*, 422.

9. Adelstein, *Up Close and Personal*.

Roddenberry's view, God is not a person, what is God? And, if religion is corrupt and untrustworthy, where is one to find God?

"I am God; certainly you are."

There are two essential aspects to Roddenberry's conception of what he called the "God thing": humanism and pantheism. These two aspects are intimately connected and are most succinctly stated by Roddenberry early in his conversation with Sweeney. "As nearly as I can concentrate on the question today," Roddenberry says, "I believe I am God; certainly you are, I think we intelligent beings on this planet are all a piece of God, are becoming God."[10]

Roddenberry said that he loved individual humans because they are part of humanity.[11] For him, neighbor love was a part of the progress of humankind. As we love one another and accept one another and work toward peace and unity with one another, we progress—not only as individuals, but as a species. This species—according to Roddenberry—is not just a collection of organic individuals, but is a participant in and is evolving toward the Divine. In essence, we are God. Loving one's neighbor, then—even loving oneself—is, ultimately, loving God. This is, of course, an extrapolation based on Roddenberry's stated beliefs, but it is a logical one and one which it is doubtful was lost on Roddenberry himself. Humans are fragile, selfish, petty, and hateful creatures. But this is not what Roddenberry believed to be our truest, best nature. It is our capacity for goodness, kindness, forgiveness, peace, and perhaps especially creativity and invention where Roddenberry saw that "we have things to be proud of."[12] It is here that Roddenberry saw in humankind the spark of the Divine.

Seeing this spark, along with the incredible order of the universe, brought Roddenberry to the clear, consistent conclusion that some form of divinity exists. Seeing the corruption, manipulation, oppression, and greed carried out in the name of religion brought him to the conclusion that the most common religious conceptions of God cannot be correct. Therefore, humanity became the anchor for his view of God. Seeing God reflected in his creation—especially in humans, who are made in his image—but rejecting the concepts of God that humans could be reflecting, he instead saw the

10. Sweeney, *God &*, 11.

11. Fern, *Last Conversation*, 28.

12. Beck, *Star Trek 25th Anniversary Special*.

reflection and the reflected as synonyms. Since he saw God in humanity and not elsewhere, humanity must be God. Since humanity is also wicked, humanity—and God—must also be in progress. Since God has already created the universe, God must also, somehow, already be fully evolved. Hence, "In some cyclical, non-time thing, we have to become God in order to create ourselves."[13]

Ultimately, it is unclear whether it was Roddenberry's concept of God that caused him to reject religion, or the religion he saw as worthy of rejection that informed his conception of God. As will later be shown in my discussion of the Original Series episode "Bread and Circuses," it is possible that he could have, under other circumstances, been a Christian, as he seems to have found his greatest philosophical kinship there. Whatever he thought of Jesus, though, the Christian religion, as he saw it, and the perception of God he perceived in it pushed him away from any kind of pursuit of Christ. But that is not to say that Christ did not pursue him. It seems, in fact, that Roddenberry may have fit Flannery O'Connor's description of the American South as "Christ-haunted." It seems that, in his Star Trek stories, Roddenberry was constantly struggling with concepts of God and religion, drawing on Edenic imagery as early as the rejected pilot episode "The Cage," and persisting in writing literal struggles with divine beings, to the point that Original Series and Animated Series writer David Gerrold remarked that "When in doubt, Gene just had Kirk get into a fight with God."[14]

It is not difficult to imagine a young man like Gene Roddenberry questioning the simple platitudes and pat answers he likely got in a West Texas Southern Baptist church in the 1930s, especially with the influence of his skeptical father. And certainly, our childhood experiences of religion and moral formation have a tendency to affect some portion of our lives into adulthood, but Roddenberry seems, strangely, at once obsessed with religion and God and not mindful of them at all.

The first example of the latter most observers point to is Roddenberry's well-documented hedonism—especially in the area of his lack of sexual fidelity to Majel. Even as he clearly loved her more than anyone in the world and remained, at heart, completely devoted to her, this never stopped him from "dipping his wick" wherever he pleased.[15] Added to his penchant for

---

13. Sweeney, *God &*, 11.

14. Tescar, "The TAS David Gerrold Interview."

15. Fern, *Last Conversation*, 111.

drink, his sailor's vocabulary, his dabbling in drugs, and his contempt for religion, this made Roddenberry the consummate, classic heathen.

All of this, however, seems at least partially rooted in his official rejection of Christianity and the pursuit of an essentially moral life—in terms of seeking justice and walking humbly—without a stern religion and a vindictive God towering over him and threatening to punish him if he got out of line. As we hear echoed in the dialogue from the episode "Bread and Circuses" ("The words are true"), there was clearly something undeniable to Roddenberry about the wisdom of Jesus. Equally undeniable to him seems to have been the existence of some form of creator and deity, even if he could ultimately pinpoint it nowhere but in, as Kirk puts it in *Star Trek V*, "the human heart."

His hedonism, then, may have been a kind of reaction against a perceived insufficiency of religion to encompass the greatness of the divine, or to satisfy the human heart. All the pleasures he sought—perhaps especially sex—were rooted in the belief that, if humanity was divine, then it is also basically good, and further, if it is basically good, then so are its basic desires. So, a desire for pleasure and sexual fulfillment was seen as simply the desire to connect with another human being in a mutually pleasurable way. From the external signs, he may have been completely vindicated in this belief, as Majel seemed to accept this aspect of her husband's personality. One wonders, however, if the detectable sadness on the surface of her demeanor when she discussed this subject might hint that she was more hurt by his behavior than she let on.

In reacting against religion, however, it would seem that Roddenberry was, in a certain sense, questing for a divinity he did not find with the walls of a church. In fact, there is more than a small amount of evidence to suggest that biblical narratives and Christian ideas and imagery had made an impression on Roddenberry and imbued him with a kind of "indelible Christian imagination"[16] that colored his work. "I used religion several times in *Have Gun, Will Travel*," he recalled. "Once in a penitentiary where a pastor was trying to keep a fellow from being hung, I wrote that the pastor grabbed a hacksaw blade, was cut by it, and was bleeding. I had him make some comment about blood and salvation." While his familiarity with Christianity from his time in church certainly contributed to his ability to use this type of imagery, he included it, in part, with an awareness of how

---

16. This is something of a paraphrase of the book title, *Afterimage: The Indelible Catholic Imagination of Six American Filmmakers*, by Richard A. Blake.

it would be received. "It's not that I actually believed in blood and salvation being connected," he continued, "but that was the way the audience believed and I can remember going out of my way not to deal directly with what my thoughts [on religion] were for several reasons."[17]

These references Roddenberry consistently brushed off as incidental flukes of imagination. However, his humanistic philosophy seems thoroughly rooted in his rejection of religion (and, conversely, in the moral foundation he received from religion) and talk of God seems to have been never far from his lips. Time and time again, Roddenberry—of his own volition, with no one else even mentioning the subject—brings up the topic of the divine, whether as creator of all things or in the collective human spirit or with reference to religion. In some form or another, Roddenberry the creator seemed to be also on his own journey of discovery.

17. Alexander, "Interview of Gene Roddenberry."

4

Questor

S tar Trek was intended as and is often celebrated as an allegorical exploration of human morality and political/social issues, but perhaps there are also even somewhat unconscious allegories with Roddenberry's own spiritual quest. Most notably, perhaps, this quest is embodied in the precursor of the Data character from *The Next Generation*, an artificial life form known as Questor. In the television movie *The Questor Tapes*, a lone android seeks his creator, only to find that his creator is one like him and that he has been tasked with the Godlike duty of monitoring the entire world and setting wrongs right to help humanity along in its progress out of infancy. In this narrative, we see Roddenberry exploring a theme that would be frequently visited throughout Star Trek, especially in Original Series stories: the search for the creator. As in Roddenberry's own theology, the creator is both mysterious and unknown and to be found within.

Like Questor, Roddenberry left conventional structures behind and struck out, consciously or not, on his own quest for the Divine—for his origins, his place in the world, and for his ultimate destiny. This deeply personal quest, though sometimes underplayed by Roddenberry, was never far below the surface of his work—especially *Star Trek*. It is also a quest we all share, perhaps giving a clue to the deeper reasons for Star Trek's widespread appeal, and reflecting the words of Carl Rogers, "What is most personal is most general,"[1] or would "speak most deeply to others."[2]

It is in Roddenberry's hedonism that we find his deepest convictions and his moral core, and in his rejection of religion and commitment to

1. This sentence is often quoted, perhaps more elegantly, as "That which is most personal is most universal."

2. Rogers, *On Becoming a Person*, 26.

humanism that we find his quest for God. If, as Scripture tells us, human-kind was indeed created in the image and likeness of God, then it should come as no surprise to us that an exploration of humanity would be bound up in and include a quest for the Divine. It should also come as no surprise that, if the gospel is truly the cure for and aim of the human heart, an ex-ploration of humanity would bump up against the gospel along the way. If the truths of Scripture are really true, we should discover them as part of universal, human truths. Indeed, Roddenberry was continually inspired to affirm and embrace as true the teachings of Jesus and fundamental truths about humanity, the universe, and our relationship to God. His predisposi-tion against any form of God he saw in religion (and in particular, Christi-anity) led him to draw different conclusions than Scripture, but he observed the same conditions inherent in those conclusions.

Where Roddenberry saw human beings as a part of God, Christians see the fingerprints of God on his creation—a creation made in his image. Where Roddenberry concluded that God could not be a person, Christians see that he is a person unlike any other. Where Roddenberry saw humanity evolving and improving on its own, Christians see the plan and design of God for humankind coming to fruition. Where Roddenberry saw human-ity as its own Savior—if indeed it needed saving at all—Christians see hu-man beings as participants in their own salvation, partners with Christ, in the outworking of the grace of God.

It all has to do with perspective. Roddenberry saw all the elements of the gospel and had a hunger in his heart for the culmination of salvation, but since his predisposition was to reject the gospel itself, he never saw the connection between the longings of his heart, the observations of his mind and the fulfillment they would find in Christ. As a result, the elements of his philosophy and theology remained, at certain crucial points, pieces of a puzzle he could never fully solve.

In Roddenberry, we see someone who, while he rejected Christ, ultimately lived largely by Christian values. Of course, there were many Christian values by which he did not live, but those are perhaps less im-portant than essential issues of character. Certainly the substances he chose to put into his body and how he chose to behave sexually and his general hedonism connote a bit of a rebellious spirit, but that rebellious spirit—that restless heart—was a deeply human trait that sought rest in that which ul-timately would give it completion. As Augustine writes to God, "Our heart is restless, until it rests in you."[3] In its own way, Roddenberry's restless heart was ultimately questing for God. If his conception of God was not in keeping with a Christian understanding of the Divine and if he rejected Christ in a general theological sense, this had more to do with the abuse of those images and abuse through those images that have been carried out in the name of Christ than with Christ himself. It is clear that Roddenberry admired Jesus and tried, in his own way, to live like him. And it is possible that, were he helped to understand that the true gospel offered exactly the vision, hope, and future for humankind that he sought, that his theological perspective might have changed. Ultimately, though, his heart seemed oriented toward the things of God and toward the heart of grace. That he rejected Christianity in name may not matter in the end. After all, man sees what is on the outside, but God looks at the heart. Therefore, I have hope for Gene Roddenberry. And that gives me hope for my own restless, stumbling self as well.

3. Augustine, *Confessions*, 3.

SECTION 2

The Gospel According to the Original Series

1

More Than a Wagon Train to the Stars

Star Trek, now known as the Original Series (TOS), was totally revolutionary for 1966 television. Amidst a sea of cop shows, Westerns,
courtroom dramas, and even other, more conventional, ray gun science
fiction, *Star Trek* brought thoughtful stories, exciting new worlds, philosophical and ethical explorations, and relevant social commentary to the
screen as nothing had before. Gene Roddenberry had famously sold the
series to network executives as a "wagon train to the stars," intentionally
name-checking the popular Western *Wagon Train* in his pitch. And, while
there was a certain amount of this element to the series and fans have long
romanticized the phrase as a descriptor of *Star Trek*, the fact of the matter
is that the series was more about ideas than adventure. Certainly its scripts
kept enough fistfights, ship battles, and (mostly offscreen) bodice ripping
in its stories to make them exciting and please network executives, but it
never strayed far from the philosophical inquest into the human condition
that was the true dilithium for its warp engines.

Despite its reputation for being antireligious, this conversation frequently touched on issues of religion and faith and the scripts regularly
borrowed imagery and language from religious traditions and texts—especially the Bible. In contrast to popular evaluations, the series is also surprisingly open toward religion, even as it condemns the use of religion as a
means of controlling people and hiding truth—something to which Christians should similarly object. Given all we've discussed in the previous section regarding Gene Roddenberry's religious background and theological
beliefs, and the fact that every episode of the series passed his scrutiny and
constant rewrites, TOS' discussion of these ideas is particularly interesting

as an outgrowth of Roddenberry's own spiritual journey. Similarly, the Original Series set the tone for much of the attitudes toward religion that would exist throughout future series and films.

Beyond its specific discussions of religion and gods, though, the Original Series established the humanistic worldview of the Star Trek universe and the central focus of its stories on understanding humanity—its successes and failures, its beauty and ugliness, its potential and its nobility. The struggle and promise of what it means to be human is the core focus of TOS, and of the entire Star Trek franchise. In this, Star Trek hardly goes afield of a conversation relevant to a Christian worldview. Humanity is, after all, something God designed and chose to bear his image. This makes understanding our humanity of deep importance to understanding who and what God intends us to be. As stated earlier, if the gospel truly is the cure and completion for the human condition, then as we discuss the human condition, we ought to find ourselves bumping up against the gospel. In *Star Trek*, we certainly do, and we also find ideas that can be importantly instructive for how we are to live as followers of Christ.

2

The Way to Eden: The Edenic Imagination of the Original Series

The Original Series (TOS) is a bit of an easy target for episodes that deal directly with religion and God concepts. It is also rife with biblical allusions—particularly to the book of Genesis and the garden of Eden. In 1978, this recurring theme led author Betsy Caprio to her persistent theme of "the paradise within" as a central idea in *Star Trek*.[1] [2]

She has a bit of a point. TOS seems almost obsessed with debunking various models of paradise—largely, it would seem, because Roddenberry himself was seeking to define and depict a true paradise as he saw it. In his view, of course, this must be an entirely human paradise, created by humans, for humans. His cosmology of alien races is certainly grounded in his belief that alien civilizations exist and that humankind will one day be interacting with them. However, from a more practical writing standpoint, these alien races stand in for various types of humans. The paradise he seeks, then, is a human one—first and foremost. It would seem that Roddenberry believed that this "child race"[3] of humanity must prepare itself to be ready for an encounter with alien life. It is therefore through imagining how we will interact with those aliens that he shows us how to interact with

1. Caprio, *Star Trek: Good News in Modern Images.*

2. Caprio's book holds the distinction of being the first (and before this book, the only) traditionally published book by a single author specifically discussing the relationship between Star Trek and Christianity (though Caprio veers from that concept somewhat). It was also published in the year of this author's birth.

3. Fern, *Last Conversation*, 12.

one another, thus providing a real and immediate human impact, as well as a hope for future growth and development.

Human growth and development are at the heart of TOS and of Star Trek itself, and particularly come to the fore in TOS' paradise narratives. Consistently, we see that growth and development are essential to our humanity, but that we must work in order to grow. If we are to have a paradise, we must earn it. If we cheat by using technology in an unethical manner, we will undermine our own efforts and the paradise we make will be unsustainable. If we trust in a higher authority to create and sustain our paradise for us, we will become prisoners and slaves. ("The Cage," "The Apple," "Who Mourns for Adonais," and other episodes highlight the instinct against human imprisonment.) Therefore, a paradise for humans can only be built by human hands. Here, we see Roddenberry clearly reacting against his evangelical upbringing and the concepts of God and humankind's relationship to God that he grew up with.

The vision of God and the concept of religion that Roddenberry rejected seem to have been rejected on the basis of two or three essential concepts which Roddenberry could not accept: (1) a personal, authoritarian God, (2) helpless humans conscripted to lifelong worship, and (3) submission to a manipulative ruling class of religious leaders as a means of salvation. These overtones, rooted more in Western religion than in the Biblical narrative, served to distance Roddenberry from the gospel, muting the significance of Christ's suffering and death, not to mention humankind's role as co-creators, or, perhaps more accurately, as cultivators of creation. It is, however, this very theme of humankind's participative role in creation that could have caused Eden to fire Roddenberry's imagination in more positive ways. Distracted by his disgust at the idea of humans being driven out of paradise for seeking knowledge (his assessment of the story), he missed the depth of the human calling contained in those earliest Biblical passages. Whether one reads the book of Genesis as a historical account or as a metaphor, the image of the garden of Eden is profoundly important because it highlights as central to the human narrative our role as cultivators of creation. This idea seems one that would have been very attractive to Roddenberry. If it had been presented to him as the central calling of the Christian life, he might have had a very different feeling toward the idea of being a Christian.

In this light—as original destiny and contemporary calling—Eden can be viewed as the central narrative of the human condition. It should therefore come as little surprise that, as Star Trek seeks to find meaning in the human experience, its most common recurring theme is Eden. Eden is the primary literary and narrative thread that runs from "The Cage" (*Star Trek*'s original, rejected pilot episode) throughout the run of the series.[4] Here, then, are a few brief examples:

1. "The Cage": In this very first *Star Trek* episode, the Talosians seek an Eve for Pike's Adam, but Pike doesn't want to be Adam and doesn't want to have an Eve. In fact, any sexual desire he might have for Vina is relegated to his dark, lonely fantasies and giving in to that temptation is equated with giving in to a baser lust and failing to seek the moral high road. The Talosians offer a paradise, but at a cost—the cost of perpetual captivity and illusion. Throughout TOS, paradise is depicted as a tempting, dangerous illusion. This is particularly noteworthy since, biblically, it is a tempting, dangerous illusion that leads to the expulsion from paradise. This inverted narrative—in which Eden is the temptation and expulsion is freedom—is played upon in many episodes, including "The Apple."[5]

2. "The Apple": The seeming paradise offered by Vaal is based on ignorance and technological manipulation. Worship is again associated with slavery. Salvation is offered specifically (if metaphorically) by the "apple" of the Genesis narrative.[6]

3. "Where No Man Has Gone Before": The desire of a human to be like God, to create his own Eden (complete with Kapherian apples and an Eve), is destructive to himself and others. Unrestricted power without conscience or virtue makes him a bringer of death, masquerading as the Author of Life.[7]

---

4. We will also see that this theme follows the original crew through all of their cinematic journeys, even down to Spock's painting of "The Expulsion from Paradise" in *Star Trek VI*. It could also be said to be subtly present in the film *Star Trek: Generations* (which will be covered in the next book), if nothing else, in the depiction of a misguided attempt to attain (or regain) paradise.

5. Butler, "The Cage."

6. Pevney, "The Apple."

7. Goldstone, "Where No Man Has Gone Before."

4. "The Way to Eden": A group of "space hippies" make and ill-fated attempt to find the planet Eden, a supposed paradise. Instead, the fruit of a tree on the planet brings death. Paradise is barred to us.[8]

5. "This Side of Paradise": The spores offer perfect health, longevity, and happiness, but at the cost of individuality, challenge, and the quest for personal improvement. No matter what good things they provide their hosts, their hosts are clearly slaves, their very thoughts and desires altered to serve the purposes of the spores. This, as Kirk insists, is no paradise, but the squelching of the human soul.[9]

Paradise is most often seen in *Star Trek* as incompatible with humanity—that is, at least certain concepts of paradise are. Any paradise that is nothing but leisure, that is free of "negative" emotions, is ultimately shown to be corrupt—a choking out of the human soul. The apparent perfect garden is, in reality, filled with unseen weeds.

These paradise impostors are often exposed through the introduction of disorder, anger, unpredictability, or other disruptive forces. In "The Cage," the Talosians cannot maintain their mental control against anger, hatred, and thoughts of violence. Such "primitive" impulses give Pike his first doorway to freedom and, ultimately, it is the primitive and violent aspects of the human race that cause the Talosians to decide that humans are not good candidates for their purposes. Again, in "This Side of Paradise," Kirk discovers that anger and violent emotions counteract the effects of the spores and it is ultimately through inspiring aggression in the entire crew that he and Spock are able to free them from "paradise."

Time and again in the Original Series, humankind's failings, faults, and primitive nature are its saving grace. In "The Enemy Within," a Kirk without anger and aggression finds himself incapable of summoning the gumption and wherewithal to effectively execute the responsibilities of command. Only by re-absorbing his "animal" side can good Kirk hope to survive. Indeed, neither version can survive on his own. Unbridled fury and debauchery must be contained and controlled by the more rational side. The resulting intermix is virtue. Kirk's good side and his evil side must literally embrace one another in order for the captain to be made whole again.[10]

---

8. Alexander, "The Way to Eden."
9. Senensky, "This Side of Paradise."
10. Penn, "The Enemy Within."

In the episode "This Side of Paradise," the *Enterprise* goes to Omicron Ceti III, a planet settled by a colony of humans seeking a simpler life. Here, the landing party encounters spores that, when inhaled, protect their human hosts from the lethal Berthold radiation on the planet, providing them with health, longevity, and a new attitude—freedom from all want. In a thematically central scene, after almost the entire ship's complement has decided to stay on the planet, Spock (under the influence of the spores) and Elias Sandoval, the leader of the Omicron colony, attempt to convince Kirk to join them.

ELIAS: Captain, why don't you join us?

KIRK: In your own private paradise.

ELIAS: The spores have made it that.

KIRK: Where did they originate?

SPOCK: It's impossible to say. They drifted through space until they finally landed here. You see, they actually thrive on Berthold rays. The plants act as a repository for thousands of microscopic spores until they find a human body to inhabit.

ELIAS: In return, they give you complete health and peace of mind.

KIRK: That's paradise?

ELIAS: We have no need or want, Captain.

SPOCK: It's a true Eden, Jim. There's belonging and love.

KIRK: No wants. No needs. We weren't meant for that. None of us. Man stagnates if he has no ambition, no desire to be more than he is.

ELIAS: We have what we need.

KIRK: Except a challenge.

SPOCK: You don't understand, Jim, but you'll come around sooner or later. Join us. Please.

KIRK: I'm going back to the ship.[11]

This need for challenge is presented here in the context of a common theme in *Star Trek*: humankind's desire to grow and advance. Note Spock's

11. Senensky, "This Side of Paradise."

reference to Eden. If his assessment is to be taken as correct, then Kirk's words may be seen as a rejection of the concept of Eden (and, by extension, heaven) as a human paradise—at least, as it is popularly understood. *Star Trek* answers this with its own idea of paradise in twenty-third–century society. While Roddenberry's earthbound utopia may be free of war, disease, poverty, and illiteracy, the challenge set before humans is found in the stars. This concept allows the presence of both a kind of paradise and a continued human journey. Earth as created, though, could not have been dull, and heaven (or, rather, the new earth) will almost certainly be an adventure. But the concept of challenge without a struggle against our ills is difficult for our current perspective to encompass. It is against this cognitive dissonance that Roddenberry seemed to constantly battle, living in both hopeful expectation of the achievement of an ideal and in constant appreciation of the struggle it takes to get there.

In this sense, Roddenberry's imagined future tells us something about the essential necessity for life-affirming challenge to define our humanity. In essence, if we cease to challenge ourselves, to progress or advance in some form, we cease to be human. While, at our best, we strive to improve ourselves and to advance as a species, our humanity is a tarnished one and can give rise to the kind of lethargy and contentment with mere existence that "This Side of Paradise" warns against. It is perhaps for this reason— our ability to lose our own humanity by inches—that some of Star Trek's notable nonhuman or part-alien characters (Spock, Data) are best able to articulate and demonstrate what it means to be human. In "This Side of Paradise," freedom from the illusion of the spores—and thereby, freedom from a kind of bondage to them—is reached through the fostering of anger and negative emotions. The too-perfect world of the spores cannot contain the full depth and breadth of human experience and expression. Struggle, anger, and dissatisfaction: these are all essential, if unpleasant, elements of the human experience. Without them, this episode postulates, we are merely half human, too willing to give up against the promise of happiness at the cost of living truly valuable lives.

For Spock, especially, this transition is a difficult one. He gives up a sense of belonging and the chance for romance in order to return to his true self, his chosen path, and his ultimate calling. The world of the spores on Omicron Ceti III is an enticing one, but ultimately it is empty. In the same way, it is often difficult for us to abandon the things that attract us, but which pull us away from Christ. As Jesus says in the ninth chapter of Luke's gospel, "If anyone wants to become my follower, he must deny himself, take up his cross daily, and follow me. For whoever wants to save his life will lose it, but whoever loses his life for my sake will save it. For what does it benefit a person if he gains the whole world but loses or forfeits himself?"[12] Faith itself is its own adventure—its own challenge with its own sacrifices and struggles. And, though we tend to see struggle in a negative light, it is an essential element of a true, deeply engaged humanity. In that sense, the notion that either heaven or Eden is a paradise that presents no challenges or opportunities for advancement is not in harmony with the biblical concept of a restored, redeemed humanity.

In the fullness of restoration, our humanity will not be abolished like that of the inhabitants of Omicron Ceti III. Instead, it will be brought to its truest, most robust expression. Though we will no longer struggle against the deleterious effects of sin, our curiosity will be ever piqued and the world of possibilities ever open for new expressions of creativity and adventures of discovery. When we become truly restored as human beings, our human experience will be the greatest adventure we've had yet. As the closing words of *Star Trek: The Motion Picture* remind us, "The human adventure is just beginning . . .".

12. Luke 9:23–25.

3

Our Many Beliefs: Openness Toward Religion

I s the Original Series truly antireligious? Certainly, it spends a great deal of time dispelling and debunking false religions. Note, however, that the theme of these religions is consistently a manipulative, controlling, authoritarian structure. This structure is usually maintained by an imposed ignorance—through hidden information, unapproachable authority, suppression of curiosity, and even mind control, as is notable in the quasi-religious nature of the penal colony/rehabilitation center in "Dagger of the Mind." However, when it comes to sincere faith that benefits the human experience and is in harmony with basic human principles, TOS is notably tolerant and respectful, even while coming just short of embracing these religions. In "Balance of Terror," for example, Kirk conducts a wedding ceremony "in accordance with our laws and our many beliefs,"[1] one of several statements in the Original Series reflecting a variety of religions aboard the *Enterprise*. To examine this idea of religious tolerance in Star Trek, we can look at a number of key episodes of the Original Series that deal with religion and even at times with Christianity.

Roddenberry once cited "The Return of the Archons" as one of his ten favorite episodes of *Star Trek*.[2] Upon reflection, it is easy to see why. The episode manages to deal with human social structures, technology, and religion, all while staying true to Roddenberry's idea of using Earth

1. McEveety, "Balance of Terror."
2. Roddenberry, "My Favorite Voyages," 12.

analogues to tell Star Trek stories.[3] In discussions of religion in Star Trek, the episode is often cited as an example of the series and Roddenberry making a broad statement rejecting all religions as the kind of soul-killing machines of control and intimidation that we see on Beta III, the planet depicted in the episode.

Certainly Roddenberry and others have leveled such accusations at religion—Christianity in particular—at many times, often with much clear justification. However, if the episode is to be read as an outright, universal condemnation of religion, it must also be read as a similar condemnation of technology. After all, Landru is ultimately shown to be a computer that, however advanced it may be as a technological achievement, is ultimately incapable of sustaining a truly flourishing society. Dependence upon this computer has gutted the life from the planet's society. Perhaps the greatest mistake Landru ever made was leaving his people in the hands of a machine. They are free from war, but they are in bondage nonetheless. The curse of Beta III is the domination of technology—a curse that is broken when the supercomputer is destroyed. Freedom for the soul, it seems, comes in freedom from technology.

Of course, it is difficult, if not impossible, to believe that *Star Trek* would make such a blanket statement against technology. Technology is what allows its characters to function in their environments, pursue their goals, and solve many of their problems. In fact, some have claimed that Star Trek praises technology above all else. This is also an incorrect analysis, since Star Trek's stories frequently portray the perils and disastrous consequences of technology and the many inhuman goals for which it can be used. In the Trek universe, technology is neither unconditionally praised nor wholly dismissed. Therefore, a technophobic reading of this episode seems unwarranted. Instead, the episode (like many in the Trek universe) is better understood as a warning about what happens when technology is used without virtue and is too greatly depended upon.[4] Certainly warning about a particular use of technology is not the same thing as disparaging all technology.

By the same token, it seems blunt to interpret "Archons" as a universal indictment of religion. Certainly most of the religion Roddenberry had been

3. Cushman and Black, *These Are The Voyages: TOS: Season Two*.

4. The greatest working out of this lesson in Star Trek is, of course, the Borg. In fact, there are interesting resemblances to the Borg in this episode, with individuals being consumed by a mechanized collective, the Body. The phrase "You will be absorbed" seems a precursor to "You will be assimilated."

exposed to probably seemed much like Spock's description of the society on Beta III as "a soulless society" with "no spirit, no spark."[5] There is no creativity—no heart—and, therefore, a complete lack of flourishing. Kirk says as much when he counters Spock's suggestion that the Prime Directive prohibits them from interfering with the planet's social structure. "That refers to a living, growing culture," he says. "Do you think this one is?"[6] Spock's silence indicates the withdrawal of his objection. Notice that an essential missing element is creativity. Indeed, we are created to be creators.

It is also interesting to note that something as difficult—if not impossible—to scientifically describe and quantify as "spirit" could be so obvious to Star Trek's characters as important to the flourishing of a society. Because of its strongly scientific focus, it is often assumed that Star Trek is only interested in the purely rational. In reality, time and again, such ephemeral notions as "spirit" and "heart" are appealed to in Star Trek. That is because, ultimately, Star Trek is not about science or technology, except as aspects of its real focus—humanity and human nature. It doesn't take long to see that concepts like spirit, imagination, faith, courage, consciousness, love, and even justice are essential to humanity, though none of them is particularly rooted in a purely scientific understanding of humans as a species. We'll examine more of that in future chapters.

While "The Return of the Archons" is almost certainly a critique of communism, the religious imagery of the episode is impossible to miss and is arguably the prevailing tone of the society on Beta III. The Lawgivers wear monk-like, hooded robes, while followers of Landru praise his name, revere him, and speak of his gifts of peace, love, and tranquility. Some observers have gone so far as to assume this episode is a direct attack on Christianity,[7] with parallels being drawn between the "Body" of Landru and the biblical image of Christians as the Body of Christ.[8][9] Though some intentional criticism of Christianity is likely present, a direct metaphor is never clearly drawn. Still, read in this specific context, the episode is notable for its attitude toward Landru. Even as the soulless system that imposes what purports to be Landru's will is obviously viewed as evil, Landru himself is never denigrated. Landru's wisdom and his importance in Beta

---

5. Pevney, "The Return of the Archons."

6. Ibid.

7. Muir, *A History and Critical Analysis of Blake's 7*, 43.

8. Higa, "#669."

9. Mooney, "The Return of the Archons."

III's society are never questioned. In fact, Kirk's central criticism of the computerized Landru is that he lacks Landru's insight and wisdom. "I am Landru," the computer says, "I am he. All that he was, I am. His experience, his knowledge."[10] Kirk counters, "But not his wisdom. He may have programmed you, but he could not have given you a soul. You are a machine."[11] In other words, the problem with the religion of Beta III is that it has lost touch with its founder in trying to create a perfect system that rids the world of flaws by, in essence, stripping it of its humanity.[12] The people of Beta III no longer truly follow Landru. Instead, they worship a projected image of him, an echo of who he really was.

This episode seems to be saying that Christian religion often suppresses the spirit, rather than restoring it, and that the rigidity of religion misses the point of Jesus' teaching. It would also seem to suggest that our image of Christ is often merely and icon and does not reflect Jesus himself. In very brief, much of the criticism Christians have leveled at their own faith is reflected in this episode, as is the cure to which they have frequently returned. The remedy for the "frozen chosen," locked in soul-killing religion, is to return to the heart and teachings of Christ as closely and as purely as possible. Indeed, Star Trek was produced in the earliest years of the Jesus Movement, which sought just such a return to first-century Christian faith. So the critique of religion here is not only accurate, but also timely.

Beyond the mechanized formality of the religion of Beta III, though, there is another element that is equally prevalent—fear. The Lawgivers use intimidation to keep the citizens of Beta III under control and the rule of fear is frequently apparent. Reger cowers before the image of Landru, burying his head in his arms on the table, pleading to be spared from the punishment he and the *Enterprise* crew receive. Ultimately, he even recants his role in the resistance against Landru, desperately shouting, "No, no, I was wrong! I submit! I bear myself to the will of Landru!"[13] as Kirk, Spock, and Marplon plan to confront Landru in the Hall of Audiences. Marplon himself has to be persuaded against his fears by Kirk and only very hesitantly leads Kirk and Spock to Landru. These and other moments reflect

10. Perhaps intentionally, the Landru computer's words here mirror Jesus' words, "I am he," in John 18:6 and God's words to Moses, "I Am that I Am," in Exodus 3:14.

11. Pevney, "The Return of the Archons."

12. Though these are aliens, who don't technically have "humanity," they look and act human and are ultimately meant to mirror humanity.

13. Pevney, "The Return of the Archons."

a common image of American Christianity as a religion based in fear and punishment—an image to which the Jesus Movement was strongly opposed, choosing instead to focus on the love of God. This focus not only reflected a Christian resonance with the philosophical direction of the hippies, but a return to the biblical admonition against punishment and fear as hallmarks of the Christian life. In a well-known passage, shortly after his assertion that "God is love,"[14] the author of 1 John says that "There is no fear in love, but perfect love drives out fear, because fear has to do with punishment. The one who fears punishment has not been perfected in love."[15] While there is no specific appeal to love in the episode, fear is confronted head on and the affectation of peace and love is abolished along with fear on Beta III when the Landru computer is destroyed. Describing several domestic disputes and fights that have erupted on the planet since the end of Landru's control, Lieutenant Lindstrom remarks, "It may not be paradise, but it's certainly human," a description which Kirk finds to be "most promising."[16] [17] Certainly, the people of Beta III have not yet been "perfected in love," but they are at least human again and that's a start.[18] "You will know the truth," Jesus said, "and the truth will make you free."[19] The people of Beta III now know the truth and they are learning to be free.

In the same way, while Christians become understandably defensive when criticisms are leveled at Christian religion, the ability to recognize the truth that is often present in critiques such as those found in "The Return of the Archons"—and indeed, throughout the Star Trek universe—can only lead to improvement. It is very possible for an insular system like much of Christian culture to become corrupted and wayward without those on the inside ever realizing it. The ability, then, to look at one's faith and faith community objectively can help to ferret out inconsistencies and failures. As Lindstrom's remarks illustrate, the human equation is never without foibles, but a striving toward righteousness is something that both a Christian

14. 1 John 4:8.

15. Ibid.

16. Pevney, "The Return of the Archons."

17. This moment, of course, also serves as another example of the Original Series questioning the value of the concept of paradise, choosing a more human existence, rather than a "perfect" one.

18. Again, these are presumably Betans we are dealing with in this episode. But, even Lindstrom's description of their burgeoning culture as "human" leaves some question as to how much effort was put into truly making this an alien race.

19. John 8:32.

worldview and Star Trek recognize as fundamentally important to human progress. In this way, learning the truth of our own failings can help Christians—and all humans—become free.

While it is unlikely that such a detailed and specific critique was intended in this episode, the lesson is there to be mined and is one that echoes the words of Jesus, who strongly criticized religious leaders of his time for loving their rules more than God's true law and missing the point of everything God had called them to do.[20] Faith without works may be dead,[21] but works without love are pointless.[22] "The Return of the Archons," like many episodes in *Star Trek* that deal with overtly religious themes, was originated by Gene Roddenberry (he received story credit for the episode). As such, there is some evidence that a return to the teachings of Jesus and a movement from fear to love is a remedy (apart from simply abandoning religion altogether) that Roddenberry himself might have suggested for the Church in his own time—namely, in another episode that originated with Roddenberry, "Bread and Circuses."[23][24]

Conventional wisdom about "Bread and Circuses" says that the episode is about television in some way, that it's a parody of television or poking fun at television.[25] That certainly is an element of the story, however, it's honestly a very small amount that is relegated to a few lines of dialogue and the presence of the television studio and the gladiatorial combat that occurs therein. The primary focus of the story doesn't even hinge on the strange qualities of planet 892-IV, where the story takes place. Its eerie similarity to Earth is brushed off after the opening scene and its merging of twentieth-century technology and the Roman Empire is not explored very convincingly. For the most part, 892-IV looks like any other planet Starfleet might explore that happens to borrow from Roman culture. It doesn't actually feel very twentieth century at all except in the newsreel footage and in the presence of television. When the crew encounters the refugees in the desert, they have rifles, but that is really the most modern thing about them,

20. Matt 23:1–36.

21. Jas 2:26.

22. 1 Cor 13: 1.

23. Though some sources credit John Kneubuhl with writing the story for "Bread and Circuses," the story actually originated with Roddenberry. The idea that Kneubuhl wrote the story arises from a dispute over the work he did on the writing of the episode, as is made clear by Cushman and Black, *These Are the Voyages.*

24. Cushman and Black, *These Are The Voyages.*

25. Clark, *Star Trek FAQ.*

apart from the magazine Kirk flips through and the mention of cars being present. Even though Spock mentions that the planet has "power transportation" and "an excellent road system,"[26] we never see a road outside the television broadcast, or a car outside the magazine print ad.

Otherwise, it's just like a biblical epic or anything else that happens on a planet that appears in the Original Series. There is no vehicular transit. When our characters want to go somewhere, they walk there. This ends up greatly playing down the twentieth-century aspect of the episode. Certainly, there must have been production reasons for these things to be the way they were, but as a planet, except in those descriptions in the dialogue, there's nothing terrifically unique about it. It actually doesn't do a very good job of living up to the hype of merging the twentieth century and the Roman Empire. So, while observers have frequently discussed the episode in terms of the television angle and the merging of the twentieth century and the Roman Empire, these don't seem to be the focus of the episode.

In reality, the episode is about the relationships between the characters. It's about what makes Kirk and company different from Merik and his crew. Ultimately, it's really about sacrifice and redemption and the script's infamous wordplay between the words "sun" and "son." The Children of the Sun that we meet in the beginning of the episode, assumed by the *Enterprise* crew to be sun worshippers, are revealed to be the Children of the Son (of God)—that is, early Christians. They therefore bring with them an enormous package of Christian symbolism that can be read throughout the episode. Their exemplar is Flavius, the former gladiator.

Upon his arrest, we learn that he has a reputation in gladiatorial combat as a fighter and a killer. When Maximus, the centurion, tells Flavius that his first fight has been scheduled, Flavius protests, "I will not fight. I'm a Brother of the Son." Maximus cavalierly replies, "Put a sword in your hand, and you'll fight. I know you, Flavius; you're as peaceful as a bull."[27] This is an interesting exchange between these two men about the narrative that will define Flavius as a person. Maximus believes Flavius is going to be defined by fighting and killing, by being a gladiator, and Flavius insists that he will not fight.

He is forced to fight, just as Kirk, Spock, and McCoy are, but he makes a different choice. He chooses to sacrifice himself and save the strangers who he was ready to kill earlier in the episode. This is a distinctively

26. Senensky, "Bread and Circuses."
27. Ibid.

Christian act, rooted in the deepest of Christian ethics. Much the way it has in the history of biblical cinema, the sacrifice of a Christian—Flavius—mirrors the sacrifice of Jesus and one wonders if this is this is a conversion story we are seeing. Flavius, at the beginning of episode, appears to be a new believer, learning to be fully committed—a possibility suggested by his desire to kill the strangers from the *Enterprise*. "I didn't harm them, Septimus," Flavius tells the group's leader when he delivers Kirk, Spock, and McCoy, "as much as I wanted to." Septimus replies with a gentle admonishment he seems to have given Flavius many times, "Keep always in your mind, Flavius, that our way is peace."

This scene provides the first moment of identification between the philosophy of these early Christians and the crew of the *Enterprise*. McCoy remarks that they are grateful that the Children of the Son follow the way of peace, "for we are men of peace ourselves." Septimus immediately takes this as a possible sign that they are fellow believers and asks, "Oh? Are you Children of the Son?" McCoy then affirms the pluralistic nature of the Federation, in a rare discussion of its religious makeup. "Well, if you're speaking of worships of sorts," he says, "we represent many beliefs." As such expressions often do with modern Christians, McCoy's statement of pluralistic values immediately draws anger from Flavius, who retorts, "There is only one true belief!" and concludes that these outsiders must be "Roman butchers, sent here by the First Citizen." Septimus, the older and wiser believer, consistently responds to Flavius' outbursts by gently insisting on peace. "I know killing is evil," Flavius tells Septimus, "but sometimes it's necessary." Septimus simply responds, "No."

The central struggle of Flavius' character, then, is repeatedly shown to be a conflict within himself, between a warlike nature and a peaceful nature. Is he a fighter, or a man of peace? In other words, when he is pressed, will he follow the words of the Son or not?

> FLAVIUS: For seven years, I was the most successful gladiator in this province
>
> KIRK: Then you heard the word of the sun?
>
> FLAVIUS: Yes. The words of peace and freedom. It wasn't easy for me to believe. I was trained to fight. But the words, the words are true.[28]

---

28. Ibid.

Later, Flavius again refers to the words of the Son, and to his difficulty believing them. "The message of the Son, that all men are brothers, was kept from us," he says. "Perhaps I'm a fool to believe it. It does often seem that man must fight to live." But Kirk encourages him, "You go on believing it, Flavius. All men are brothers." Flavius then goes on to live—and die—as though those words are indeed true.

"The words that I have spoken to you," Jesus said, "are spirit and are life."[29] Like the words of the Son depicted in "Bread and Circuses," his words both drew people to him and repelled them. When many of his disciples left him because of what he taught, he asked the twelve, "You don't want to go away too, do you?" to which Simon Peter replied, "Lord, to whom would we go? You have the words of eternal life."[30] Flavius lives between the poles of Peter and the disciples who left Jesus. While he is drawn to the Son by "the words of peace and freedom," they are difficult for him to accept because they challenge him to fundamentally change how he views the world and his place in it. Ultimately, though, Flavius chooses to follow the Son because "the words are true."

While Flavius struggles to accept the words of the Son and questions his salvation, more lost than Flavius by far is former Federation Merchant Marine captain R. M. Merik, known on the planet as Merikus. Merik has surrendered to Proconsul Claudius Marcus, allowed himself to be bullied and his crew to be killed. He has failed in his duty as a captain and has become the whipping boy for the proconsul. The proconsul has won a victory over him and he has accepted defeat. "Would you leave us, Merikus?" Marcus says during a conversation with Kirk. "The thoughts of one man to another cannot possibly interest you." Merik quietly accepts the insult and walks away, but it may in fact be a turning point for his character, a moment when he realizes just how put down he is, as he ultimately decides to make a desperate attempt to help Kirk, Spock, and McCoy escape. In so doing, like Flavius, he loses his life. He must know that this would happen, but he still makes this last effort to save not only Kirk and his crew, but also himself. He chooses to rebel against the authorities and the manipulation that have held him down, and to rebel against the weakness within himself that would allow him to sacrifice his crew.

So, again with Merik, we see a redemption, or perhaps a conversion of sorts, that moves someone from a place surrendering to evil to an act of

29. John 6:63.
30. John 6:67–68.

self-sacrifice. Flavius, even though he is a celebrated warrior, as a gladiator, is still a slave. He fights and kills because the authorities want him to fight and kill, to risk his life for their entertainment. In the same way, Merik is also a slave. He is a captive, held where he is by the proconsul. Even though he appears to be in some form of authority or position of privilege, the truth is that he is being kept where he is so that he can be controlled, manipulated, and used, his own crew relegated to death in gladiatorial combat. Since his men are all dead, Merik really has outlived his usefulness. When the proconsul encounters Kirk, he sees fresh meat and he goes after it. Seeing this, Merik chooses to act, as Flavius does, to help save Kirk and his crew. In so doing, like Flavius, he finds a kind of redemption for himself.

The narrative that the authorities want to tell about Flavius—and want him to tell himself—no longer defines Flavius. Similarly, Merik is no longer defined by the narrative with which the proconsul has controlled him. In a story that is centered around the effects of Christian faith on a Roman world, these characters are defined by salvation wrought through self-sacrifice. This is not insignificant. In fact, this seems to be the theme of the story—the victory that is won by consistently choosing peace over war. Though the *Enterprise* could have laid waste to the planet, she did not open fire. There is no rescue effort made and no attack launched. Rather, Scotty holds to the Prime Directive of noninterference. He interferes enough with events to allow Kirk, Spock, and McCoy to get free, but does not alter the course of the planet's culture. So these three characters—Flavius, Merik, and Scotty—all win victories against a very powerful opponent by holding true to their core values, regardless of what they want to do. They set aside their immediate impulses and instead stay true to a code of honor and peace, winning the victory, in spite of the odds. This, again, is a very Christian concept, that the last will be first, that the unlikely will be victorious. So, the words of the Son, the Prime Directive, and a core concept that all human beings are brothers and sisters are really at the heart of the episode. The core story comes down to the conversation on the bridge at the end of the episode.

> McCOY: Captain, I see on your report Flavius was killed. I am sorry. I liked that huge sun worshiper.

> SPOCK: I wish we could have examined that belief of his more closely. It seems illogical for a sun worshiper to develop a philosophy of total brotherhood. Sun worship is usually a primitive superstition religion.

UHURA: I'm afraid you have it all wrong, Mister Spock, all of you. I've been monitoring some of their old-style radio waves, the empire spokesman trying to ridicule their religion. But he couldn't. Don't you understand? It's not the sun up in the sky. It's the Son of God.

KIRK: Caesar and Christ. They had them both. And the word is spreading only now.

McCOY: A philosophy of total love and total brotherhood.

SPOCK: It will replace their imperial Rome, but it will happen in their twentieth century.

KIRK: Wouldn't it be something to watch, to be a part of? To see it happen all over again?[31]

It is seems as if Kirk encourages Flavius' religious belief because it contains a humanistic truth, possibly in the hope that it will lead Flavius into humanism. Isn't it interesting that most Christians don't seem to encourage beliefs that are in line with Christian values, regardless of what worldview they come from, in similar hopes? "There are many good, helpful values contained in [religious] beliefs," Roddenberry said. "How could I condemn them?"[32]

From these examples, it is clear that the kind of religion TOS admires and respects is the kind that is life-giving, peacefully oriented, and essentially humanistic. It also most often resembles or directly mirrors Judaism and "pure," first-century Christianity. TOS, it seems, always comes back to biblical essentials, with the possible exception of its conception of God.

31. Senensky, "Bread and Circuses."
32. Fern, *Last Conversation*, 123.

4

We Find the One Quite Adequate: God and God Figures

Very technically, the Original Series' conception of God is the human heart, or the human spirit. TOS never claims this, but given the undergirding of Roddenberry's own theology, this is a safe assumption. The gods of Earth's religion and mythology are constantly dispelled. Though Apollo is a very powerful alien being, he is not worthy of our worship. No god is.

"Mankind has no need for gods," Kirk says in "Who Mourns for Adonais?" "We find the one quite adequate." This line is an anomaly. It could easily be construed as a statement of monotheism for Star Trek. This would, however, be an irresponsible reading. There is no other statement in all of Star Trek that espouses monotheism. In fact, there are plenty of statements that put theism and religion squarely in the realm of mythology.

However, it should not be dismissed out of hand. If nothing else, it shows that, to some level, someone involved with the episode wanted at least a passing reference to monotheism. The important question here is: was this a function of NBC's Standards and Practices, as is generally assumed? As this episode is the fourth of the second season, when Roddenberry still had final say on and rewrote, to some extent, every episode, it would be interesting to know exactly why this line was approved by him for the final episode, or if he was overruled.

There is also the matter of the language of the line to be considered. Kirk says, "We find the *one* quite adequate," but fails to specifically identify who (or what) "the one" is. While the line may exist in order to satiate nervous network brass (who famously objected to Spock's "satanic" appearance), it is a concession that could easily be made with the unspoken caveat that "the one" is nonspecific enough to fit within the bounds of acceptable Star Trek theology. "The one" could very well be the creative force or "God-thing" to which Roddenberry ascribed the creation of the universe and the origin of the human imagination. It could also refer to the human spirit, humanity as a whole, or "the All," to which Roddenberry frequently referred as the ultimate destiny of all human beings. Whether "clout" or "socio-organism," "the one" could easily be understood as a reference to Roddenberry's god-concept, regardless of its description or manifestation.

Similarly, the reference to "the Maker of all things" in the episode "Metamorphosis" is ambiguous, even if a largely Judeo-Christian audience would easily interpret it as a reference to Yahweh. Roddenberry himself said that our growing scientific understanding of the universe revealed an order that was unlikely to have happened by accident. "To me," he said, "it would be more incredible that all of this precision of mathematics and astronomy and down to the quark and wherever it goes beyond that, could just have . . . happened."[1] The god-thing of his theology is not just a spiritual essence and muse for creative endeavors, but a creative force responsible for causing the cosmos to be. Therefore, even if his god is not a person to be worshipped, "Maker of all things" is an apt description of it.

If indeed these fleeting references to a true deity are concessions to network pressure, they are made in such a way as to be interpreted according to the viewer's beliefs. To a Christian, then, they are a glimmer of Christian monotheism. To a pagan, they can refer to a personification of nature or Gaia. And, to an atheist, they are anomalous by-products of a church-dominated, conservative culture, to be discarded as outweighed by the numerous false gods and destructive religions of Star Trek's narrative body.

I would contend, however, that, were they wholly antithetical to Star Trek as Roddenberry saw it, he would have fought vehemently against their inclusion in the scripts of these episodes, as he famously did when it was suggested that the *Enterprise* have a chaplain.[2] It is easy to read TOS' repetition of the theme of a false god as a universal statement of atheism, but a more careful analysis suggests that these false gods and the destructive religions they inspire are attacks against certain conceptions of God. In fact,

1. Adelstein, *Up Close and Personal.*
2. Alexander, "Interview of Gene Roddenberry."

it may be more accurate to say that these gods are incidental to a critique of religion.

Consistently, there is room in Star Trek for some form of spirituality, religion, and even God, as long as it is not destructive to—and, more importantly, is beneficial to—the human spirit. What Roddenberry reacts against, time and again, is the idea of God as religion and, by extension, the kind of God he feels religion represents. Therefore, if the God of an alien religion is a malevolent computer, it is because the kind of religion practiced (controlling, soul-killing, joyless) suggests such a deity as its focus.

A tormenting, demanding religion can only come from a tormenting, demanding God. Roddenberry rejected such a view of God because it resulted in religion that was opposed to the flourishing of the human spirit. He judged the deity of a religion on the basis of the religion it produced, concluding that any truly divine essence could not possibly create an environment that was hostile to human growth and development. The takedown of the gods in Star Trek is a process of rejecting what God is not and, in a quite unspoken fashion, embracing what, in Roddenberry's view, God is.

It was Roddenberry's conception of God that led to his rejection of most all religion and the understanding of God that, in his view, must necessarily undergird them. The all-creative force in which he believed and which he saw reflected in the universe and in the human race, could not be the author of a humanity-phobic religion. It was therefore not Roddenberry's atheism that caused him to reject religion, but his theism.

The only "atheist" statements Roddenberry ever made were really anti-religious and the only statements he ever made about God were defining his own conception of God and rejecting more common ones. While his rejections of religion are frequently pointed to as evidence of his atheism, the truth seems to be that he rejected religion precisely because was a theist.

These episodes rejected religion—particularly of a certain type—but would seem to, in small ways, leave the door open to some form of theism. Of course, the obvious exception to the rule is "Bread and Circuses." While it is easy to dismiss a faint appeal to monotheism in "Who Mourns for Adonais?," "Bread and Circuses" is much harder to ignore or explain away—though most commentators usually do. If it is the fluke such sources as the book *Star Trek FAQ* claim it to be, why is it coauthored by Roddenberry himself? And though, as *FAQ* points out, the ringing endorsement of Christianity in the episode is "reserved for the episode's epilogue,"[3] this is no reason to set it aside as meaningless. In fact, the final scene of "Bread and Circuses" serves as an interpretive lens for the rest of the episode. Taken in the context of the concluding revelation, several elements of the episode take on new meaning—the commitment to nonviolence among the followers of the Son, Flavuis' insistence that "the words are true," Kirk's admonition that he "go on believing them," and Flavuis' willingness to sacrifice himself for Kirk and company, to name a few.

In fact, in light of the final scene, the entire episode becomes an endorsement of Christian virtues. It is important to note, however, that while the episode identifies Christ as "the Son of God," it does so only with reference to the beliefs of Christians. What it espouses are the ways in which the teachings of Christ are in harmony with Star Trek's philosophical grounding. "A philosophy of total love and total brotherhood," McCoy calls it, emphasizing the core values with which Star Trek whishes to associate over against later religious developments. "The words are true," Flavuis says, and Kirk agrees: "All men are brothers," he affirms. It is the burgeoning, first-century Christian hope with which Star Trek here identifies. Rather than, as even the episode's director Ralph Senensky has done, relegate the episode's inclusion of Christian imagery to a circumstantial glitch of historical happenstance,[4] let us consider that, with Star Trek's creator's name on its byline, "Bread and Circuses" represents an intentional commentary on the teachings of Jesus, their harmony with Star Trek philosophy and, by extension, their dissonance with religion as Roddenberry saw it. Unlike the aforementioned passing reference to the doctrine of salvation in which he did not believe in *Have Gun, Will Travel*,[5] "Bread and Circuses" stands as an entire episode whose narrative is constructed, in no small part, around ideas in which Roddenberry clearly did believe, which also goes to particular lengths to specifically link those values with the teachings of Jesus. In light, again, of the dichotomy between the religion and its central figure that is drawn in "The Return of the Archons," it seems perfectly consistent with Roddenberry's worldview and methods that he could praise the good that he saw in the teachings of Jesus and the civilizing influence they had on the world without decreasing one degree his distaste for and dissatisfaction with religion—and, in particular, the Christian religion.

3. Clark, *Star Trek FAQ*.

4. In a telephone interview with the author.

5. Recounted in the previous chapter.

Ultimately, the episode is not at all dissimilar to many others in the series. Firstly, it is one of many "Earth analogue" episodes, wherein the Enterprise crew encounters a planet similar to Earth—usually so similar as to seriously strain credibility. While this is usually an excuse to reuse sets, props, and costumes from other productions in order to save money, this episode also uses the Earth analogue trope to comment on modern television, as well as to explore Christianity.

Secondly, and perhaps more importantly, "Bread and Circuses" mirrors other *Star Trek* episodes in terms of its overall narrative and thematic structure. Specifically, it mirrors the structure commonly used in antireligious episodes; the crew beams down to a planet and finds it in the grip of an inhumane, totalitarian regime. They try not to get involved, but are captured and thrown in with the planet's few dissidents. The crew then mounts some level of rebellion in order to escape and either destroys said regime or religion, or sets things in motion so that the rebellious faction has a good chance of doing so.

While it shares many qualities with any number of nonreligious, oppressive forces against which Kirk and company contend, it is not insignificant that the Roman Empire depicted in this episode reflects many attitudes and actions often seen in the series' various false religions. While it could be argued that the opposing force in this episode is Christianity as a matter of historical reality, it seems unnecessary to tell a story about a Roman planet, except to make this very comment. Indeed, on a planet where imperial Rome rules in the age of television, any rebellious group could have been invented. However, the episode's script hinges on the dichotomy of "S-U-N" vs. "S-O-N" and goes to great lengths to highlight the philosophical similarities between Star Trek and the earliest forms of Christian faith—particularly the teachings of Jesus regarding nonviolence and love of one's neighbor.

Interestingly, the values and actions of the Roman Empire in the episode echo exactly the actions of the religious groups that Roddenberry so frequently condemned, which actions are exemplified by a Christianity forged in the crucible of the Holy Roman Empire. Could the concept of an Imperial Rome that persists into the twentieth century be a commentary on the ways in which such authoritarian mentalities have infected and corrupted "pure" Christian faith and the original teachings of Christ? If so, it might be helpful to understand Roddenberry's perception of Christ and his teaching. In 1985, Roddenberry described Jesus to Terrance Sweeney in this way:

> To me the whole joy and glory of Jesus is the fact that he is one of us. It seems to me that the whole statement of the New Testament is, "Hey, man, you can too, because I was born like you. I died like you. There's nothing special about me that's not special in you. And I'm offering you both." And I think the divinity thing is bullshit because they've taken away from the glorious, divine message that he kept saying over and over again. Divine, yes. But so are we. I think that's what he was saying: "So are you."[6]

Clearly, Roddenberry had some level of admiration for Jesus, but this episode should hardly be read as a wholesale endorsement of religion. Certainly, he praises Jesus' core philosophy and the positive role religion had in the formation of Western civilization. The civilizing influence of religion was similarly praised in the episode, "Who Mourns for Adonais?" After sending the alien being worshipped on Earth as Apollo to his apparent demise by refusing to worship him, the victory rings hollow, as the crew's act of fighting for their own survival has resulted in the loss of an ancient and unique alien being.

McCOY: I wish we hadn't had to do this.

KIRK: So do I. They gave us so much. The Greek civilization, much of our culture and philosophy came from a worship of those beings. In a way, they began the Golden Age. Would it have hurt us, I wonder, just to have gathered a few laurel leaves?

While the episode was written by Gilbert Ralston, it seems to reflect something of Roddenberry's own relationship to religion. Though he had no problem rejecting it for the most part, he seems to have held, to some degree, what Italian film director Pier Paolo Pasolini referred to as "a nostalgia for a belief."[7] While concepts of God in *Star Trek* may stray further from biblical constructs than its discussions of religion, a sense of humankind's grappling with the concept of the Divine is a frequently visited idea and one which lands less in the realm of atheism than is often perceived. Like its focus on paradises and religions, *Star Trek* tears down the false gods, while perhaps leaving room for whatever true Divinity may remain.

---

6. Sweeney, *God &*, 19.

7. Flatley, "One Man's God, Another Man's Devil," D15.

5

False Gods,
False Paradises,
and False Religions

The existence of false paradises in Star Trek does not mean that paradise does not and cannot exist, but the consistent theme of these episodes is that a true paradise cannot come at the cost of our humanity. A path that leaves our humanity intact, however less ideal, is always preferable to a paradise arrived at by artificial or totalitarian means. Ultimately, a garden that asks us to be submissive, docile, or tame, to be dependent upon anyone but ourselves, is unacceptable in Star Trek. It also appears to be ultimately unattainable. No matter what ills our society can rid itself of, there is always our stubborn, imperfect humanity, making a mess of paradise again. But that, it seems, is preferable. Roddenberry would rather have us living in a paradise in process that is truly human than in one that kills our lovely, limited humanity. It is that paradox that makes the promises of Star Trek's future seem both grounded and hopeful, and so far out of reach. As youth pastor and writer Scott Higa notes,

> Star Trek's version of a utopia built solely by human hands is great, but it's more fictitious than [Star Wars'] invisible force holding the universe together. Humanity isn't capable of curing its ills and creating paradise; only Jesus can do that, which is why we look forward to his return.[1]

The sense in Star Trek that humans must attain paradise on their own connotes distrust in a divine entity. This distrust is likely rooted in a tendency to

1. Higa, "#1245."

ascribe human faults to God. It seems impossible to Roddenberry that a God who is outside us and is all-powerful can be trusted. Whatever he promises us, if it entails our submitting to him in any way, it is a dangerous compromise that will lead to soul-killing totalitarianism. Roddenberry seems unable to conceive of a God who is both wholly loving and omnipotent. He fears that God is not good and will abuse any power we give him. The only divinity he trusts is that which resides in us. This, again, does not reject the idea of God, but simply defines God differently. In the same way that false paradises do not necessarily mean that paradise is unattainable, false gods do not necessarily mean that God—in some form—does not exist.

In that context, Star Trek's false god episodes are not necessarily atheistic. They don't necessarily say that God does not exist, just that the being in question is not God. Therefore, one could see these episodes as depicting various ways in which a being may fall short of qualifying as God. One could then theoretically begin to construct a Star Trek definition of God from the opposites of each false god's flaws. But perhaps it's simpler than that. Perhaps they represent a more unified picture based on what they all have in common: they all present God as a person. Perhaps all the false gods of Star Trek are a continued, consistent declaration that God—whatever "it" is—is not, cannot, and must not be a person. For Roddenberry, personhood was a limitation that could not possibly describe the "god-thing" of his imagination. He simply could not conceive of a God who is a person, but is not also flawed and limited. A limitless, perfect, personal, and wholly good God seems to have been simply beyond his imagination.

Also rooted in this essential distrust of the external Divine—or, perhaps more accurately, the cause of this distrust in Roddenberry's own experience—is a distrust of religion. Roddenberry saw religion as primarily manipulative—a man-made method for reaching a divinity that could be found within. Again ascribing human foibles to God, Roddenberry asked, "How can I take seriously a god-image that requires that I prostrate myself every seven days and praise it? That sounds to me like a very insecure personality."[2] Of course, Jesus addressed this very idea when he admonished the religious leaders of his day that "The Sabbath was made for people, not people for the Sabbath."[3] In other words, the practice of resting and worshipping every seven days was established by God as a means of

2. Van Hise, *The Man Who Created Star Trek*, 7.
3. Mark 2:27.

regularly renewing the human soul, not of stroking God's fragile ego, as Roddenberry imagined.

As discussed in the previous chapter, even as Roddenberry was puzzled by Christian doctrine and largely turned off by religion, he still saw its benefits. He even imagined that the good things he saw in religion might one day exist without the beliefs and doctrines he saw as superstitious. "I would hope," he told Yvonne Fern, "that [churches] would go away of their own volition. That people would find it in themselves to write great music and gather and sing and look at lovely pictures and statues and such . . . . Or bow and kneel because they felt like it. Or do any of those other things I admire in Catholic and Jewish ceremonies."[4] This, of course, raises the question of why Roddenberry thought people might want to bow or kneel if he had no concept of a God that should be worshipped. He seemed to want the results of religion without its central purpose and aim—namely, worshipping God.

Roddenberry saw bowing and worshipping a god as demeaning. Scripture sees worship as elevating, as followers of Christ are made sons and daughters of God and encouraged to "boldly approach the throne of Grace."[5] But worship is not just confined to religion, nor is Star Trek's relevance to a Christian life and worldview. Indeed, it is perhaps when Star Trek is not discussing religion at all that it has its most important connection to Christian faith.

4. Fern, *Last Conversation*, 120.

5. Heb 4:16.

6

Last Battlefields and Neighbor Love

In 1959, Gene Roddenberry was honored by the American Baptist Convention with an award for "skillfully writing Christian truth and the application of Christian principles into commercial, dramatic TV scripts."[1] Roddenberry graciously accepted the award, despite having had no such intentions. Long predating *Star Trek*, the honor was likely inspired by his work on *Have Gun, Will Travel*, a series for which he had, as mentioned in the previous section of this book, made at least one overt allusion to Christianity. Still, the mention of "the application of Christian principles" seems to allude to the idea that it was not just outright religious references that caught the eye of the convention, but a philosophical and moral grounding with which its members clearly resonated. That moral parity with Christianity was echoed again shortly thereafter. Following Roddenberry's recognition by the American Baptist Convention, and possibly based on the assumption that Roddenberry's acceptance indicated that he was a Christian, John M. Gunn, head of the National Council of Churches' broadcasting and film commission, began a long correspondence with Roddenberry about creating a television series based on that very idea of teaching Christian principles through broadcast media. Roddenberry seemed to entertain the idea, so long as he could focus on values he shared with those of a Christian perspective. But he was interested in making a living as well and, perhaps uncomfortable with the fact that he might be leading Gunn on with regard to his actual beliefs, he penned a clear statement to Gunn. "But you must understand," he wrote, "that I am a complete

1. Alexander, *Star Trek Creator*, 167.

pagan, and consume enormous amounts of bread, having found the Word more spice than nourishment, so I am interested in a statement couched in dollars and cents of what this means to the Roddenberry treasury." This ended his exchange with Gunn.[2]

Perhaps this was an act of self-sabotage on Roddenberry's part—a mercy killing for a project that was, if he was honest with himself, a step beyond what he was comfortable with in terms of religious association. Still, the "spice" of the Word was one with which he continued to season his scripts, all the way up through *Star Trek*. Biblical references abound in the Original Series, only a few of which have been recounted here. Still, as likely noticed by the American Baptist Convention, it is not just these allusions that echo a Christian worldview, but also much of the series' core philosophy. Of course, that philosophy is a dirty word in today's evangelical subculture—humanism.

For most evangelicals and many other Christians, Christianity and humanism are seen as utterly incompatible, with many going so far as to paint humanism as Christianity's chief enemy. All humanism is immediately labeled as "secular" and "atheistic." But this very limited perspective forgets that many of the great Christian thinkers and theologians—from Origen and Justin Martyr to John Locke and John Calvin—were part of a movement known as Christian humanism, a Christian worldview grounded in "the belief that human freedom, individual conscience, and unencumbered rational inquiry are compatible with the practice of Christianity or even intrinsic in its doctrine," thus representing "a philosophical union of Christian faith and classical humanist principles."[3] Those principles, such as human dignity and beauty (reflected in the Christian doctrine of humans as *Imago Dei*—the image of God) and human potential (reflected in Christ's words that his disciples would do greater things than he had done[4] and achieve great unity[5]), are reflected in much of Christian thought, from the very foundations of the Protestant reformation, up through modern Christian scholars like G. K. Chesterton and C. S. Lewis.[6]

For many modern Christians, any positive emphasis on humanity is, at the very least, uncomfortable. The schismatic view of contemporary

2. Ibid., 169.
3. "Christian Humanism."
4. John 14:12.
5. John 17:20–21.
6. "Christian Humanism."

religion separates spirit from flesh and "secular" from "sacred," failing to see the beauty of God at work in all creation, especially and chiefly in humanity. Obsessed with the fallen, broken state of humanity, Christians often forget that—fractured and marred though it may be—the image of God still resides in human beings. So repugnant to many of us is our human nature that we live in a state of constantly denying its needs, its beauty, and its purpose. A deeper, more holistic view, however, recognizes that God created us as humans to be humans and not anything else. If we can deeply explore what it means to be human, then and only then can we discover what it means to be human to the glory of God.

This far more positive view of our humanity can be traced back, not just to Christian theologians and philosophers throughout the centuries, but to Paul and even to Christ himself. Paul's emphasis on human liberty under Christ and freedom from the "curse of the law"[7] reflects the reaction of Renaissance humanism against Catholic authoritarianism, favoring individual freedom above religious dogmatism. Paul emphasized equality under Christ[8] and the inclusion of the Gentiles,[9] an act of radical openness in what was then viewed as an exclusively Jewish group. This inclusion of the outcast reflects Jesus' parable known as the story of the Good Samaritan,[10] often cited as an example of Jesus' humanistic teachings. Certainly, a view of universal human dignity leads to a philosophy that even the most despised (such as the Samaritans) are capable of deep human kindness and that those in need (such as the man beaten and left for dead in the story) are worthy of help, even if they are ones who despise you. But, most simply, this belief in human dignity, beauty, and potential is reflected in Jesus' most essential teaching: "Love the Lord your God with all your heart, with all your soul and with all your mind," and "Love your neighbor as yourself. All the law and the prophets depend on these two commandments."[11]

Star Trek certainly teaches neighbor love, as identified by Yvonne Fern in her *Last Conversation* with Gene Roddenberry. "I can't believe we're comparing *Star Trek* to a religious ceremony," Roddenberry said of Fern's tack at one point, "You're driving me crazy . . . we don't tell people *what* to think." But Fern insists that Roddenberry does. "You tell them to love thy neighbor.

7. Gal 3:13.
8. Gal 3:28.
9. Rom 3:29.
10. Luke 10:25–37.
11. Matt 22:37–40.

You really do, Gene. That's a commandment if I ever heard one. You tell them that violence is wrong, that handicaps are acceptable, that unity is a better goal than divisiveness. All precepts I learned as part of Catholicism." Roddenberry objects to the idea that *Star Trek* teaches precepts. "No," he replies, "We point out to them that the consequence of loving thy neighbor is that a more loving world results. They can choose to participate in the creation of that world or not. We tell them that violence breeds violence and that doing unto others as they would be done by produces different results. We don't," he insists, "tell them that they must do this or that."[12] This statement shows us that Roddenberry indeed saw *Star Trek* as a conduit for the biblical idea of neighbor love, but it also demonstrates his assumption that the "Christian" way to teach this idea is "do it or else." This unfortunate misunderstanding of Christian morality as a list of strictly enforced rules drove Roddenberry away from the faith, but his moral core, formed by family and church, remained largely intact and he found it reflected best in humanism. This should come as no surprise, as both Christian ethics and humanism resolve to a single idea: neighbor love. And neighbor love is essential to Star Trek—so essential, in fact, that Original Series and Animated Series writer David Gerrold once wrote, "The primary philosophy in Star Trek, stripped of everything else, was 'Love one another.' I think Jesus might have said something like that once too."[13] Indeed, he did.[14]

In recent times, however, Christians have frequently failed miserably at this central calling. As author and Biola University President Barry H. Corey recently wrote, evangelical culture "has too often opted for boycotts over reconciliation and culture wars over common-good collaborations. We're often more interested in building revengeful walls than relational bridges. When we could be on the streets serving neighbors, we are on social media rattling sabers. We have used our hands less to serve than to shake our fists. We've used our voices far more than we've used our ears." Christians, Corey says, "have disregarded God's call for his people 'to do justice, and to love kindness, and to walk humbly with your God' (Micah 6:8). Sadly we have often been perpetrators of injustice, exemplars of unkindness and citadels of hubris . . . .When we bypass or devalue a relationship in favor of being right, we cheapen the image of God in our fellow

---

12. Fern, *Last Conversation*, 121.

13. Gerrold, email message to author, July 29, 2013.

14. John 15:12, John 15:17.

human beings."[15] Corey's Christian and humanistic call against "the caustic course of our culture" is for priority to be placed on "the virtue of kindness in the context of relationships." "If the followers of the one who said 'love your enemies and pray for those who persecute you' (Matt. 5:44) do not take the higher road of countercultural kindness," Corey asks, "who will?"[16]

In Star Trek, all the various groups of humans and even a number of alien species, in all their varieties, have a remarkable unity in the Federation, a unity which comes from gathering around common ideals and a common purpose. It is the kind of unity Jesus himself prayed that his followers would have, and that Christians have failed at horribly for centuries. If Christ really is the one who will ultimately bring all of humanity together, shouldn't his followers be able to find more camaraderie amongst themselves, as they come together around Christ? Perhaps it is not Christ who fails to unify us, but we who fail to seek and embrace the unity to which we are called. Star Trek peoples are able to work together because of shared values of mutual understanding. They focus on the common good, personal liberty, and respect for all life forms, no matter how different they may be. Or, in very brief, they love their neighbors.

Neighbor love is so fundamental to what it means to be a follower of Christ that Jesus places it second only to love of God, though, by implication, he seems to say that they are inextricable, one from the other. In this sense, Star Trek may have a better grasp on, and be a more potent example of, a lived-out gospel than much of the modern church world has been able to muster. Where Star Trek demonstrates neighbor love, the institutional church lashes out at its neighbor. Where Star Trek seeks to defend others, the institutional church seeks to defend itself. Where Star Trek's fundamental vision is a better world for all, the institutional church fails to show how it improves the world for anyone. The Christian gospel is failing in our culture because we do not believe it. In fact, we don't even know what it is. We've so strongly focused on how faith in Jesus saves individuals from hell, that we have failed to show what he saves them to—that following Jesus here and now is beneficial to the individual and to the broader human community. We've failed to learn and demonstrate how the gospel makes us better human beings and better neighbors, largely because we've forgotten that it's supposed to.

15. Corey, "'I'd like to punch him in the face.'"
16. Ibid.

The ideas driving *Star Trek* come to the core of universal, human struggles and values. Because of that, and because the times, places and technologies of *Star Trek* are mostly unencumbered by immediate historical references or cultural trends, the stories and characters reach out and meet us where we are in unique and sometimes surprising ways. This timelessness was designed into the show from Gene Roddenberry's initial conception for that very reason—when we can view issues of human relevance apart from cultural trappings and political ideologies, we can often see them through entirely new eyes.

The vibrancy and immediacy of the *Star Trek* narrative was demonstrated to me years ago as I spoke with a magazine editor about his experience of the movement for the civil rights of black Americans in the 1960s. As a boy growing up in white America during that period, his television continually brought him images of protests, riots, and armed police forces with dogs and batons turning fire hoses on men, women, and children because of their race. Confronted with such disturbing imagery, my friend asked the nuns at his conservative Catholic school, "What's going on? What's this all about?" The nuns emphatically replied, "Those niggers just don't know their place."

But later at home, on his family's black-and-white television, he saw the original broadcast of the now-classic *Star Trek* episode "Let That Be Your Last Battlefield." In the episode, a species is divided between those whose faces are white on the right and black on the left and those who are black on the right and white on the left. Bele, black on the right side, is pursuing Lokai, black on the left. To the *Enterprise* crew, these facial distinctions are inconsequential. "I fail to see the significant difference," Kirk says.[17] But Bele and Lokai are locked in mortal hatred of one another. Even after they arrive at their home planet to find that no one is left alive, they refuse to give up fighting one another. I asked my friend if the episode changed his perspective on racism and civil rights. "Oh, you bet it did!" he exclaimed, "Right then and there!" And, thanks be to God, he hasn't been the same since.

As he described watching that episode and reading in it a deeper message of justice and peace that spoke to his heart, the power of that moment for him seemed as immediate as the day he saw it. In that moment, *Star Trek* was not a fifty-year-old television program. It was a message of human compassion that changed my friend's heart and its effect was as present

17. Taylor, "Let That Be Your Last Battlefield."

and current in his life as ever. As I thought more on my friend's story, I had to wonder what would have happened if those nuns, who likely shielded themselves from such "secular" fare, had watched "Let That Be Your Last Battlefield." Would they have been moved as my friend was? Would their hearts have been pricked as was his? I would hope so. Because at that time, *Star Trek* was doing a better job of representing the gospel to its culture than were that school's cloistered sisters, who were supposed to have dedicated their lives to Jesus.

While racism is still with us, it would be instructive to consider who the "other" might be in our world, in our culture, in our personal lives and prejudices. Who might be the person we see as so different and detestable, who, to an alien visitor, might appear to be just another human? How can we disagree with them, but behave in a compassionate manner? Are our actions promoting justice and equality or injustice and disparity? Any time Christians rejoice in reduced rights or injustice or inequality for our neighbors, we fail to love our neighbors as ourselves, to do to them what we would have them do to us. In so doing, we fall short of Christ's call to love—a call we can find anew in a science fiction television program called *Star Trek*. Perhaps the central human value Star Trek discusses is how we as humans deal with "the other." This core philosophy, which David Gerrold articulated with the words of Jesus ("Love one another"), is the central calling of the Christian life. This simple shift of moving from "othering" to "one-anothering" will not obliterate our differences, but it will help us to see the image of God in every human being, to see neighbors instead of enemies, to "seek out new life" in "new civilizations" of compassion and kindness.

SECTION 3

The Gospel According to the Animated Series

1

Star Trek, Season Four

S*tar Trek: The Animated Series* (or *The Animated Adventures of Gene Roddenberry's Star Trek*, as it was originally known) is rarely mentioned in discussions of Star Trek. The franchise is frequently described as comprising "five television series." If the oft-ignored sixth series (second, chronologically) is discussed at all, it is in passing, as a small curio, an anomaly hardly worth serious discussion. Writer and associate producer Dorothy "D.C." Fontana, a veteran of the Original Series, feels differently. "I've always felt it was part of *Star Trek*," she says, "And a very important part that has been long overlooked . . . . It was the further adventures. It was the fourth season, that we didn't get to do in live action, but we did get to do in animation."[1] The cast and crew of TAS did not set out to make a parody or a kids' show, but to make *Star Trek*. All the core actors from the Original Series (except Walter Koenig, the victim of a small budget) reprised their roles. Many of the same writers returned, including Fontana and David Gerrold. Several of the series' writers, such as Samuel A. Peeples, had already written for the Original Series, while others—some, respected science fiction writers—had been selected to write *Star Trek* episodes or had wanted to write for *Star Trek* before the first series was canceled, with some of the TAS scripts having even been slated for production as part of the live action series.

Of course, there were significant differences that presented new challenges, but these often opened up new opportunities. The series is short—just twenty-two episodes—and each episode is twenty-four minutes in length. This made for much more efficient storytelling with less exposition. Its quicker pace delivers a lot more excitement, with stories that are just

---

1. Fontana et al., *Star Trek: The Animated Series* DVD special features.

as interesting as those in the Original Series. The fat has certainly been trimmed, often for the better. The series contains not a single turbolift ride—and they are hardly missed. Another advantage was that the series was animated. Because the studio, Filmation, used their limited animation technique, which reused character plates and stock movements for similar scenes (of running, talking, etc.), there was a great deal of latitude in the series' tiny budget for innovation—the kind of innovation that often eluded TOS. (Though TAS' budget was the highest for a cartoon at the time, it was still small by TOS standards.)

In the Original Series, sets and costumes were frequently borrowed from other productions at Desilu and Paramount in order to cut production costs. This resulted in sometimes interesting but often tiresome "Earth analogue" episodes. Instead of encountering anything resembling an alien on anything like an alien planet, the away team would meet humanoids living on, say, a 1930s Chicago gangland planet, an avant-garde Old West planet, a Nazi Germany planet, and so on. While some of these episodes still manage to be fun and even thought provoking, these episodes have the sum total effect of starving the imagination for the "strange new worlds" promised at the beginning of each episode. Not so in TAS. Here, our intrepid *Trek* writers could imagine aliens that looked like Aztec snake gods or strange, wormlike Snuffleupagi, or, as in the famous David Gerrold-penned episode "Bem," a being who could dismember himself at will and operate his body parts independently. Notably, the episode "Bem" was originally considered for the third season of the Original Series but was abandoned due to the technical difficulties of bringing that character to the screen.[2] The Animated Series, however, greatly expanded opportunities for the kinds of strange creatures and aliens that could be depicted and allowed ideas that could previously only be imagined to come to life. Bizarre, beautiful, physics-ignoring ideas could be spun, as each episode was limited only by the boundaries of ink and paint. This also meant the opportunity to meet countless new characters and marvel at the vocal talent of James Doohan (who voices over sixty of them) as well as those of Nichelle Nichols, Majel Barrett, and George Takei, who also supply numerous character voices. The adventures are exciting and fun, unburdened by the constraints of live action and the orders of up to twenty-nine episodes in a season. "None of us

2. Gerrold, "Audio Commentary for 'Bem.'"

ever said 'cartoon,'" Fontana recounts. "Never. So, we were going to do *Star Trek* in animation."[3]

The series has its weak episodes. "The Jihad" and "The Slaver Weapon" go too far afield of typical *Star Trek* stories and manage to be painfully dull in the process. (Fontana and company may have never said "cartoon," but it's hard to describe these episodes as anything but cartoonish.) At its best, though, TAS allows further exploration of themes from the Original Series and insights into its characters. Most famously, the time-hopping, causal-loop–creating "Yesteryear," written by Fontana, gave viewers the opportunity to learn about Spock's childhood on Vulcan and provided the most detailed vision of Vulcan culture and society since the Original Series episode "Amok Time." The episode is so well respected that Mike Sussman, writer and producer for *Star Trek Enterprise*, leaned heavily on its design elements and story components when writing episodes on Vulcan for his series.[4] The Animated Series also introduced an early version of the holodeck, a staple of twenty-fourth–century Trek,[5] and Kirk's middle name, Tiberius.[6] For my purposes, there are a few episodes in the series that stand out as exemplars in discussions of religion and human progress. They also happen to feature some of the series' most unusual and interesting alien life forms.

---

3. Fontana et al., *Star Trek: The Animated Series* DVD special features.
4. Ibid.
5. Reed, "The Practical Joker."
6. Reed, "Bem."

2

Gods and Monsters

How do we respond in Star Trek when met by a far advanced species—even one that claims to be a god? In the Animated Series, at least, we do it with a surprising amount of humility and respect. That is, unless said being is calling for our worship. Attitudes toward advanced beings and encounters with gods in space color the narratives of three notable episodes of the Animated Series: "The Eye of the Beholder," "Bem," and "How Sharper Than a Serpent's Tooth."

The giant, slug-like, and tentacled Lactrans of Lactra VII are highly intelligent, telepathic zookeepers. And Kirk, Spock, and McCoy are the latest additions to their zoo. Like many episodes of the Original Series, "The Eye of the Beholder" emphasizes the limited nature of humans, in comparison with other more advanced species. Rather than demeaning humans, however, this story device seems designed to open up the future potential of humanity, and to emphasize the importance of our tendency toward growth and progress. While humbling us in the face of supremely advanced intelligence, it also tells us that we have something to strive for and the ability to reach greater levels of advancement than we currently have. This may seem, at first blush, counter to a humanistic philosophy that focuses on and exalts the best traits of humankind. However, it actually illustrates the importance of a human trait that is sometimes underappreciated: humility. Arrogance is the surest route to complacency. When we believe we already have all we need and already are all we need to be, we close ourselves off to possibilities for learning and growth. This is true both socially and spiritually, in both corporate and individual contexts.

In Star Trek, when encountering a life form that forces us to recognize our own limitations, we can choose to rebel against that idea and prove our might, or humbly accept that we are not as powerful as we like to think we are. Indeed, it is often through surrender and submission that we find freedom. Kirk, Spock, and McCoy's journey on the planet begins with three encounters with alien creatures—all of whom pose a threat, and all of whom can be overcome, either by phasers or by force fields, or simply by being outrun. When they encounter the Lactrans, however, the tables are entirely turned. As Kirk notes, "On this planet, Bones, they seem to be the people and we are the animals."[1]

Star Trek stories about humans being captured and placed into a zoo go back to the first, unaired *Star Trek* pilot, "The Cage." In that episode, humans are deemed to be too violent, too primitive, and too resistant to captivity for the Talosians' purposes. The assessment of humans as primitive is echoed repeatedly in "The Eye of the Beholder," such as when Spock theorizes that their communicators and phasers were taken away "for the same reason you would take a sharp object away from a child."[2] Importantly, however, emphasis is placed on the fact that humanity is in progress and shows great potential. "We are considered simplistic," Spock says of the Lactrans' perspective on humans, "but in the process of evolving into a higher order."[3] A central concept of humanism is the potential of humankind and our continued advancement. Pursuing this advancement, however, requires a balance between understanding our unique and exceptional qualities and a humility regarding our place in the larger universe. Only by understanding how much room we have to grow can we reach for progress and only by understanding our capabilities for exceeding expectations can we know we have the ability to grow.

Scripture strikes a similar balance, reminding humans of their smallness and weakness, but also pointing out their remarkable beauty and complexity. "Where were you when I laid the foundation of the earth?" God roars at Job, "Tell me, if you possess understanding! Who set its measurements—if you know—or who stretched a measuring line across it?"[4] And later, God asks Job, "Will the one who contends with the Almighty correct him? Let the person who accuses God give him an answer!"[5] Job responds in utter humility. "Indeed," he says, "I am completely unworthy—

1. Sutherland, "The Eye of the Beholder."
2. Ibid.
3. Ibid.
4. Job 38:4–5.
5. Job 40:2.

how could I reply to you? I put my hand over my mouth to silence myself. I have spoken once, but I cannot answer; twice, but I will say no more."[6] The psalmist is similarly humbled by the works of God's hands. "When I look up at the heavens, which your fingers made," he writes, "and see the moon and the stars, which you set in place, Of what importance is the human race, that you should notice them?"[7] But the psalmist recognizes also that humans, since they are so small in the face of the Almighty, must also be greatly blessed because they are given such authority on Earth. "Of what importance is mankind," he continues, "that you should pay attention to them, and make them a little less than the heavenly beings? You grant mankind honor and majesty; you appoint them to rule over your creation; you have placed everything under their authority . . . ."[8]

In the New Testament, Peter writes that God's divine power "has bestowed on us everything necessary for life and godliness through the rich knowledge of the one who called us by his own glory and excellence."[9] And further, he writes that God has "bestowed on us his precious and most magnificent promises" so that human beings may "become partakers of the divine nature."[10] [11] Paul also points to ongoing human advancement, writing to the church at Corinth, "And we all, with unveiled faces reflecting the glory of the Lord, are being transformed into the same image from one degree of glory to another, which is from the Lord, who is the Spirit."[12] As these biblical passages speak of the greatness and exaltation of humankind, they do so couched an understanding of the fact that this is a demonstration of the greatness of God. They begin with humankind's smallness before God and culminate in the greatness of humanity because of how God made us and what God has equipped us to do and become. So, cultivating humility is an important first step for the humanist, and especially for the Christian humanist. Without it, recognition of human greatness leads only

---

6. Job 40:4–5.

7. Ps 8:3–4a.

8. Ps 8:4b–6.

9. 2 Pet 1:3.

10. 2 Pet 1:4.

11. It is worth noting that, while not exactly the same idea, this passage recalls Roddenberry's belief that all human beings "are a piece of God, are becoming God" (Sweeney, *God &*, 11). As usual, Roddenberry's hopes and beliefs about humanity in some way mirror the biblical narrative.

12. 2 Cor 3:18.

to arrogance and skips over learning and growth, leading to foolhardiness and failure.[13]

The importance of learning is perhaps the central theme of the TAS episode "Bem." Ari bn Bem, the aforementioned modular being, learns the importance of both humility and pride in oneself. And, thanks to Gene Roddenberry, he does so through the teachings of a godlike entity. According to writer David Gerrold, Roddenberry was somewhat scattered at the time, apparently due to health issues, and was constantly changing his mind about things.[14] Through many meetings about the episode, Gerrold reports that Roddenberry introduced many different ideas. "Somewhere in the middle of that," he recounts, "Gene said, 'How about they meet God on this planet?' And my gut-level was, 'Haven't we done that one enough?' But Gene liked it and I said, 'Well, let's see what we can do with it.'"[15] Though he initially was not fond of Roddenberry's suggestion, once he embraced it, Gerrold found that he liked the story it helped him tell because "now our characters have to solve a problem with their wits instead of violence, and that was really in theme with where I was starting, anyway . . . . They get to show that they are heroes because of who they are as people, not because of the weapons they carry."[16] Gerrold explains the story this way:

> There are two stories in this episode. One, of course, is Bem, who's testing Kirk and Spock, and the second is the action down on the planet—these lizard people and the god, the alien intelligence, who is protecting them. And that's the action story. So, you always have your action story, and then you have your philosophical dilemma. So, Bem represents the philosophical dilemma: Are our characters gonna behave like the good guys? And the lizard people who've captured them represent the action dilemma: And how does our behavior relate to our core beliefs, that we are the good guys and we're not gonna interfere with other, with primitive peoples? So, this was an episode that truly tested the Prime Directive in a lot of different ways.[17]

More than just the Prime Directive, the episode also tests how Kirk and Spock will respond to a godlike being that rules a planet. Based on the many

13. Prov 16:18.
14. Tescar, "The TAS David Gerrold Interview."
15. Gerrold, "Audio Commentary for 'Bem.'"
16. Ibid.
17. Ibid.

encounters with god figures the *Enterprise* crew has in the Original Series, the assumption with such a setup might be that our heroes would end up destroying, undermining, or in some way thwarting said god. But the god of Delta Theta III is quite different from those often encountered in the previous series. The gods dethroned or destroyed by the *Enterprise* crew in episodes like "The Return of the Archons," "The Apple," or "Where No Man Has Gone Before" are computers, machines, and megalomaniacal beings who seek to crush, conquer, oppress, and enslave. Not so on Delta Theta III. This god being is a benevolent protector who watches over her "children" on the planet, seeking to keep them from harm and outside interference. In a sense, the being acts as an embodiment of the Prime Directive, seeking to avoid contamination of the natural evolution of the native species. When Kirk understands the relationship of the lizard people to their god, he does nothing to interfere. "We apologize for intruding," he tells the entity. "We did not realize the situation. We will leave. We will tell others of our kind not to bother you here."[18] This humility before the god being is in stark contrast to Kirk's bold challenging of god figures in the Original Series. But this being is also in stark contrast to those oppressive forces. When Bem realizes he has overstepped his bounds and interfered with the mission by testing Kirk and Spock, he is overcome with shame. But it is the god being who teaches him otherwise.

> BEM: This one has greatly erred. The mission was to judge, and right of judgment was not conferred. This one must disassemble unity.
>
> KIRK: Disassemble?
>
> BEM: Never to exist again as a cooperation. This unity is defective. This unity must cease to exist.
>
> ENTITY: No, do not destroy yourself.
>
> BEM: But this one has erred. This one has tried to judge Kirk and Spock and been found wanting himself. This one has acted badly.
>
> ENTITY: Yes. You have erred, but if you disassemble, you cannot learn from your error. Errors demand recognition so that they will not be repeated.[19]

18. Reed, "Bem."
19. Ibid.

Bem is ready to destroy himself for his failure. He operates on a sense of punitive response to bad behavior that expresses humility, but without room for growth or improvement. His self-worth is bound up in his actions and he cannot see himself as worthy of life when he has made a great error. The entity, however, teaches him that failure is an opportunity for growth. Yes, justice says that we must humbly acknowledge wrongdoing, but grace and mercy say that we must not live in guilt and shame.

> BEM: You do not demand punishment?

> ENTITY: Punishment? What is punishment? Revenge? Intelligent beings need no revenge. Punishment is necessary only where learning cannot occur without it. You are behind that.[20] My children here are not. That is why you must leave, so as not to corrupt their development with concepts that they are not yet ready for.[21]

Here, the entity echoes Scripture. John the Evangelist tells us, "There is no fear in love, but perfect love drives out fear, because fear has to do with punishment. The one who fears punishment has not been perfected in love."[22] Bem has not been perfected in love. He fears punishment. But, at this moment, he seems to be changing. Throughout the episode, Bem demonstrates a kind of self-effacing humility in his speech, referring to himself, not with personal pronouns, but as "this one" and "this unity." This reflects his nature as a cooperative being, but also seems to express his lack of value of himself as an individual. In his response to the entity's words, for the first time, we hear him refer to himself in the first person: "I am humbled." As the *Enterprise* leaves orbit, the entity sends a message: "Go in peace. Yes. Go in peace. You have learned much. Be proud."

Still, a sense of humility permeates the script. When Spock calls the entity they encountered on the planet "almost a god," Kirk replies, "Mister Spock, the difference is meaningless. In comparison, we're all still children." For Gerrold, this is the point of the episode. "We all still have so much left to learn," he says. "And I think that it's when we forget that we're still children, when we forget we still have lessons to learn, that we start making

---

20. This is a mistake in the episode. According to David Gerrold, the line should be "You are beyond that." Gerrold, David, email to the author, April 22, 2016.

21. Reed, "Bem."

22. 1 John 4:18.

serious and stupid mistakes . . . . I think Gene, if he were still around today, he would agree with that assessment of *Star Trek*."[23]

Human beings are once again referred to as children in the episode "How Sharper Than a Serpent's Tooth," but with very different results. When the *Enterprise* encounters a "god" in space, this time it appears to be, for all intents and purposes, a "real" god. That is to say, it is the alien being who appeared as the god Kukulkan (amongst others) in ancient Earth history. Co-writer David Wise explains that the idea arose from trying to work in co-writer Russell Bates' ancestry as a full-blooded Kiowa Indian into the story, an idea to which associate producer Dorothy Fontana seemed quite attracted. "So, at that time," Wise recalls, "there was a book that was very popular, a crackpot book called *Chariots of the Gods* by Erich von Däniken, which basically claimed that, you know, all these Indian sites in Peru and what not were actually made by aliens and they were communication methods, and we thought, 'Well, there's science fiction and Indians in one package.'"[24] Wise continues,

> What if the ancient gods of the Aztecs and the Mayans and the rest of the world was this one god, this one alien who came to Earth, spreading the seeds of knowledge, and all of the cultures of Earth were attracted to a certain portion of his knowledge, but none of them got the complete picture? They all missed it. So he's, in essence, been waiting around for thousands of years for his phone call from his students on Earth, and never receives it. So he has come back to see how Earth has turned out. And, at the start of this episode, he's not happy with what he sees.[25]

What Kukulkan sees is a humanity that no longer worships him or follows the religions he established. Thankfully (and only for this episode), the *Enterprise* crew includes Ensign Dawson Walking Bear, a Comanche relief helmsman, who recognizes Kukulkan. "I was angered because I believed you had forgotten me," Kukulkan says. "But one in your midst knows my name. You will be given one chance to succeed where your ancestors failed. Fail me again and all of your kind shall perish."[26] Clearly, Kukulkan differs greatly from the benevolent, protective being encountered by Kirk and Spock in "Bem." Kukulkan is a demanding, punishing god who, whatever

23. Gerrold, "Audio Commentary for 'Bem.'"
24. Wise, "Audio Commentary for 'How Sharper Than a Serpent's Tooth.'"
25. Ibid.
26. Reed, "How Sharper Than a Serpent's Tooth."

wisdom or knowledge he may have, demands submission and threatens destruction if he is not obeyed. This is the sort of god Star Trek universally reacts against. A god that seeks to confine or oppress is, in Star Trek's view, no god at all.

Kukulkan indeed seems intent upon confining humanity. Like the Talosians and many other species in the Original Series and the Lactrans in the Animated Series, Kukulkan is a zookeeper. His vessel houses hundreds of species from around the galaxy, all kept in small cages, with barely enough room to move. "What you cannot see," Kukulkan tells Kirk, "is that each of them, mentally, is in its own natural environment. They eat, breathe and live in worlds created by my machinery, worlds only they can see. They do not know they are in cages."[27] Like the Talosians' psychic illusions in "The Cage," the imprisonment these creatures experience has the added cruelty of ignorance. Perhaps a greater crime than keeping these creatures from their natural environment is keeping them from the truth of their reality. Though Kukulkan, like the Talosians, sees this as a benevolent act, Star Trek values have consistently railed against the confinement of innocent beings, no matter how apparently magnanimous the intentions of the captors. "This zoo of Kukulkan's," Wise remarks, "again sort of shows his desire to create environments for people and keep them. In that, his plans for Earth were, in essence, a cage for us that we, fortunately, broke free from."[28] Despite Kukulkan's stated intentions of teaching "peaceful ways" to warlike humans, Kirk objects to his methods and his view of humanity. "No one being," he insists, "not even you, has the right to interfere with other cultures."[29]

But Kukulkan's determination to capture any creature he wishes is apparent. In one cage, McCoy finds a Capellan power-cat, a creature he says no one has ever been able to capture alive. "They hate captivity," he explains to Kirk. "You try to put more than one hand on them and they throw off a charge of two thousand volts." In this, the power-cat symbolically reflects humanity's aversion to captivity—and Kukulkan seems well aware of that fact. "How did you ever capture it?" McCoy inquires of Kukulkan.

> KUKULKAN: It was an infant and easily controlled, as you were when I visited Earth. You still are children to me, to be led and shown how to live.

27. Ibid.
28. Wise, "Audio Commentary for 'How Sharper Than a Serpent's Tooth.'"
29. Reed, "How Sharper Than a Serpent's Tooth."

> KIRK: But if children are made totally dependent on their teachers, they will never be anything but children.

> KUKULKAN: Enough! This is useless. Despite what I have shown you, you still cling to your disobedient ways. My dream is ending and all of you are to blame![30]

Kukulkan's interest is in compliance. He sees humankind as perpetually limited. As opposed to the acknowledgement in "The Eye of the Beholder" and "Bem" that humans are, in many ways, still children, Kukulkan's view of humankind seems to have no room for growth. He underestimates human potential, intending to make human beings dependent upon him forever. Where previously, the *Enterprise* crew had to embrace humility, here they must stand up for what humankind has accomplished. When Kukulkan describes human beings as "warriors," Walking Bear protests, "But we work only to create peace." Kukulkan is completely dismissive, refusing to believe that humanity has been able to grow without his guidance. "Nothing you have done so far," he retorts, "makes me believe that is true."[31]

While they probably never fully convince Kukulkan they are peaceful, the crew of the *Enterprise* does manage to show him that they aren't so helpless as he imagines. As the *Enterprise* breaks free of Kukulkan's force field, Kirk and McCoy are able to free the Capellan power-cat, who goes on a rampage and smashes open several of the other animals' cages. Kirk taunts the ancient god. "Kukulkan, can't you control one of your own creatures?" "I cannot," replies Kukulkan, "Your ship has disabled my central power source."[32] Facing the risk of high-voltage shock, Kirk subdues the creature with McCoy's hypospray tranquilizer. "We thought, there has to be a sort of wild, ferocious, very dangerous creature," explains Wise, "so that when they smash all the cages, it'll threaten Kukulkan. Our guys can handle it and Kukulkan can realize maybe we're more grown up than he thought."[33] Kirk uses this moment of Kukulkan's weakness to make a case that humanity doesn't need to be caged and controlled in order to live.

> KIRK: You think of us as being small creatures like this one. Are we really that inferior to you?

30. Ibid.
31. Ibid.
32. Ibid.
33. Wise, "Audio Commentary for 'How Sharper Than a Serpent's Tooth.'"

KUKULKAN: No. But the violence of your kind surpasses even that of the power-cat.

McCOY: We'd be fools if we didn't know that. But we also have been using our minds and trying to learn to live in peace.

KIRK: Because we have minds, we can't be what you wanted us to be. If we fail or succeed, it has to be our own doing. Intelligent life is too precious a thing to be led by the nose.

KUKULKAN: But you are my children. I hoped I could teach you, help you.

KIRK: You did, long ago, when it was needed most. Our people were children then. Kukulkan, we've grown up now. We don't need you anymore.

KUKULKAN: I will let you go your own way. I have already done what I can.[34]

This moment might seem to contradict the statements in the previous episodes that humans are children—a view, according to David Gerrold, which Gene Roddenberry would likely endorse. However, the vision of perpetual childhood and dependence that Kukulkan espouses is not the view of humankind that the previous episodes presented. There is a view of humans as children that sees us growing and learning and progressing toward greater things and a view that sees us as simple, unintelligent, and needing to be, in Kirk's words, "led by the nose." Kirk explains to Kukulkan in terms he can understand that humankind does not need to be controlled in order to grow, but to be set free. Dependence may have once marked humankind's progress, but now we have grown beyond that need. Whether humankind is truly independent in Star Trek is debatable. Certainly, there are still those who are religious ("Well, if you're speaking of worships of sorts," McCoy says in "Bread and Circuses," "we represent many beliefs"[35]), but oppressive, domineering religion is certainly set aside.

Christians, too, should be glad to see humankind move beyond vengeful, manipulative god images. Roddenberry himself was held back from truly exploring Christian faith because he viewed God in this way. Much of these kinds of episodes in Star Trek are his reaction against the God of the "terrible, swift sword." And rightly so. Such a God is not Christ. Just as

34. Reed, "How Sharper Than a Serpent's Tooth."
35. Senensky, "Bread and Circuses."

the animals in cages in Kukulkan's vessel were broken free from captivity and ignorance, so Christ came to "proclaim the release of the captives and the regaining of sight to the blind, to set free those who are oppressed, to proclaim the year of the Lord's favor."[36] "Where the Spirit of the Lord is present," Paul writes, "there is freedom."[37] In these three animated episodes, we can see the importance, both of humility and of pride—not the sinful pride of arrogance, but the sense of accomplishment and capability that comes from recognizing growth and progress. Our progress must always be toward greater freedom, expanding knowledge, and deeper understanding. We don't know everything, but we have accomplished much, and the humility to ask for help will lead to greater progress and growth, especially as we live in relationship to a God who does not despise our weakness, but understands it and understands just as deeply the potential with which he created us. As the author of the book of Hebrews writes,

> Therefore since we have a great high priest who has passed through the heavens, Jesus the Son of God, let us hold fast to our confession. For we do not have a high priest incapable of sympathizing with our weaknesses, but one who has been tempted in every way just as we are, yet without sin. Therefore let us confidently approach the throne of grace to receive mercy and find grace whenever we need help.[38]

We do need help, and we must admit our weakness. But in our weakness, we are made strong.[39] "We are no longer children," the Apostle Paul wrote, "to be tossed back and forth by waves and carried about by every wind of teaching."[40] We can throw off the yoke of oppression and embrace the liberty of Christ. This is a deeply humanizing thing. As Star Trek shows us, the human heart is oriented toward growth and advancement. As Scripture shows us, that trait is designed to bring us closer to God and to who he has made us to be. Kukulkan seeks to control. Christ seeks to set us free. That is the difference between God and a monster.

36. Luke 4:18–19, Isa 61:1–2a.
37. 2 Cor 3:17.
38. Heb 4:14–16.
39. 2 Cor 12:10.
40. Eph 4:14.

3

Sympathy for the Devil: "The Magicks of Megas-Tu"

" The Magicks of Megas-Tu" is an admittedly odd episode, but one with an important message about respect and fairness. It is also rife with religious references, though they are largely references to the occult and to demonology. This was not the case when the episode was first pitched. It actually started out as yet another divine encounter in space. Episode writer Larry Brody explains.

> I had some ideas—that I'd always had, for years—about what *Star Trek* as a series should have, so I was ready to go with them. I decided to lead with my favorite, which was, "Why can't the *Enterprise* encounter God in space?" Gene thought that was the greatest thing he'd ever heard of. He said, "I've been trying for years to just get that out in that way. I never really thought about just doing it. So, alright, let's do that." You know, "Go home; we're gonna make a deal." Well, a week later, Dorothy called me and said, "The good news is that we're making a deal and you're gonna write that episode we talked about. The bad news is we can't use God, but we can use the devil." So it became "The Magicks of Megas-Tu," which was a story about a planet of devils.[1]

So, a story about God became a story about the devil. Why this took place is uncertain. It could be that the network was uncomfortable with the concept of meeting God in space (though one wonders why the devil would be more acceptable). Or it could be that the concept was too close to Roddenberry's own work in progress, "The God Thing," which bore similarities to the later film *Star Trek V*, as the *Enterprise* went on a quest for God. In any case, the

---

1. Fontana et al., *Star Trek: The Animated Series* DVD special features.

transition was made and the *Enterprise* enters an area of space where matter is being created, only to find the planet Megas, where magical beings live in a world limited only by the imagination.

There are a surprising number of real occult references throughout the episode, beginning with that strange title. One of the characters in the story is Asmodeus, who is mentioned, amongst other places, in a work called *The Magus: A Complete System of Occult Philosophy*, originally published in 1801. Asmodeus appears in Book Two of *The Magus*.[2] So, it would seem, *The Magus*, Book Two, became "Megas-Tu." Asmodeus' most well known appearance is as the main antagonist in the deuterocanonical[3] book of Tobit. This reflects the episode's odd mix of occult and biblical references.

Of course, the key figure in the story is Lucien, whose name could refer to the Greek writer and rhetorician Lucian of Samosata. Lucian was a satirist who began as a public speaker, probably also pleading court cases.[4] Lucien in "The Magicks of Megas-Tu" certainly loves to talk and is called to testify in the climactic courtroom scene. Whether the character's name and attributes are in any way based upon Lucian of Samosata is unclear, but the connections are striking. In fact, in an unused line from the episode's script, Lucien says he visited Babylonia, Mesopotamia, and Greece while he was on Earth, though the script also describes him as "the image of all the goat gods of supernatural mythology."[5] In any case, Lucien is said by Asmodeus to actually be Lucifer. But that will come in later.

In this episode, Spock realizes that the crew of the *Enterprise* is in a realm where belief is as powerful as any physical force. To test his hypothesis, he sets up a space from which to conduct magical incantations. This scene contains one of the few overt uses of a religious symbol from Earth in Star Trek, as Spock draws a pentacle on the floor of the *Enterprise*.[6] "It must work, Doctor," he tells McCoy. "It is logical here. Power of this universe, enter my being. I know I can. I believe I can."[7] An aura forms around his body and a chess piece moves on its own. It can make

2. Barrett, "VIII: The Annoyance of Evil Spirits," 49–52.

3. Catholic, Eastern Orthodox, and other Christian traditions recognize deuterocanonical books as biblical canon (Scripture). However, they are not in the Hebrew Bible or in Protestant Bibles.

4. "Lucian," *Encyclopædia Britannica*.

5. "Lucien," *Memory Alpha*.

6. It is strange indeed to see Spock, who I will later discuss as a Christ figure, engaging in an occult ritual!

7. Sutherland, "The Magicks of Megas-Tu."

Christians uncomfortable to see the idea of faith as effective portrayed as normally false. However, the episode is not dismissing all faith and belief. From a Christian perspective, faith is real and powerful and miracles do happen, but believing very strongly will not suddenly endow a person with telekinetic powers or the ability to conjure up any desired object or force, as happens on the planet of Megas-Tu. Such magic is not even believed in by occult practitioners and Wiccans. So, at the end of the episode, when McCoy says, "No more magic for us, Jim. It's all back there," it is not a statement that faith has no power. Certainly, we know faith is an essential part of any human endeavor. But it does mean that the kind of whimsical magic practiced on Megas-Tu does not exist in the real world.

The Megans, Asmodeus says, came to Earth as friends, not evildoers, and were simply misunderstood. Can we believe him? Can we trust the word of a devil? In any case, Asmodeus claims that the Megans were the victims of the Salem witch trials, hence the colonial trappings of the trial at which Kirk and company stand.

> ASMODEUS: We came to your world as friends. But wherever we went, the story was invariably the same. Some humans would attempt to use us to gain power, to serve their own greed and lust. When we refused to serve them, they turned against us and taught other humans to fear us, to hate. They called us devils, warlocks, evil sorcerers. Those of us who survived came to the town of Salem in Massachusetts, as settlers, and tried to live like other men.
>
> SPOCK: But you made mistakes, used your powers.
>
> ASMODEUS: And burned for it. Burned!
>
> KIRK: As witches.[8]

And here, I must respond to Star Trek with history. Salem, Massachusetts was the center of one of the most tragic instances of religious persecution in American history. "The Magicks of Megas-Tu" follows the commonly portrayed idea that real witches, who were viewed at the time as magical beings, were executed there. Historical evidence, however, shows that no witchcraft was ever proven in Salem, beyond some folk fortune telling. In reality, those who died were innocent citizens—most likely Christians—persecuted by other Christians because they were social outcasts, or for land interests.[9]

8. Ibid.
9. Boyer and Nissenbaum, "Enlarged Salem Covenant of 1636," 31, 90–91.

Writings from the period following the Salem trials suggest that the guilt of those who were famously executed as witches could not be established and that their deaths were a "great wrong," based on invalid evidence.[10] In Salem, motives of fear, distrust, and greed drove to lethal action those who had pledged in their town covenant[11] to "walk with our brethren, with all watchfulness and tenderness, avoiding jealousies and suspicions, backbitings, censurings, provokings, secret risings of spirit against them; but in all offences to follow the rule of our Lord Jesus, and to bear and forbear, give and forgive, as he hath taught us."[12]

Beneath the surface in Salem was a bubbling cauldron of misplaced religious zeal, self-righteous indignation, discrimination, and greed—qualities which read like a description of the social and political climate of today's Western world. Because we are fallen, broken human beings, the same fear, intolerance, avarice, and social stigmatization that plagued that infamous Massachusetts town will never be far from us. Our challenge, then, rests not in avoiding them wholesale, which is impossible, but in how we deal with them when they arise. Will we have the humility to recognize our shortcomings, as in "The Eye of the Beholder?" Will we, as Bem does, have the wisdom to learn from our errors? Have we, as Kirk claims in "The Magicks of Megas-Tu," truly grown beyond the barbarism of Salem? Even if we do not execute those with whom we disagree at the gallows or the stake, do we still condemn, marginalize, and vilify our fellow humans? Or can we, in the words of Scripture, "do justice, love mercy, and walk humbly" with God[13] and with our neighbor?[14] The chaos of Salem is the explosion into the light of day the biases and desires for personal gain that had been kept hidden in the dark. Perhaps it happened so loudly so that future generations might see the horrible depths into which an ungenerous, unloving heart can lead humanity and learn a better way.

"Tell the court, please," Spock entreats Captain Kirk, "Would you say that since Salem, humans have changed?" Kirk replies, "I think we've been trying to, Spock. Humans have their faults—greed, envy, panicky fear.

10. Faulkner, "The Petition of Francis Faulkner, et al.," in Boyer and Nissenbaum, *The Salem Witchcraft Papers*, SWP No. 172.5.

11. This covenant for the Church of Christ in Salem was essentially a covenant for Salem itself, as church membership was required for civic participation.

12. Pierce, ed., *Records of the First Church in Salem*, 4.

13. Mic 6:8.

14. Phil 2:3.

But in the centuries since the Salem witch trials we have learned. We try to understand and respect all life forms." Appealing to Starfleet's General Order Number One, "No starship may interfere with the normal development of any alien life or society,"[15] and opening the *Enterprise*'s record for inspection, Kirk argues that humans have changed and needn't be feared. It is interesting to note that Kirk acknowledges that many of the human failings that fueled the Salem witch trials still exist in the twenty-third century. While Star Trek is often cited as promoting a near-perfect version of humanity, it is actually constantly pointing to human faults and failings. Though Earth is practically paradise in the Star Trek universe, humans are still imperfect. They are advancing, growing, and learning, but it is a long, slow process.

Asmodeus ultimately agrees that humans pose no threat to Megas-Tu, but pronounces judgment on Lucien. "For his betrayal of his people," he declares, "he shall be confined in limbo for all eternity, to live with only himself." Kirk objects. "No. To isolate someone like Lucien, that's the same as sentencing him to death." It is then that Asmodeus claims to reveal Lucien's true nature. "Do you realize who you defend?" he asks. "He has told you his name is Lucien. Would you defend him still if you knew he had another name too? The Rollicker, the Tempter—Lucifer!" Kirk is unimpressed by this accusation. "We're not interested in legend. He's a living being, an intelligent life form. That's all we have to know about him. We will not join in harming him." Asmodeus then unleashes the magic of the Megans on Kirk, engaging him in a sorcerer's battle. "You cannot beat an entire planet," he tells Kirk. "There is no way you can win." Kirk remains determined. "I have to," he replies, "or you'll become as bad as the Earthmen you fear. You're acting out of terror instead of out of thought or respect." And here we come to a central theme of the episode: Fear as a destructive force. To truly show that humans have changed, Kirk had to demonstrate that he would not submit to fear. "The Megans had to have proof that mankind had grown and learned wisdom since they last saw Earth," Spock observes, after Asmodeus relents and reveals his actions as a test. "Your compassion was that proof, Captain."[16] As the *Enterprise* flies away from Megas-Tu, Kirk, Spock, and McCoy discuss the magnitude of what may have just taken place.

15. Sutherland, "The Magicks of Megas-Tu."
16. Ibid.

> McCOY: You think Lucien really was the demon some men call Lucifer?

> KIRK: Does it really matter?

> SPOCK: It just might, Captain. If he was, this would be the second time Lucifer was cast out, and thanks to you, the first time he was saved.[17]

Did Kirk save Lucifer? Is that even possible? Biblically, it's highly unlikely, but the implications addressed here are more for effect than message. The challenge of the "sympathy for the devil" shown in "The Magicks of Megas-Tu" is less about kindness to the person of Lucifer himself, and more about kindness to the devils we make of others in our world, through misunderstanding, self-righteousness, ignorance, and fear. When we come to know the feared "other" as our fellow human and neighbor, we can see, instead of a broad caricature or abstraction, a person—made in the image of God and needing to be loved, whether we may deem them worthy or not. In these instances, it will do us good to have the humility to recall our own unworthiness. Knowing that we can learn and grow from our mistakes, as well as that we still have much learning and growing to do, can help us to find the compassion that convinces the Megans to no longer fear humanity. That same compassion is the key by which we will learn to no longer fear one another.

17. Ibid.

SECTION 4

The Gospel According to the Original Series Films

1

Star Trek: The Motion Picture

"The Creator must join with V'Ger."

—The Ilia Probe

For all its irreligious sensibilities, Star Trek constantly finds itself asking the same questions, and seeking the same kinds of answers, as are found in the human spiritual quest. In that sense, then, Star Trek is consistently spiritual. In *Star Trek: The Motion Picture*, this quality of the Original Series and the overall Star Trek narrative is demonstrated on a grand scale. V'Ger, having consumed all the information it can amass, is empty—still seeking answers, but finding none. It cannot complete its quest for meaning because it has lost the context of its original programming: its relationship with its Creator.

V'Ger is, as Kirk puts it, "an alien object with unbelievable destructive power" and also, the *Enterprise* crew will learn, a conscious entity that has amassed incredible knowledge. But, for all its power, for all its knowledge, it is, as Spock later describes it, "a child—evolving, learning, searching, instinctively needing." Certainly, this describes not only children, but all human beings, as individuals and as a species. In children and infants, we find a concentrated microcosm of the human experience—all our most essential needs distilled and on constant display. Perhaps this is why the Scriptures say, "out of the mouths of children and nursing infants, you have prepared praise for yourself."[1] Children know deeply and instinctively what they need and they seek it with absolute, unwavering focus. This seeking instinct of children, combined with their trusting nature and willingness to

---

1. Matt 21:16, Ps 8:2.

depend on others when they are weak led Jesus to say, "I tell you the truth, unless you turn around and become like little children, you will never enter the kingdom of heaven!"[2] This essential desire to seek, learn, and grow, alongside the trust, the faith, that there is something to be found, is at the heart of the human journey and also at the heart of Star Trek. Roddenberry himself liked to refer to humankind as "a child race" and "an adolescent species."[3] This seems to have been a reference both to our as yet-developing state and to our insatiable hunger for knowledge and growth. But the quest alone is not enough. Even though V'Ger has far surpassed humans in knowledge, there is an emptiness to its existence.

It is a feeling Spock knows well. Having pursued the Vulcan ritual of Kolinahr, to purge himself of all emotion, Spock telepathically senses "a consciousness of a force more powerful than I have ever encountered— thought patterns of exactingly perfect order." He hears V'Ger's searching and knows that he, too, is somehow not complete. He proceeds to rejoin his companions aboard the *Enterprise* as an act of faith, hoping to connect with V'Ger. "I believe," he says, "it may hold my answers."[4] He too is driven by an insatiable need to know. He seeks to reach V'Ger in hopes of understanding his own sense of incompleteness. With typical self-sacrificial abandon, he embarks on a thruster suit-enabled journey into V'Ger. In so doing, he clearly embraces the possibility that he will not return alive, recording his observations for Captain Kirk as he will likely be unable to relay them himself.[5] He engages in a mind meld with V'Ger that almost kills him, but gives him vital insight into V'Ger's thoughts and motivations. As he recovers in sickbay after Kirk rescues him, he recounts to the captain, in uncharacteristically emotional terms, what he has learned.

> SPOCK: I saw V'Ger's planet, a planet populated by living machines. Unbelievable technology. V'Ger has knowledge that spans this universe. And, yet with all this pure logic, V'Ger is barren, cold, no mystery, no beauty. I should have known.
>
> KIRK: Known? Known what? Spock, what should you have known?

2. Matt 18:3.

3. Fern, *Last Conversation*, 12.

4. Wise, *Star Trek: The Motion Picture*.

5. As he releases the thruster portion of the suit, his arms briefly mimic the extended arms of Christ on the cross, an unintentional foreshadowing of similarly unintentional symbolism in future films.

SPOCK: *(taking Kirk's hand)* This simple feeling is beyond V'Ger's comprehension. No meaning, no hope, and, Jim . . . no answers. It's asking questions: "Is this all I am? Is there nothing more?"[6]

"As I was when I came aboard," Spock tells Kirk later, "so is V'Ger now—empty, incomplete, searching. Logic and knowledge are not enough." V'Ger has fulfilled its programming to, in Decker's words, "learn all that is learnable" and it is lost, lonely, and needing purpose. "Is this all I am?" it asks, "Is there nothing more?" While we can relate to this journey emotionally, it is, for V'Ger, a function of its basic programming. "I sense no emotion," Spock says, "only pure logic." What some may consign to the realm of emotion and irrationality, V'Ger sees as not only reasonable, but essential. For all that it lacks—even down to the understanding of a "simple feeling"—it knows that it needs something more in order to be complete. It does not seem to intend to be malicious in the destruction it brings. It is hungry—deeply hungry—longing for something it cannot find and disinterested with all the useless things in its way. Its purpose is singular and unwavering. Yet, even without emotional context, it reflects a deep yearning in the human soul.

ILIA PROBE: V'Ger and the Creator will become one.

SPOCK: And who is the Creator?

ILIA PROBE: The Creator is that which created V'Ger.

KIRK: Who is V'Ger?

ILIA PROBE: V'Ger is that which seeks the Creator.[7]

V'Ger is defined by its desire to know its Creator, just as we are defined by a desire to know ours. Humankind has been described by philosophers from Hegel to Kierkegaard, and Schleiermacher to Tillich as *homo religiosus*—the religious human—that is, a being defined by an innate quest for the Divine, an innate need to seek higher meaning and a higher power.[8] Spock, in particular, connects V'Ger's longing with that of all humans. "It only knows that it needs," he tells Decker, "But, like so many of us, it does not know what."[9] V'Ger's Creator (more than once referred to as its God) is defined in the same ineffable manner as the need for God—expressed in

---

6. Wise, *Star Trek: The Motion Picture*.

7. Ibid.

8. Dubose, "Homo Religiosus," 827–30.

9. Wise, *Star Trek: The Motion Picture*.

a need for a sense of completion, wholeness, and meaning—that is felt by all humans.

While V'Ger defines itself in terms of its deepest desire, it defines its Creator only as the satiation for that desire. In the same way, as Spock points out, "Each of us, at some time in our life, turns to someone, a father, a brother, a God, and asks 'Why am I here?' 'What was I meant to be?'" And, just as we do, he says, "V'Ger hopes to touch its Creator to find its answers." This desire to find meaning and purpose perhaps most often expresses itself not so much in a desire to be religious as in a quest for meaning and purpose in our lives. It is this quest that lies at the core of all human pursuits—in our spiritual journeys and our scientific inquiries. But knowledge is not enough. After spanning the universe, V'Ger asks, "Is this all I am? Is there nothing more?" With all its knowledge, V'Ger still has, in Spock's words, "no answers."

> SPOCK: What it requires of its God, Doctor, is the answer to its question, "Is there nothing more?"
>
> McCOY: What more is there than the universe, Spock?
>
> DECKER: Other dimensions, higher levels of being.
>
> SPOCK: The existence of which cannot be proved logically. Therefore, V'Ger is incapable of believing in them.
>
> KIRK: What V'Ger needs in order to evolve is a human quality: our capacity to leap beyond logic.[10]

Spock says that other dimensions and higher levels of being cannot be proved logically. They require, as Kirk points out, an act of faith. Since general relativity makes a strong argument for other dimensions—dimensions to which Star Trek itself has journeyed—the "other dimensions" Spock says cannot be logically proven must not be of the relativistic sort. Similarly, "higher levels of being" have certainly been encountered by the *Enterprise* and therefore must have been discovered by V'Ger as well. In fact, the inhabitants of the machine planet seem to fit that bill nicely. Still, V'Ger does not seek a being higher than humans, but one greater than itself and greater than all that it has discovered in its journeys. In all its scope of knowledge and scale of size, what is greater than V'Ger? The answer, it would seem, lies in a realm that is deeper and vaster than the universe itself—what we would call the Divine. In Star Trek, the seat of the Divine is consistently located in

10. Ibid.

the human heart. And the human heart, with all its questing, searching, and exploring, longs for God. In truth, it is not just its own Creator—its own God—that V'Ger seeks. V'Ger represents the true longing of our human quest for knowledge, the true hunger of the human heart—unity with our Creator. V'Ger has been the embodiment of the human quest for knowledge. Now, having accomplished that quest, it comes back to the longing for something more—something greater than the universe itself. It arrives—logically—at the deepest longings of the human soul.

"What more is there than the universe, Spock?" McCoy asks. Decker comes close to an answer. Certainly for humans, the answer includes other dimensions and higher levels of being, but in a scientific context, those are still something that can be found within the universe. The only thing truly beyond the universe is its Creator—our Creator. V'Ger may seek humans as its God, but it reflects our own quest for God. Its robotically stated programming is actually a deep desire—a desire we humans share. With our capacity for emotion and for faith—for more than mere cognition—we hold the key to V'Ger's advancement, even as we continue to seek our own.

V'Ger is the product of the human drive to know, to explore. The very drive for knowledge, expansion, and improvement upon which Star Trek is based has turned against humanity itself. On paper, V'Ger has completed the quest at the heart of Star Trek. It has traversed the universe and learned all there is to know. But it has done so without the human spirit, and as such, it has come up empty. Pure research, cold information, is nothing without the human capacity for meaning. "What V'Ger needs in order to evolve," Kirk realizes, "is a human quality: our capacity to leap beyond logic." In other words, what V'Ger needs is faith. Decker brings that quality.

DECKER: And joining with its Creator might accomplish that.

McCOY: You mean that this machine wants to physically join with a human? Is that possible?

DECKER: Let's find out.[11]

Through Ilia, V'Ger seems to find the beginnings of an emotional connection to its purely logical pursuit. Decker frequently looks into the Ilia probe's eyes, seeking the connection he had found there before. At times, she seems to respond, but then her faint expression falls, and she looks robotically away. That is, until V'Ger cuts off the transmission of the final

11. Ibid.

code sequence. "The Creator must join with V'Ger," the Ilia probe insists. The demand may sound robotic, even ominous and threatening, but it is also the demand of a child, insisting on satiation for its deepest needs. At last, Decker sees what he has longed for—the desire for connection in the probe's eyes. V'Ger's own deep need, it seems, merges with and finds expression in Ilia's desire to be reunited with Decker. Finally, the bride longs for the bridegroom—and he responds to her plea.

> DECKER: I'm gonna key the sequence through the ground-test computer.
>
> McCOY: Decker! You don't know what that will do to you.
>
> DECKER: Yes, I do, Doctor.
>
> KIRK: Decker, don't!
>
> DECKER: Jim, I want this. As much as you wanted the *Enterprise*, I want this.[12]

Decker is a person of faith. Specifically, he has faith that Ilia is somewhere inside the probe and, therefore, inside V'Ger. He has faith that he can join with V'Ger and that his "bride" can be saved, that he can be reunited with her, somewhere underneath all that has taken her soul away from him. Throughout the film, he has frequently been cautious, only to be countermanded by Kirk's brash, bold instincts. In this instance, he is willing to take a risk that even Kirk is unwilling to broach. He steps forth, with something of Spock's self-sacrificial abandon, and offers himself in order to make his lost, broken bride whole, to resurrect her spirit and bring life from death.

In fact, in following the lead of faith, Decker himself may have experienced "the next step in our evolution," not an evolution of the body so much as an evolution of the soul. As V'Ger begins to merge with Decker, Decker seems to visually represent the divinity of the exalted human form. In this way, the union of Decker and the Ilia probe reflects the merging of the human and the Divine, in an image that recalls the joining of the first man and the first woman, in a new kind of Eden, that gives birth to a higher level of existence. This new being is so far beyond our understanding that we cannot even see it. It is beyond our plane of existence. Such is also the case as we seek union with God. Decker embodies V'Ger's Creator and gives himself completely and willingly to join in unity with it, to rejoin his lost "bride," much as Christ rejoins his Church. He sacrifices himself to save

12. Ibid.

her and live with her on a higher plane of existence. They are not casualties, as Kirk corrects himself. They are "missing"—no longer on this plane of existence, but together, somewhere—far beyond the stars.

> KIRK: Spock! Did we just see the beginnings of a new life form?
>
> SPOCK: Yes, Captain, we witnessed a birth—possibly a next step in our evolution.
>
> KIRK: I wonder.
>
> McCOY: Well, it's been a long time since I delivered a baby, and I hope we got this one off to a good start.
>
> KIRK: I hope so, too. I think we gave it the ability to create its own sense of purpose. Out of our own human weaknesses, and the drive that compels us to overcome them.
>
> McCOY: And a lot of foolish human emotions. Right, Mister Spock?
>
> SPOCK: Quite true, Doctor. Unfortunately, it will have to deal with them as well.[13]

The film opens with a long, forward motion through the stars that is returned to at its end. Demonstrating the cold vastness of space, filled with the warmth and wonder of Jerry Goldsmith's music, these moments apply the vision, imagination, and hope of the human heart to the calculable but almost incomprehensible distance between the stars. It is this hope and wonder that sustains us, that braces us against the crushing reality of the smallness of our being. As the human form becomes ever smaller throughout the film, outsized by space stations and starships, and ultimately utterly dwarfed by V'Ger, V'Ger itself is shown to be small—a child—in the face of the vastness of its questions of purpose, meaning, and belonging in the universe. Without its Creator, V'Ger can be filled with the knowledge of entire worlds and still be completely empty. Similarly, without this purpose, this knowledge of our relationship to our Creator in our hearts, we humans will also fall into the loneliness, despair, and isolation V'Ger represents. We may mask it, ignore it, or try to escape it in some other way, through some facsimile of relationship with our Creator, but we are always questing for the essential qualities of a relationship with God. It is this desire that, like V'Ger's programming, drives us—out into the stars, and right back to where we came from.

13. Ibid.

2

Star Trek II: The Wrath of Khan

"How we deal with death is at least as important as how we deal with life."

—ADMIRAL JAMES T. KIRK

S *tar Trek II: The Wrath of Khan* begins on March 22, 2285. While this is not stated explicitly in the film, when Star Trek historians Michael and Denise Okuda later officially established the Star Trek timeline, the year of this film was determined to be 2285.[1] Importantly, the film takes place on the occasion of Admiral James T. Kirk's birthday, which is similarly established as March 22, probably because it coincides with actor William Shatner's birth date.[2] In the Western Christian liturgical calendar,[3] Easter is a movable feast, occurring on a Sunday anywhere between March 22 and April 25.[4] March 22 is the least common date on which Easter can fall (a 0.483 percent likelihood), most recently occurring in 1818. Amazingly, the next time Easter will fall on March 22 will be in the year 2285.[5] Therefore, *Star Trek II* begins on Easter Sunday.

Further, it begins on the very next Easter Sunday to fall on the birthday of James Kirk and the only one that will do so during his (fictional) lifetime. This fact cannot possibly have been in the mind of anyone connected with the creation of *Star Trek II*, as these dates had not yet been established

---

1. Okuda and Okuda, *Star Trek Chronology*, 84.
2. Ibid., 39.
3. That is, as reckoned according to the Gregorian calendar.
4. Brokhoff, *Lectionary Preaching Workbook*, 133.
5. Van Gent, "Distribution of Easter Sundays."

in 1982 and would not be established for more than a decade. Even still, in Star Trek history, the fact remains that a film that begins on Easter Sunday is the first in a cycle of films concerning death, resurrection, and restoration, a trilogy that inaugurates one of the most visible and potent icons of pop culture—Spock—as a Christ figure.

In his audio commentary for *Star Trek II*, writer and director Nicholas Meyer says, "You get an idea and you say, 'Oh my God, this is great,' and you know it's great, but you can't say why. Other people will tell you why."[6] *Star Trek II* is great, and I humbly suggest that I know at least one reason why—it tells the story of Jesus. In conjunction with its two following sequels, in perhaps the greatest unplanned trilogy in film history, it tells that story very well and in surprising detail. The fact that all of this is entirely unintentional is perhaps the most amazing part of the story, and may in fact indicate that something sacred is at work here.

But *Star Trek II* isn't all unintentional symbolism. It also hinges on a prominent literary reference, which provides the spine of its narrative. Structurally and thematically, the film is the story of *Moby-Dick*—from the perspective of the whale. Khan is Ahab, and Kirk is Moby-Dick. In his script, writer/director Nicholas Meyer (a great admirer of Melville's classic epic) clearly casts Khan as Ahab, going so far as to put Ahab's words in Khan's mouth. When Khan declares of Kirk, "I'll chase him round the moons of Nibia, and round the Antares maelstrom, and round perdition's flames before I give him up,"[7] he alters a quote from Ahab that instead lists Good Hope, the Horn, and the Norway Maelstrom.[8] His last words, similarly, are quoted from Ahab: "To the last, I grapple with thee; from hell's heart, I stab at thee; for hate's sake, I spit my last breath at thee."[9] This is no coincidence. Meyer made sure Khan was familiar with Ahab, putting a copy of *Moby-Dick* on his shelf inside his makeshift cargo container home, alongside *Paradise Lost* and the Bible.

The film's story revolves around the slow creep of death Kirk feels as he ages. The past, in Khan, is trying to overtake and consume him. Kirk is on the run from his past mistakes, but if we take Melville more to heart, we can see that Kirk is dealing with the weight of even more.

---

6. Meyer, "Audio Commentary" for *Star Trek II*.

7. Meyer, *Star Trek II*.

8. Melville, *Moby-Dick*, 135.

9. Ibid., 468.

> All that most maddens and torments; all that stirs up the lees of things; all truth with malice in it; all that cracks the sinews and cakes the brain; all the subtle demonisms of life and thought; all evil, to crazy Ahab, were visibly personified, and made practically assailable in Moby-Dick. He piled upon the whale's white hump[10] the sum of all the general rage and hate felt by his whole race from Adam down; and then, as if his chest had been a mortar, he burst his hot heart's shell upon it.[11]

To Ahab, Moby-Dick was all evil, all that weighs upon the human heart—in theological terms, the whale had become, in his mind, the very embodiment of sin. In the biblical narrative, human misery and pain, age and death, are introduced into the world through the selfish, prideful desires of the heart. The sinful nature is the deadly virus that has infected the entire human race. For this—the misery and ugliness within himself—Ahab blames Moby-Dick. In a similar way, Khan also blames Kirk, and Kirk is doomed to die, in terms of the Moby-Dick metaphor, for all the sins of the world.

Khan has the perception that Kirk has wronged him, and he has a point. It is reasonable to assume that Kirk or someone from Starfleet should have checked in on him. Kirk is at least somewhat culpable. He did make a mistake. And Khan is taking that mistake from Kirk's past and stabbing at Kirk at a point when he feels, in Meyer's words, "the cells in his body aging,"[12] as he is feeling old and useless, threatening, in Bones' words, to join his own collection of antiques. On his fifty-second birthday, Kirk is dealing with perhaps the greatest challenge he has ever faced—promotion. The rank of admiral, for Kirk, is less an honor to be embraced than a burden to be borne, his aversion to it having been made clear in his pursuit of the *Enterprise*'s center seat in the previous film. By this time, the rank has become an inescapable prison for him. It stands as a signal from Starfleet that he has outlived his usefulness. Gone is his brash bucking for a return to command. Kirk is defeated. Seeing the demise of his career as a starship captain, he sees the demise of the best part of himself. Feeling his own mortality in the mortality of his captaincy, he is dying before he is dead.

---

10. Astute observers may be having a sense of recognition here, as Jean-Luc Picard invokes a version of this part of the quotation in a pivotal scene in *Star Trek: First Contact*. Unfortunately, the normally studious Picard misquotes the passage.

11. Melville, *Moby-Dick*, 153.

12. Meyer, "Audio Commentary" for *Star Trek II*.

McCOY: Dammit, Jim, what the hell's the matter with you? Other people have birthdays. Why are we treating yours like a funeral?

KIRK: Bones, I don't want to be lectured.

McCOY: What the hell do you want? This is not about age, and you know it. This is about you flying a goddamn computer console when you wanna be out there hopping galaxies.

KIRK: Spare me your notions of poetry, please. We all have our assigned duties.

McCOY: Bull. You're hiding—hiding behind rules and regulations.

KIRK: Who am I hiding from?

McCOY: From yourself, Admiral!

KIRK: Don't mince words, Bones. What do you really think?

McCOY: Jim, I'm your doctor and I'm your friend. Get back your command. Get it back before you turn into part of this collection. Before you really do grow old.[13]

"It was the best of times, it was the worst of times," Kirk reads from the copy of *A Tale of Two Cities* Spock gives him as a birthday gift. "Message, Spock?" Kirk inquires. "None that I'm conscious of," replies Spock, "except, of course, 'Happy Birthday.' Surely, the best of times."[14] Despite Spock's insistence that it contains no intended message, this famous Dickensian sentence is an apt description of many relevant ideas. Though Spock says a birthday is "the best of times," it is apparent in Kirk's inability to embrace the joy of the occasion that it is the worst of times for him, as he feels the end of his life ever nearer. The admiralty is, in the eyes of the world, the best of times. It represents ascension to the highest rank in Starfleet. For Kirk, though, it is perhaps the worst time of his life, as he sees his usefulness and calling taken away from him. It is this point—the point of perhaps his greatest vulnerability—at which Khan comes to challenge Kirk.

Khan represents the past haunting Kirk, condemning him to a future marked by age and death, which were introduced into the human race by the curse ("from Adam down," in Melville's words). Khan is an anti-Kirk, a fractured mirror image, reflected in his clothing—an open Starfleet jacket,

13. Meyer, *Star Trek II*.
14. Ibid.

stolen from a dead officer; a broken Starfleet insignia around his neck—and even in his vessel. The *Reliant*, with its saucer section above its warp nacelles, was designed as an inverted *Enterprise*, representing Khan's fundamentally oppositional orientation toward Kirk.[15] Star Trek captains are routinely used as symbols for the best of humanity, often standing trial in defense of humanity itself. The *Enterprise*, similarly, may be viewed as an avatar for humankind, reaching out into the stars in search of new discoveries. The symbolic effect, then, of Khan as a fractured reflection of Kirk and the *Reliant* as an upturned *Enterprise*, seeking vengeance instead of knowledge, is an embodiment of the worst humankind can be, a total perversion of everything Star Trek (and Scripture) tells us humanity was meant for. The conflict between Khan and Kirk, then, is one of large proportion and significant implication. But the victory in this battle will come in an unexpected way. The Dickens quotation presages this as well, as it comes from the beginning of *A Tale of Two Cities*, "Book the First: Recalled to Life."[16]

With this context in mind, let us return to the opening scene of the film, which begins on the central character of the story, Spock, and introduces the Kobayashi Maru, the famously unwinnable scenario that plagues all Starfleet cadets. In her novel, *The Kobayashi Maru*, Julia Ecklar imagines just how impossible the challenge was for Kirk. "It was," she writes, "like trying to win a war against God."[17] Saavik, of course, loses this war, leading to the first in a string of "religious" moments. First, when Saavik asks Kirk for suggestions, the Admiral recommends prayer, because "the Klingons don't take prisoners."[18] Spock, who had seemed to have been killed before the scene was revealed to be a training exercise, then opens his eyes, "dying" and "resurrecting" in the first scene of the film, a foreshadowing, as well as a kind of Easter passion play. Rumors that Spock would die in *The Wrath of Khan* had been circulating for some time and Meyer saw this as a way to "kill" Spock in the opening scene,[19] giving viewers the idea that, in the words of Mark Twain, "The report of my death was an exaggeration."[20] Lastly, Kirk says to McCoy, "Physician, heal thyself," a reference to Luke 4:23, when Jesus says that the people of Nazareth were likely to use this

15. Meyer et al., "Special Features" for *Star Trek II*.

16. Dickens, *A Tale of Two Cities*, 5.

17. Ecklar, *The Kobayashi Maru*.

18. Meyer, *Star Trek II*.

19. Meyer, "Audio Commentary" for *Star Trek II*.

20. Fishkin, *Lighting Out for the Territory*, 134.

Jewish proverb against him, wanting miracles as proof after Jesus claimed to be the messiah by reading from Isaiah. The chief priests and others later echo this same sentiment during the crucifixion of Jesus, mocking him by saying, "Save yourself! If you are God's Son, come down from the cross!"[21] In both instances, the entreaty seeks for Jesus to prove his messiahship, which he proves instead by sacrificing himself and rising from the dead.

The Edenic imagery (carried right over from the Original Series) sneaks in early in the film. Chekov and Captain Terrell beam down to what they believe is Ceti Alpha VI (actually Ceti Alpha V), which is being considered as the planetary test site for the Genesis device, in order to investigate the possible presence of life forms. Amidst a blinding sandstorm, Terrell asks, "Are you sure these are the right coordinates?" "Captain," Chekov replies, "This is the garden spot of Ceti Alpha VI." Terrell replies, "I can barely see it."[22] The "garden spot" is now a desert. If Eden existed as a geographical location on Earth, it is likely now in a place (whether in Turkey or Iraq) barren of vegetation. In any case, the garden is inaccessible. We can't see it. We are cut off from Eden.

But Genesis stands ready to bring, in Carol Marcus' words, "life from lifelessness." The Genesis effect, she says, takes something that is dead and "reorders its matrix, with life-generating results." Indeed, the biblical narrative of Genesis contains just this story. "The earth," the biblical account says, "was without shape and empty"[23] before God brought life. Life from lifelessness and a restoration of youth and Eden is a central theme of this film, illustrated by the Genesis effect animation and Carol Marcus' narration. The first stage, she says, will take place "in a laboratory," the second stage in a "lifeless underground," and the third stage "on a planetary scale."[24] This oddly mirrors the biblical story of the bringing of new life. It, too, comes in stages. First, in the garden of Eden (the laboratory), then in Christ's resurrection from the tomb (the lifeless underground), and then in the restoration of all creation (on a planetary scale). This is also the story of life from lifelessness that is followed in *Star Trek II, III*, and *IV*. After watching Carol Marcus' Genesis Project proposal video, Kirk refers to Genesis as "the power of creation."[25]

21. Matt 27:40.
22. Meyer, *Star Trek II*.
23. Gen 1:2.
24. Meyer, *Star Trek II*.
25. Ibid.

It is at this point that Khan first arrives, in his inverted *Enterprise*, to attack Kirk. Khan certainly represents Ahab, and therefore a reflection of Kirk, twisted by sin and hatred. But director Nicholas Meyer describes him as "Ahab, Lear, Lucifer, all rolled into one."[26] Certainly, he demonstrates a Lear-like descent into madness, but his similarity to Lucifer is most notable. When we meet Khan, he is a hissing, serpentlike presence, ruler of his desert garden. And, in this scene, he comes as a deceiver, posing as a friend, but striking out with lethal force. The attack badly damages the *Enterprise* and results in the death of Midshipman First Class Peter Preston, who we learn in the director's cut of the film is Scotty's nephew. Peter Preston is portrayed as a young, green, boyish figure. He is pure, untested, and innocent. As Scotty mourns over the young man's dead body, he tearfully recalls, "He stayed at his post . . . when the trainees ran."[27] Peter Preston represents nobility and courage. All these things the deceiver, Khan, has struck down. In Peter Preston, we see the death of innocence. And, just as a serpent approached Adam and Eve in the garden, appearing to be a friend, but deceiving them into a loss of innocence, so Khan has struck down innocence in this attack. In his dying moment, Preston reaches up and grasps the front of Kirk's uniform. The stain of a bloody hand (the symbol of guilt) on white cloth (a symbol of purity) remains over Kirk's heart. He has encountered the death of innocence and he wears the stain of guilt—guilt which Khan is placing upon him and condemning him for, and from which Kirk ultimately cannot, of his own power, be released.

"Who is Khan?" Carol Marcus asks. Kirk doesn't want to talk about it. He is trying to avoid everything that Khan represents—age, death, regret, and mortality. Kirk tells Carol he feels "old" and "worn out." Carol replies, "Let me show you something that will make you feel . . . young, as when the world was new."[28] She literally offers to show him Eden. This is a deep desire of humanity. The fact of our fallen state is that our bodies age, die, and decay. Because of this, we are constantly chasing after youth, vitality, and longevity. What we want is to return to Eden and recapture what we've lost. Throughout Star Trek, there are attempts at creating Eden, but they fail because those making the paradise are trying to play God. In the next film, a similar story will play out, but for now, the Genesis cave represents the hope of new life. The Genesis cave is a paradise, a green and lush garden,

26. Meyer, "Audio Commentary" for *Star Trek II*.
27. Meyer, *Star Trek II*.
28. Ibid.

flowing with water and growing with fruit. Kirk has met his son, David, a reason to hope for the future. To further the Edenic imagery, he even bites into an apple. But this represents the goodness of the garden, not the infamous bite of fruit from the Genesis narrative. For the first time in the film, we see Kirk begin to come alive, to show his old spark and vigor. Kirk has glimpsed Eden and he begins to be restored. He recounts the story of his defeat of the Kobayashi Maru test, a feat he accomplished essentially by cheating. "I changed the conditions of the test," Kirk says. "I don't like to lose." He recalls his youth and his escape from the consequences of the Kobayashi Maru. He feels hopeful. Saavik points out the obvious. "Then you never faced that situation, faced death." "I don't believe," Kirk replies, "in a no-win scenario."[29] After his encounter with Eden, Kirk is moving toward restoration. He receives a new uniform jacket, no longer wearing the sign of death, guilt, and shame. And he feels ready to face Khan once and for all. Little does he know that the battle ahead is one he can only lose.

The battle is indeed fierce. Destructive blows are landed on both sides. But Khan has a final gambit—the Genesis device. Khan, broken and marred, bloodied and disfigured, will pervert Genesis, destroy the power of creation, and bring death and destruction instead of life. He has come, in the words of Jesus regarding the Adversary, "to steal," (the *Reliant* and the Genesis device), "kill" (Kirk and the crew of the *Enterprise*), "and destroy"[30] (the power of Genesis, the *Enterprise*, and himself). The *Enterprise* is crippled, unable to escape under her own power, and Khan, the destroyer, stands ready to obliterate it by undermining and distorting the promise of Genesis. Recall here that, throughout Star Trek, the *Enterprise* has always been symbolic of humankind itself, reaching out into the stars in hope and freedom. Now there is no hope, no escape, and Khan is about to destroy the symbol of humanity itself. Khan, in his dying moments, sets the Genesis device into motion and once again quotes Ahab. "From hell's heart," he hisses, "I stab at thee. For hate's sake, I spit my last breath . . . at thee."[31] Khan comes from hell's heart, to reverse Genesis and bring destruction and death. But Spock has another plan.

> SPOCK: Admiral. Scanning an energy source on Reliant. A pattern I've never seen before.

---

29. Ibid.
30. John 10:10a.
31. Meyer, *Star Trek II.*

DAVID: It's the Genesis Wave!

KIRK: What?

DAVID: They're on a build-up to detonation!

KIRK: How soon?

DAVID: We encoded four minutes.

KIRK: We'll beam aboard and stop it.

DAVID: You can't!

KIRK: Scotty, I need warp speed in three minutes or we're all dead!

UHURA: (on intercom): No response, Admiral.

KIRK: Scotty!

KIRK: Get us out of here, best speed possible!

SULU: Aye sir.[32]

At this moment, Spock quietly leaves the bridge. In the confusion, no one notices. There is only one way to provide escape for Kirk and the *Enterprise*, only one way to thwart Khan's plan—and only Spock can do it. Only he is strong enough to withstand the radiation in the engine room for the length of time needed to make the repairs. Only he can set himself aside and die so that others might live. But, before he goes, he performs a mind meld on an unconscious Dr. McCoy and says a single word, "Remember," the same word Jesus used just before his death when he took bread and broke it, passed the wine cup and called them his body and blood. "Do this," he said, "to remember me."[33] No one forces Spock to die. No one kills him. In fact, his friends try to stop him. "No one takes [my life] away from me," Jesus said, "but I lay it down of my own free will."[34] Grace and mercy both happen. With a sudden burst of speed, the *Enterprise* is delivered from that which is coming from hell's heart to stab at it. "Bless you, Scotty!"[35] Kirk exclaims, but Scotty had nothing to do with it. McCoy's voice—the voice that, at the beginning of the film, encouraged Kirk to embrace what Spock called his "first, best destiny," before truly growing old, crackles through the

32. Ibid.
33. Luke 22:19, ESV.
34. John 10:18.
35. Meyer, *Star Trek II*.

intercom. "Jim, I think you'd better get down here . . . Better hurry."[36] Kirk looks over and sees Spock's empty chair. And it is only now that he knows what has happened. His feet can't carry him fast enough.

The scene intercuts between new life forming as the Genesis planet emerges and Kirk's hurried approach toward death and grief—the best of times and the worst of times. Kirk tries to get to Spock, to save him, but he is as incapable of stopping Spock's death as he was of saving himself from Khan. "He's dead already," says Scotty, helping McCoy hold Kirk back. And it is clear to Kirk now. Spock is dying in his place, accepting the death that he and all the crew would have faced because of Kirk's own past mistakes and because of the attacks of the Accuser and Deceiver. He's dead already. Indeed, it is said that Christ was "born to die," that his destiny was always before him. Kirk can see and talk to Spock through the glass, but he cannot touch him. Spock's skin is peeling, his green blood seeping through. He looks like a man who has been beaten within an inch of his life. "I never took the Kobayashi Maru test," Spock confesses. "What do you think of my solution?" His solution certainly differs from Kirk's. Kirk changed the conditions of the test by cheating death. Spock changed the conditions by embracing death, and in so doing, allowed Kirk to escape death yet again, but not by his own wits—by a sacrifice he could never earn or repay. "Don't grieve," Spock says. "It is logical. The needs of the many . . . outweigh . . ." Kirk completes the sentence for him: "The needs of the few." Spock nods and, with effort, adds, "Or the one."[37]

And now, let us take a moment for some rather deep-dive symbolism. Spock is a real surname, most famously held by renowned pediatrician Dr. Benjamin Spock. The spelling is an Americanization of the Dutch surname Spaak. Even though it refers to someone in the wheel-making trade, when we remember that the Scriptures refer to Christ as the Word,[38] it is interesting that the name Spock means "spoke."[39] Additionally, and perhaps at less of a stretch, Kirk is a Scottish, northern English and Dutch surname,[40] and is the Scottish word for "church."[41] Add these together and, in *Star Trek II*, Spock (spoke, the Word, Christ) saves Kirk (the Church).

36. Ibid.
37. Ibid.
38. John 1:1–18.
39. "Spock Name Meaning."
40. "Kirk Name Meaning."
41. "Kirk n.1, v.1," *Dictionary of the Scots Language.*

In a similar vein, the Vulcan salute, Spock's famous hand gesture, is something actor Leonard Nimoy pulled from his own Jewish heritage. It is a gesture used by Jewish priests called Cohanim during a ceremony that is said to bring the congregation into the Shekinah, or dwelling presence of God. Its shape, thumb extended, four fingers separated in a V-shape between the middle and ring finger, represents the Hebrew letter *shin*, the first letter of Shalom, Shekinah, and Shaddai, one of the Hebrew names of God.[42] [43] It is this symbol that Spock presses against the glass in his final moments with Kirk—a symbol of blessing in the name of the Most High, with the words, "I have been and always shall be your friend. Live long and prosper."[44] Again, Jesus' words: "But I have called you friends, because I have revealed to you everything I heard from my Father."[45] "I am with you always, to the end of the age."[46] And, finally, "I have come so that they may have life" (live long) "and have it abundantly"[47] (and prosper). "Live long and prosper," Spock tells Kirk. And because of Spock's sacrifice, Kirk is able to do just that.

> We are assembled here today to pay final respects to our honored dead. And yet it should be noted that in the midst of our sorrow, this death takes place in the shadow of new life, the sunrise of a new world, a world that our beloved comrade gave his life to pro-tect and nourish. He did not feel that sacrifice a vain or empty one, and we will not debate his profound wisdom at these proceedings. Of my friend, I can only say this. Of all the souls I have encoun-tered in my travels, his was the most . . . human.[48]

Kirk's words at Spock's funeral speak volumes. Spock was indeed human—half human, at least. His dual nature, both human and Vulcan (or, if you will, human and superhuman, with superior strength, intellect, and lifes-pan, along with a deeply spiritual, elevated existence) is the subject of many Star Trek stories and is at the core of his character's journey. It also echoes, though it certainly cannot perfectly illustrate, the dual nature of Christ as both human (having, like Spock, a human mother) and Divine (having

42. Gershom, "The Jewish Origin of the Vulcan Salute."
43. Yiddish Book Center, "Live Long and Prosper," Wexler Oral History Project.
44. Meyer, *Star Trek II*.
45. John 15:15.
46. Matt 28:20.
47. John 10:10b.
48. Meyer, *Star Trek II*.

God as his father, reflected somewhat by Spock's Vulcan and "superhuman" father). Kirk refers to Spock's soul, an idea that will be most important in the next film, and calls it "human." In Star Trek terms, where its creator believed that humans were "a piece of God" and "becoming God,"[49] it can be said that the word "human" is almost interchangeable for the word "Divine." So, in a certain sense, Kirk calls Spock both human and Divine. But the story of Christ is not complete without the resurrection, and neither was this film. Executive producer Harve Bennett tells the story.

> The original ending of the picture was grimmer, more final. It said, "Spock is dead." The picture ended over the feelings of Kirk in that wonderful moment when he says, "Of all the souls I have encountered in my travels, his was the most . . . human." That's how we were leaving the picture. The preview audience was aghast. There was silence in the theatre. And "What have I done?" crept into my mind. "What have we all done?" And people walked slowly out . . . . It was leaving a funeral. So, we had a couple of meetings and we said, "You know, it's a great ending; it's a dramatic ending, but it's a downer of the worst sort and it may end the franchise. There may not be another *Star Trek*."[50]

Something had to be done. "And what we did," Bennett explains, "was to modify the ending by adding one word: hope." The last scene was rewritten and reshot. Industrial Light and Magic filmed the scene of Spock's burial torpedo tube resting on the surface of the green and growing Genesis planet. And, finally, Leonard Nimoy recorded Spock's voice reciting the opening prologue of the Original Series: "Space, the final frontier . . .". Referring now to the *Enterprise*'s "ongoing mission," there was little doubt left for the audience that Star Trek—and Spock—would return. "I think the final argument," Bennett recalls, "was [Spock's voice-over] was too much, folks. That was too much. If you do that . . . they know you're gonna bring him back. And those of us who were for that said, 'Yeah. So?'"[51] Christ's victory is on the cross, but that victory is a victory over death. It takes the resurrection to demonstrate that the victory has taken place. In a film about life from lifelessness, death cannot win. The audience knew it and Harve Bennett and company knew it too. So, they decided to not shy away from it, to let hope emerge. And perhaps it is no accident that the music playing at

---

49. Sweeney, *God &*, 11.

50. Meyer et al., "Captain's Log."

51. Ibid.

Spock's funeral and in the film's score as his torpedo casket is shot toward the Genesis planet is "Amazing Grace,"[52] a piece of music that was, incidentally, also played at the funeral of one Gene Roddenberry.[53] Now, as Kirk, McCoy, and Carol Marcus observe the Genesis planet from the bridge of the *Enterprise*, McCoy asks Kirk, "How do you feel?" Kirk replies, "Young. I feel young."[54] The story has come full circle. Kirk has been restored to youth, released from the pangs of mortality, and now stands looking on a new creation—new life springing forth from death.

When the new ending was shown to a second preview audience, the response was entirely different. "The audience rose as one," Bennett says, "tears in their eyes and applause on their hands, and I felt like I'd—I felt like all of us had done something right and noble. And I know that's corny, but I walked out of the theatre that night saying, 'Yeah. Yeah, that's the way it should be.'"[55] Or, in the words of *New York Times* film critic Janet Maslin, "NOW this is more like it."[56]

When the story is right, everyone knows it. *Star Trek II* is great. And it's the story of Jesus. And, at the end of the film, the story is only beginning.

52. Meyer, *Star Trek II*.

53. Okuda, Michael, "Text Commentary" for *Star Trek II*.

54. Meyer, *Star Trek II*.

55. Meyer et al., "Captain's Log."

56. Maslin, "New 'Star Trek' Full of Gadgets and Fun."

3

Star Trek III: The Search for Spock

"The Genesis effect has in some way regenerated Captain Spock."

—Lieutenant Saavik

In the original six Star Trek films, there exists a phenomenon, to which fans refer as the "Odd Number Curse." The idea is based on the widely held notion that the second, fourth, and sixth films of the series are the most exciting, most interesting, and best made installments in the series. Fans often bemoan the long running time and slow, tedious pace of *Star Trek: The Motion Picture* and the weak structure, poor visual effects, and somewhat recycled plot of *Star Trek V: The Final Frontier*, but, while it is included among the derided "odd" films, *Star Trek III: The Search for Spock* rarely receives such specific or vociferous complaints. In fact, when one looks at the film anew, one finds that, while it may lack the spectacle and thrills of the surrounding films, *Star Trek III* is, for the most part, skillfully written, dramatically compelling, and even surprisingly funny. It is, in fact, a solid, well-made entry into the franchise that, while it may be understated, seems in no way "cursed." The truth seems to be that, between the slam-bang action and iconic narrative of *Star Trek II* and the comedic whirlwind and delightful antics of *Star Trek IV*, *Star Trek III* gets a bit lost in the shuffle. While it represents a strong and thoughtful directorial debut for Leonard Nimoy and a satisfying middle chapter to an ad-hoc trilogy, it is usually mentioned only in passing as "the one where Spock comes back."

Indeed, Spock does come back. Having sacrificed his life for his crewmates in *Star Trek II*, Spock returns to life in *Star Trek III*. Though, by all available evidence, never intended by the filmmakers, this process serves to further Spock's status as a Christ figure—and, almost unbelievably, a well-defined and theologically rich one, at that. But, whether one reads this film in the context of such an allegorical interpretation or not, it still stands as an important statement about faith and its role in Star Trek's universe and worldview. As Star Trek is famously rooted in scientific rationalism, verging at times on scientism, it may seem odd to claim that it contains a story of faith. In fact, however, the TV series and films contain several such stories, and faith—whether in self, humanity, or the value of ethical principles—is actually at the core of Star Trek, a key example of which is *Star Trek III*.

The film begins with a recapitulation of the death of Spock from *Star Trek II*. The first words we hear are Spock's: "Don't grieve." But this wish will prove difficult for Kirk to fulfill. In the first new footage for this film, we see the same star field as at the beginning of first film, but in reverse. It has the feeling of returning to the way things were before. As the ship enters view, the stars appear to be pulling against the momentum of the battle-damaged *Enterprise*, heading back to Earth after a near-fatal conflict with Khan Noonien Singh, her crew still mourning the loss of Spock. Even as the ship is going away from the newly created Genesis planet, in the backward pull of the stars, there is something already drawing it back. While the previous mission was certainly a personal one for Kirk, it was also a large-scale adventure that dealt in sweeping narrative and urgent, high stakes. It is clear from the outset of *Star Trek III*, however, that this is a more character-driven film, as it opens with an emotionally exposed log entry from James T. Kirk:

> USS *Enterprise* Captain's personal log. With most of our battle damage repaired, we're almost home. Yet, I feel uneasy and I wonder why. Perhaps it is the emptiness of this vessel. Most of our trainee crew have been reassigned. Lieutenant Saavik and my son David are exploring the Genesis planet, which he helped create. And *Enterprise* feels like a house with all the children gone. No, more empty even than that. The death of Spock is like an open wound. It seems that I have left the noblest part of myself back there, on that newborn planet.[1]

From the vantage point of the Christ figure analogy, Kirk has been saved by Spock's sacrifice and given new life. In the previous film, Kirk had felt weighed down by age and haunted by death. In contrast, the Genesis device

1. Nimoy, *Star Trek III*.

brought references to Earth's creation and the cave in which it had been tested was compared with Eden. Carol Marcus even told Kirk the cave would make him feel "young . . . as when the world was new." And, in the film's climactic moment, after Spock's sacrifice, Kirk had answered McCoy's question, "How do you feel?" with "Young. I feel young."[2]

In his log, however, Kirk now says he feels "uneasy." This might be seen as an example of what has been called the "already, not yet"[3] salvation of Christ. Christ accomplishes salvation on the cross, but there is a full completion yet to come. Also, it could be seen as reflecting the grief of those who knew Jesus in the days following his crucifixion and preceding his resurrection. Indeed, this film seems to live in an extended version of that time period, carrying a melancholic ache throughout that have led some to label it a "downer." In reality, it exposes—as good Star Trek does—a truth of the human heart and experience, the truth that, even when we win, it can be hard to feel the victory, especially when we have, as Kirk says, "paid for the party with our dearest blood."[4] Kirk refers to Spock's absence like "an open wound." This recalls the wounds of Christ and the wounds of our hearts. But, amidst the pall of death come signs of life.

CHEKOV: Admiral, . . . this is not possible.

KIRK: Mister Chekov?

CHEKOV: An energy reading from 'C' deck . . . from inside Mister Spock's quarters.

KIRK: I ordered Spock's quarters sealed!

CHEKOV: Yes sir, I sealed the room myself. Nevertheless I am reading a life form there.

KIRK: This entire crew seems on the edge of obsessive behavior concerning Mister Spock.

UHURA: Sir! Security reports the door to Spock's quarters has been forced.

KIRK: I'm on my way. Sulu, continue docking procedure.[5]

---

2. Meyer, *Star Trek II.*

3. Cullmann, *Christ and Time,* 84.

4. Nimoy, *Star Trek III.*

5. Ibid.

"I'm not crazy," Chekov says to Scotty, in Russian, "There it is."[6] Chekov sees life where there should be none. When Kirk arrives, the seal is broken, the door is open, and the guards, wearing red helmets and breastplates, stand without saying a word. Jesus' tomb was similarly sealed,[7] but when the women arrived at the tomb, they found the seal was broken, and the stone was rolled away.[8] The Roman soldiers guarding the tomb, to whom the Starfleet security officers in this scene bear a striking resemblance, "were shaken and became like dead men."[9] While these officers don't seem spooked, they are certainly silent. Mary met someone at the tomb whom she thought was the gardener, but was actually Jesus.[10] In a kind of inverse of that scene, Kirk thinks he hears Spock, but finds McCoy. But Spock, through McCoy, is actually speaking. He tells Kirk to go to Mount Seleya on Vulcan. Jesus tells Mary to gather the disciples and meet with him in Galilee.[11] So, like Jesus, Spock says, in essence, "Go to the place where I am from and meet with me there."

"Absent friends."[12] Back on Earth, Kirk raises a glass as he and the other *Enterprise* crewmembers drink a toast in memory of Spock. They remember together with shared wine—a kind of communion, in remembrance of the film's Christ. The communion is interrupted by Sarek, who requests privacy with Kirk. Through a mind meld, the two relive Spock's death, repeating the words exchanged between Kirk and his dying friend. Now heard for the third time between the two films, they comprise a kind of liturgy, a ritual through which the sacrifice of Spock is experienced again. This is all too appropriate following a communion, a sacrament that is meant to reenact the sacrifice of Christ. From this experience and the investigation that follows, Kirk learns that Spock is alive in McCoy. McCoy is carrying Spock's *katra*, "his living spirit."[13] In a similar way, Christians connect with the spirit of the living Christ through communion. Kirk now has his mission. He is more determined than ever to return to Genesis and to take Spock and McCoy to Vulcan.

---

6. Okuda, "Text Commentary" for *Star Trek III*.

7. Matt 27:66.

8. Luke 24:2.

9. Matt 28:4.

10. John 20:15–18.

11. Matt 28:10.

12. Nimoy, *Star Trek III*.

13. Ibid.

In an effect that might be called "Scripture jazz," many of the symbols and biblical references in this film are somewhat scattered or jumbled. The first instance of this is that the discovery of the empty tomb happens twice. Aboard the USS *Grissom*, surveying the Genesis planet, Saavik and David Marcus discover a life sign reading—again, a life where there shouldn't be one. When they go to investigate, they find Spock's torpedo tube casket and another "decoy," like McCoy appeared to be—slug-like creatures that used to be microbes on the tube's hull. "They were fruitful," David says, "and multiplied,"[14] perhaps as a conscious reference to the book of Genesis.[15] Inside the tube, David and Saavik find nothing but Spock's burial robe, neatly folded. Indeed, Christ's tomb was visited a second time, by two of his disciples, Peter and John, and they found his burial clothes, some of them folded or rolled up and set aside.[16] The jazz here is that these discoveries happen in two locations, disconnected from one another. But, the events mirror the biblical accounts in surprising detail. In both instances, Spock is found to be alive, whether the observers know it or not. Kirk, without realizing it, encounters Spock's soul. Saavik and David, on the other hand, find Spock's living body. He is still a child, but they conclude "that the Genesis effect has in some way regenerated Captain Spock."[17]

So, both Spock's body and his spirit are alive, but they must be joined. This is obviously a science fiction plot that diverts from Scripture, but this isn't about an exact retelling of the biblical narrative. The important elements are present: Spock (Christ) is alive in both body and soul. Still, the concept that a Vulcan has a "living spirit," or soul, that might continue on after death is difficult for Starfleet to accept. It is, then, in true Starfleet fashion that Starfleet Commander Admiral Morrow responds to Kirk's request to take the *Enterprise* to the Genesis planet to recover Spock's body in order to attempt to put his *katra* back into it.

> MORROW: No. Absolutely not, Jim. You are my best officer. But I am Commander, Starfleet, so I don't break rules!

> KIRK: Don't quote rules to me. I'm talking about loyalty and sacrifice. One man who's died for us, another who has deep emotional problems.

14. Ibid.
15. Gen 9:7.
16. John 20:4–7.
17. Nimoy, *Star Trek III*.

MORROW: Now, wait a minute! This business about Spock and McCoy. Honestly, I never understood Vulcan mysticism.

KIRK: You don't have to believe! I'm not even sure I believe. But even if there's a chance that Spock has an eternal soul, then it's my responsibility.

MORROW: Yours?

KIRK: As surely as if it were my very own! Give me back the *Enterprise*! With Scotty's help, I could . . .

MORROW: No, Jim! The *Enterprise* would never stand the pounding and you know it.

KIRK: Then I'll find a ship. I'll hire a ship.

MORROW: Out of the question, my friend! The Council has ordered that no one but the science team goes to Genesis! Jim, your life and your career stand for rationality, not intellectual chaos. Keep up this emotional behavior and you'll lose everything. You'll destroy yourself! Do you understand me, Jim?

KIRK: I hear you. I had to try.

MORROW: Of course.

KIRK: Thanks for the drink.

MORROW: Any time.

(As Kirk leaves he is joined by Sulu and Chekov.)

SULU: The word, sir?

KIRK: The word . . . is no. I am therefore going anyway.

SULU: You can count on our help, sir.

KIRK: Thank you, Mister Sulu. I'll need it.

CHEKOV: Shall I alert Doctor McCoy?

KIRK: Please. He has a long journey ahead of him.

"You'll lose everything," Morrow tells Kirk. Kirk is willing to make the sacrifice because he believes he will ultimately gain something greater. "Whoever finds his life will lose it," Jesus said, "and whoever loses his life because of me will find it."[18] Certainly, Kirk found his life in the previous film. Now, he stands to lose that life for Spock. "What good will it be," Jesus asked, "for someone to gain the whole world, yet forfeit their soul?"[19] Kirk must pursue Spock's spirit, he says, "as surely as if it were my very own." Kirk's quest is not just for Spock, but for his own soul.

Kirk and company now embark on a journey that is a search for much more than Spock. Star Trek narratives are often the story of a search or a quest, particularly in their cinematic incarnations. *Star Trek: The Motion Picture* concerns V'Ger's quest for its creator; *Star Trek II* is Khan's search for revenge, and the Genesis Device; *Star Trek IV* is the search for whales and a way home; *Star Trek VI*, a search for truth and peace. And while *Star Trek V* is explicitly a search for God, *Star Trek III: The Search for Spock* might just as well have been entitled *Star Trek III: The Search for Faith*. This film is about how the crew of the *Enterprise* responds to Spock's sacrifice in the first film. Because he sacrificed himself for them, they are willing to sacrifice everything for him. It is an act of faith to keep moving forward. In the coming moments, the words of Jesus can act as markers for the steps of faith Kirk and company take.

"Ask and it will be given to you."[20] Kirk asks Morrow and it is not given to him, but he asks his crew and it is. As Kirk and crew steal the *Enterprise*, Captain Stiles prepares for pursuit in the *Excelsior*. Commanding a starship is, in Spock's words from the previous film, Kirk's "first, best destiny." When he sits in the captain's chair, the lights above come on.

"Knock and the door will be opened for you."[21] Though the spacedock doors are closed, the *Enterprise* moves forward, in faith that Scotty will get them open. At the last possible second, the doors open. As Kirk prepares to go to warp, Stiles says, "Kirk, if you do this, you'll never sit in the captain's chair again." Kirk is not a captain, but an admiral. Yet, Stiles threatens his captaincy. That is where Kirk's heart is. Kirk is prepared to make the sacrifice, telling Sulu, "Warp speed."[22] Thanks to Scotty's sabotage, the *Excelsior* is unable to pursue and the *Enterprise* is on its way.

---

18. Matt 10:3.9
19. Matt 16:26, NIV.
20. Luke 11:9a.
21. Luke 11:9c.
22. Nimoy, *Star Trek III*.

"Seek and you will find."[23] This is the search for Spock. They seek in faith and they will find him.

Back on Genesis, we learn that David changed the rules, like Kirk, but in a less than noble fashion. David's sin—his impatience, selfishness, and pride—have caused the Genesis planet to be corrupted. Saavik refers to the death his actions have caused. Spock is naked in the cold, going through the process and pain of growth. This echoes the fact that Christ came into a broken world and shared in our suffering.

Kruge, on the other hand, is an antichrist. He is arrogant, selfish, and greedy. Where Spock gave up his life to save others, Kruge will take life to further his own desires. When he arrives on Genesis, he encounters a large, snakelike creature. He squeezes the creature's neck in his hand, killing it. Unlike Spock's famously nonviolent maneuver, Kruge's neck pinch is lethal. He sees Genesis (the power of creation) as something to be used for personal gain, to bring death and not life. The power of Genesis is supposed to be life from lifelessness, but Kruge sees it as "the most powerful destructive force"[24] ever known. Kruge wants to steal Genesis, kill anyone who gets in his way, and to destroy with the Genesis device, just as the thief comes in Jesus' words. But Christ has come "that they may have life and have it abundantly"[25] (live long and prosper). Finally, in Christian tradition, sunrise is associated with the resurrection of Christ and Easter services often take place at sunrise. Recall the sun/Son wordplay of the TOS episode "Bread and Circuses." A similar wordplay likely has some role in this tradition and may often be successfully applied to sun imagery in these three films. *Star Trek III*, for example, begins with sunrise on Genesis, presaging the resurrection of Spock. When Kruge arrives on Genesis, the sun goes down.

When Kruge captures David, Saavik, and Spock, the truth comes out. "David, what went wrong?" Kirk asks. "I went wrong," his son replies, referring to his unethical use of protomatter in the Genesis matrix. David realizes the fault is not in Genesis; it is in himself. Confession is the first step toward redemption. And, ultimately, David is redeemed when he sacrifices his life for Spock and Saavik. David is a biblical name—the name of one who was after God's own heart, but who sinned, and was redeemed. David's sin is causing the turmoil on the planet, along with which Spock is

23. Luke 11:9b.
24. Nimoy, *Star Trek III*.
25. John 10:10.

also suffering, groaning along with creation, which Paul says "groans and suffers together until now."[26] Jesus comes to suffer along with us; to bear our suffering, the suffering that comes from our own sin. This is the planet Spock, in Kirk's words, "gave his life to protect and nourish. He did not feel this sacrifice a vain or empty one."[27] If we look around the world today, particularly at the followers of Christ, we might wonder what was worth saving. But Christ did not consider this sacrifice in vain. "He gave his life to save us,"[28] Saavik says. This is true of David, of Spock, and of Christ.

In the conflict with the Klingon vessel, Kirk sacrifices that which he treasures the most—the *Enterprise*—in order to, in McCoy's words, "turn death into a fighting chance to live."[29] Truly, he sacrifices everything for Spock. Kruge is so driven by his obsession that he doesn't consider the ineffectiveness of his actions. He is being completely irrational, fighting to the death with the person he wants to give him the knowledge he seeks. He is the anti-Spock. He tried to destroy Kirk—the Church. As the planet is coming to its end, he is trying to take power. But, with three kicks from Kirk—a trinity, if you will—he is cast into the lake of fire. Because these events take place in the ending moments of a dying world that, beginning with Genesis and broken by sin, is acting as a sort of symbolic microcosm of Earth, they may be seen as a foreshadowing of the ultimate victory over evil, when God (the Trinity) casts the devil and all his works into the fiery pit.[30] And immediately, the sun rises. Genesis may be falling apart, but there is hope. Evil will be overcome. Spock will rise again. Creation will be restored.

In the book of Ezekiel, the prophet is commanded by God to prophesy over a valley full of dry bones. Ezekiel obeys and the bones come together. Sinew, muscle, and skin appear on them. Then God commands Ezekiel to prophesy the breath of life. He does, and the bodies breathe and come alive. "Then you will know that I am the Lord," God says, "when I open your graves and raise you from your graves, my people."[31] It is an image of the power of the Spirit of God to bring life from death that is used in traditional gospel music. So, it is perhaps fitting that, on Vulcan at last, the resurrection comes through a man called "Bones." McCoy introduces himself to the

26. Rom 8:22.
27. Nimoy, *Star Trek III*.
28. Ibid.
29. Ibid.
30. Rev 20:10.
31. Ezek 37:1–14.

Vulcan priestess as "McCoy, Leonard H., son of David."[32] "Son of David" is a messianic title used to refer to Jesus in Scripture.[33] The term "son" here means "descendant of." Jesus is of the house and the line of David—on both sides, through Mary and through Joseph.[34] The title is messianic because the messiah was prophesied to be of the house of David.[35] Here, our Christ figure comes through someone who is of the "house of David." The living spirit of Spock resides within the son of David. "I've got all his marbles,"[36] McCoy says on Genesis. The mind is associated with the soul, but is separate from Spock's brain. This says, like the *katra*, that there is more to us than our DNA. The ceremony on Vulcan, similarly, speaks to a greater dimension of existence and is taken absolutely seriously. It is a religious event, but no one doubts that something real and efficacious is taking place. "The danger to thyself," the priestess warns McCoy, "is as great as the danger to Spock."[37] In the same way, many people around the world who risk their lives for Christ see themselves as identifying with his suffering. Embracing that danger is an act of faith. And, finally, Spock brings about his resurrection through the member of the crew who most often antagonized him, but whose heart has been converted through Spock's death. ("I've missed you,"[38] McCoy tells Spock aboard the bird of prey in the next film.) In the same way, we who were enemies of God are now friends of God.

The scene after the ceremony is quiet and reflective. Sarek approaches Kirk. "Kirk," he says, "I thank you. What you have done is . . ." Kirk cuts him off. "What I have done," he says, "I had to do." "But at what cost?" Sarek counters, "Your ship. Your son." "If I hadn't tried," Kirk replies, "the cost would have been my soul."[39] Kirk could have selfishly kept everything Spock won for him, but in relinquishing it, he has found a greater reward—Spock. It almost feels like a heavenly moment as the sun rises on Seleya. Kirk and the *Enterprise* crew have sacrificed everything. They have remained faithful to the one who gave himself for them. The body of Spock has been reunited with his soul. The Body of Christ is the name we give to

32. Nimoy, *Star Trek III*.
33. Matt 1:1, Matt 9:27–29.
34. Matt 1:1–17, Luke 3:23–38.
35. Isa 9:6–7.
36. Nimoy, *Star Trek III*.
37. Ibid.
38. Ibid.
39. Ibid.

the Church. This heavenly moment can be likened to the reward at the end of a life of faithfulness. The Body of Christ is reunited with the person of Christ, as the person of Spock is reunited with the body of Spock.

Spock stops when he sees Kirk. "My father says you have been my friend. You came back for me." Kirk replies, "You would have done the same for me." In this, Kirk reflects the calling of the Church to mirror Christ, to do what he would do. Spock is curious. "Why would you do this?" Kirk replies, "Because the needs of the one outweigh the needs of the many." Spock, like Christ, placed "the needs of the many" before his own. Here, Kirk echoes the idea that followers of Christ now put Christ before themselves, not that Christ "needs" us, but that we have a need for him and we put him and his purposes before our own. This line also begins the same liturgy we previously saw between Kirk and Sarek, with Spock now repeating the sacred words. "I have been, and ever shall be your friend." Kirk shows immediate recognition. "Yes! Yes, Spock." Spock continues the liturgy, repeating some of his last words before his death. "Ship. Out of danger?" Kirk replies, "You saved the ship. You saved us all. Don't you remember?" Again, the word "remember" returns as Kirk has a communion with Spock. "Jim," Spock says, at last. "Your name is Jim." In the book of Revelation, God gives to the one who overcomes a pure, white stone that bears "a new name that no one can understand except the one who receives it."[40] Only Kirk's closest companions, Spock and McCoy, call him Jim, and surely only Kirk can truly understand what it means to hear Spock call him Jim again. The joy on Kirk's face reflects the reward he has sacrificed his career, his ship, and his son to find. Spock remembers him. Throughout Scripture, God "remembers" his people. But it isn't that he forgot. To remember, in a Hebraic context, is to act again on someone's behalf. To remember Christ in communion is to call to mind what he has done and act accordingly.[41] When McCoy "remembers" Spock, he doesn't just keep Spock in mind; he acts. He tells Kirk where to go. Spock speaks and moves through him. When we remember Christ, we act on his behalf, as his body. At the end of a life of faithfulness, Jesus remembers us, and says that we are his. Like the crew of the *Enterprise*, we give our all to follow him. But there's one more step in the journey: the voyage home.

---

40. Rev 2:17.

41. Kaiser Jr., *The Christian and the Old Testament*, 58.

4

Star Trek IV: The Voyage Home

"Gracie is pregnant."

—Spock

A mong Star Trek films, "the funny one with the whales" is not a place most people look for deeper meaning. It certainly is not a film in which one would generally expect to find theological significance. I didn't even expect to find it, so much so that I didn't even try to look for it. But, while watching the trilogy in sequence, it found me. The story so far in this film series has been of death and resurrection, sin and redemption. This film also deals with sin, with the impending doom of Earth and with a salvation that comes through restoration, brought by our Christ figure. Director and co-story developer Leonard Nimoy explains the impetus for the film's plot.

> We were looking for what would be lost in the 23rd century as a result of unconsciousness in the 20th century—nothing intention-al, nobody setting out to just damage the planet, but just lack of consciousness. What would be lost in the 20th century that would impact in the 23rd century in a powerful, negative way that would become a problem? It was sort of a sins of the fathers visiting upon the next generation.[1]

Nimoy's reference to the sins of the fathers refers to an idea in Scripture[2] that bears out in everyday life: the effects of our wrongdoing often ripple into future generations. This is a central theme of *Star Trek IV*, as humanity

---

1. Nimoy and Shatner, "Audio Commentary" for *Star Trek IV*.
2. Num 14:18, among others.

faces its imminent demise as a result of actions taken centuries prior. At the outset of the film, however, it is Kirk who stands accused.

Standing before the Federation Council, the Klingon ambassador calls Kirk "the quintessential devil in these matters,"[3] but the ambassador himself is an accuser, much like Khan in *Star Trek II*. Here, the Accuser comes as one seeking justice, portraying himself as an "angel of light"[4] of sorts, with only the truest of intentions. Sarek, however, reveals his true nature. The Klingon ambassador appears to be outwardly honest, but is inwardly deceptive. He is trying to condemn Kirk and have him extradited and judged under Klingon law, but the president of the UFP tells him, "The Council's deliberations are over." In a certain sense, this is what God says to Satan, "The deliberation has already happened. My judgment stands. We do things here by my law, not yours." However, Kirk is still held accountable under that law. "Admiral Kirk," the president says, "has been charged with nine violations of Starfleet regulations."[5] On Vulcan, Kirk and company are aware that they have violated regulations and resolve to return to Earth to face judgment for their crimes. On the one hand, this mirrors recognition of our culpability for our sin. Confessing sin is the first step toward forgiveness and restoration. However, the actions the *Enterprise* crewmembers took were on behalf of Spock. So, in a sense, their situation at this point in the film also reflects Jesus' words, "Blessed are you when people hate you, and when they exclude you and insult you and reject you as evil on account of the Son of Man!"[6]

All vessels and planetary defenses are powerless before the probe. A probe is, in the sense depicted in the film, a vessel that searches for something. But a probe is also an investigation, an uncovering of what is hidden, a search for the truth. God probes our hearts and knows the truth of what we keep hidden. If he probes us and finds our unrighteousness, we cannot survive. This is why we need Christ to give us his righteousness to replace our own. He must stand in our stead. Like the whales, only Christ can respond to God's probe on our behalf. In this context, applying the sun/Son symbolism causes moments in this section of the film to take on new meaning. The *Yorktown*, for example, is trying to make a solar sail—their hope lies in the sun. "Mr. President," Admiral Cartwright says, "even with

3. Nimoy, *Star Trek IV*.
4. A description of Satan used in 2 Cor 11:14.
5. Nimoy, *Star Trek IV*.
6. Luke 6:22. Here, Jesus uses the Messianic title "Son of Man" to refer to himself.

planetary reserves, we cannot survive without the sun." Indeed, it is the allegorical "Son" (Spock) who will save the Earth. Cartwright says of the probe, "It's using forms of energy our best scientists do not understand." The probe has great power, but is beyond our comprehension. "There seems to be no way to answer this probe," the president worries. "It is difficult to answer," Sarek replies, "when one does not understand the question." Similarly, when we are not in harmony with God, we often cannot communicate. "Mr. President," Sarek advises, "perhaps you should transmit a planetary distress signal, while we still have time."[7] He tells the president that the people of Earth should admit that they are powerless and cannot save themselves. It is when we make this admission that we can take a step toward trusting God for our salvation.

It is this distress signal that alerts the *Enterprise* to the situation on Earth. "We cannot survive," the president says in his message, "unless a way can be found to respond to the probe." He advises those listening to "Save yourselves." Of course, Kirk and company choose instead to attempt to save Earth. Spock suggests that the probe's signal may not be intended for humans and mentions that it is directed at the oceans. It is then also Spock who, once the sound has been adapted for underwater conditions, determines that it is the call of humpback whales. He also points out that the sound can be replicated, but not the language. "We would be responding," he says, "in gibberish." It is then Spock who suggests traveling back in time to obtain whales and Spock who does the computations required to enter time warp and arrive at the correct period in Earth's history. He even devises a way to restore the bird of prey's power using photons captured from a nuclear fission reactor—and (in his spare time, it would seem) designs and builds the device necessary to do it![8] In fact, the entire plan of what the crew will do in this film comes from Spock. Of course, ultimately, it is because of Spock that the crew is even in a position to save Earth at all. After all, it was he who saved all their lives by sacrificing himself in *Star Trek II*, so the crew's very existence is owed to him. Then, in *Star Trek III*, it

7. Nimoy, *Star Trek IV*.

8. There are a number of interesting tidbits here. Reviving the crystals is yet another recapitulation of the ongoing theme of life from lifelessness. This is interesting, since the prop in which the crystals are housed is a reuse of the lid that Spock moved to save the *Enterprise* in *STII*—another moment of bringing life from death. Additionally, nuclear fission, which can be destructive and which Spock refers to as "toxic," is used to power the ship, which is bringing the restoration of life. Destructive force becomes constructive, which is just the opposite of what Khan and Kruge wanted to do with Genesis.

was for his sake that the crew stole the *Enterprise*, retrieved his body from the Genesis planet, commandeered the bird of prey, and went to Vulcan to restore his spirit to his body. Therefore, it is because of Spock that the crew was nowhere near Earth when the probe arrived. And it is because of what they did on Spock's account that they are headed back to Earth at just the right time to receive the distress signal. Everything in this film hinges on Spock. Therefore, while this is perhaps the most ensemble-based film in this series, everything that happens goes according to Spock's plan.

Much of the rest of the film concerns the carrying out of that plan. It is a marvelous adventure comedy, filled with wonderful character moments and the opportunity to see *Enterprise* crewmembers out of their element and trying to accomplish near-impossible tasks. It's great fun, but there's not a lot to discuss in the way of the Christ figure allegory with which I have primarily concerned myself in this trilogy. The real source of symbolic content in the middle section of the film is Gillian, the whale biologist. In particular, her presentation during the tour of the cetacean institute sheds light on exactly what humankind is responsible for with regard to the humpback whales. She begins by helping us relate to the whales, showing that they are not fish, but more closely related to us than we might think. "They're mammals," she says, "just like you and me—warm-blooded, needing air to breathe, and producing milk to nurse their young." A tourist in the group asks, "Do whales attack people, like in *Moby-Dick*?"[9] This should certainly call back to mind the *Moby-Dick* references and framework of *Star Trek II*. The presence of this reference is no accident. Nicholas Meyer, who co-wrote and directed *Star Trek II* co-wrote this film as well and is largely responsible for the portion of the script that takes place in the 1980s. As I mentioned in the *Star Trek II* chapter, Meyer is a great admirer of Melville's classic whale saga and the reference here was a nod to the novel it seems he couldn't resist. This moment also serves, however, as a chance for Gillian to reinforce the innocence of the whales. "No," she tells the tourist, "no, most whales don't even have teeth. They have a soft, gum-like tissue that strains vast amounts of tiny shrimp for food and that is the limit of their hostility. Unfortunately, their principal enemy is far, far more aggressive."

KIRK: You mean man.

GILLIAN: To put it mildly. Since the dawn of time, men have harvested whales for a variety of purposes, most of which can be

9. Nimoy, *Star Trek IV*.

achieved synthetically at this point. One hundred years ago, using hand-thrown harpoons, man did plenty of damage. But that is nothing compared to what he has achieved in this century. This is mankind's legacy. Whales hunted to the brink of extinction. Virtually gone is the blue whale, the largest creature ever to inhabit the Earth. Despite all attempts at banning whaling, there are still countries and pirates currently engaged in the slaughter of these inoffensive creatures. Where the humpback whale once numbered in the hundreds of thousands, today, there are less than 10,000 specimens alive. And those that are taken in are no longer fully grown. In addition, many of the female whales are killed while still bearing unborn calves.

SPOCK: To hunt a species to the point of extinction is not logical.

GILLIAN: Who ever said the human race was logical?[10]

Gillian's reference to the damage done "one hundred years ago, using hand-thrown harpoons" is a direct reference to the time of *Moby-Dick*. It is, indeed, with a hand-thrown harpoon that Ahab, in a final assault against Moby-Dick, inadvertently throws himself into the sea, much as Khan destroys himself with his final stab at Kirk in *Star Trek II*. Gillian speaks sorrowfully of the "slaughter of these inoffensive creatures," while a video screen shows the brutality of whale hunting—fishermen with large scythes slice open huge swaths of whale blubber, revealing bright red flesh, all atop a whaling ship's blood-soaked deck. Producer Harve Bennett and director Leonard Nimoy discuss the relative lack of violence in this film,[11] but this clip shows genuine brutality, not movie violence, and quietly stands as one of the most gruesome moments in Star Trek history. "This," Gillian says, "is mankind's legacy. Whales hunted to the brink of extinction."[12]

At this point, it is most instructive to return to *Star Trek II*. In this film, humanity stands on the brink of extinction because of its sin. The world is literally coming to an end because of humanity's crimes. And what is our sin? Whale hunting. In *Star Trek II*, Khan also represents the sin of humankind. He is the inverse, the fractured image of Kirk, representing the fractured image of God in sinful humankind. And he is Ahab—a whale hunter. The arc from *Star Trek II* is complete as we now see the whale hunter again portrayed as the embodiment of sin. Spock set Kirk free from Khan in *Star*

10. Nimoy, *Star Trek IV*.
11. Nimoy et al., "Future's Past: A Look Back."
12. Nimoy, *Star Trek IV*.

Trek II and now must rescue humankind from its sinful, whale-hunting heart. Just as Midshipman First Class Peter Preston was the bloody image of innocence cut down by blind obsession in *Star Trek II*, so the bleeding, eviscerated body of the whale represents humankind's destruction of innocence in *Star Trek IV*.

Gillian stands, of course, in direct opposition to that destruction of innocence. Her bumper sticker alone—"I (Heart) Whales"—says it all. When she drives up next to Kirk and Spock, she greets them with, "Well, if it isn't Robin Hood and Friar Tuck."[13] This is a direct reference to Spock's clothing and demeanor in the film. Robed, quiet, reflective, he carries a spiritual quality that is intentional, which results in a fairly humorous exchange between Shatner and Nimoy in their audio commentary for the film.

Nimoy: The whole idea was to keep him mysterious and . . .

Shatner: Monastic.

Nimoy: What?

Shatner: Monastic.

Nimoy: Monastic. Yeah. That's a good word.

Shatner: Say it again.

Nimoy: Monastic.

Shatner: Good.

Nimoy: I like that.[14]

Indeed, Spock has monastic qualities. His quiet calm and cool reserve, his bowl haircut, and especially in these films, the ceremonial robes he wears and the meditation in which he often engages reinforce that monk-like essence. It is perhaps these quirky character traits (along with Kirk's easy charm) that draw Gillian to the pair of temporally misplaced tourists. It is also Spock's quiet, undisturbed nature that makes his sudden comment all the more shocking to Gillian. After a somewhat uncomfortable exchange between Gillian and Kirk during which Spock has sat quietly between them in the center seat of the cab of Gillian's truck, the Vulcan randomly interjects, "Gracie is pregnant." Tires squeal as the truck screams to a sudden stop. No one is supposed to know that. But, as Spock later tells Gillian,

13. Ibid.
14. Nimoy and Shatner, "Audio Commentary" for *Star Trek IV*.

"Gracie does." His mind meld with the animal was most informative. At dinner, Gillian confirms to Kirk, "Your friend was right. Gracie is not just pregnant; she is *very* pregnant."[15] Gracie (Grace) is about to give birth. Gracie (Grace) is filled with new life, with hope, with a future. The return of the whales to Earth means the end of suffering, and the short-circuiting of the effects of humankind's sin. Gracie (Grace) is ripe with salvation. "Grace," the song says, "she carries a world on her hips."[16] As Paul wrote to Timothy, "Our Lord's grace was abundant,"[17] and to the church at Ephesus, "By grace you are saved."[18]

This context further highlights the sorrow evident in Gillian's words during her presentation: "Many of the female whales are killed while still bearing unborn calves." Even as she speaks those words she has probably spoken a thousand times, Gillian must feel a particular pang of grief because she holds the secret that her beloved Gracie is pregnant. Not only that, but she knows that the institute is in a hurry to divest themselves of their famous humpback couple before Gracie gives birth. This might seem to be a good thing since, in Gillian's words, "no humpback born in captivity has ever survived." But, as she explains the rest of the situation, Gillian's heartbreak bubbles to the surface. "The problem is that they won't be that much safer at sea because of all the hunting this time of year. So, you see, that, as they say, is that." She can't hold back the tears. "Damn," she says, taking a sip of her beer to recover. In these moments, Gillian mourns so much more than she realizes. Grace is at risk. George, Gracie, and the calf Gracie bears in her womb are the literal salvation of the world. In killing mothers bearing unborn calves, our whale hunters have symbolically disregarded, gutted, and murdered Grace. They have, ultimately, sacrificed their own salvation at the altar of selfish and vain pursuits. How much so have we, as a human race, turned our hearts from Grace, failed to embrace mercy, and murdered love on the altar of self-interest? "To hunt a species to the point of extinction is not logical," Spock says, to which Gillian instinctively replies, "Who ever said the human race was logical?"[19] Logic is the law of Spock's father and humanity has indeed not kept to its Father's law. Of course, logic is often Spock's cover for acts of humanity and love, and love

15. Nimoy, *Star Trek IV*.
16. U2, "Grace."
17. 1 Tim 1:14.
18. Eph 2:8.
19. Nimoy, *Star Trek IV*.

is the law of God that we have abandoned. We have been poor stewards of the Earth and all of Creation is broken because of sin. Ours sins and the scars thereof run deep. But God's Grace—God's plan to give us a hope and a future[20]—is sufficient.[21]

"Think about it," Kirk implores Gillian after telling her what Gillian calls a "cockamamie fish story" and making his proposal to take George and Gracie to the twenty-third century. She does have to think about it. He won't show her the inside of his ship. She's going to have to do this on faith. In the morning, when she finds the whales were taken away in the night without her knowledge, she is more than angry. She has lost what she cares about most in the world, and in cruel fashion. Desperately, she goes to the only person she knows might be able to help. Unsure if she even believes, she clings to her last hope—Kirk (the Church). She arrives, desperately calling for Kirk, seeking in faith for something she cannot see. The helicopter lowering the plexiglass panel into the unseen ship acts like a small miracle, bolstering her faith. She calls out all the more, is knocked down by something beyond her perception, and continues to seek in desperation, even at one point on her knees, with hands raised. It is a desperate act of faith—a faith of which she is still not entirely convinced, but to which she clings as her last and only hope. "Oh, my God!" she shouts, as she is beamed aboard the bird of prey. "And Lord haste the day when my faith shall be sight."[22] It's all real!

Now, she joins Kirk and company in their work, like a newcomer to faith becoming part of a church. When they return, though, it is clear that Kirk does not consider her as one who will stay with them. He gets the radio frequency for the whales' tracking devices from her and begins to beam away. But Gillian jumps in and embraces him. "Surprise,"[23] she says, as they dematerialize. This world is not Gillian's home anymore. Her home is the restored, renewed world—and not even Kirk (the Church) can keep her out. There are certainly many whom Christians of varying denominations deem "unworthy" or see as not having "true faith." But the surprise they are likely to experience is when they enter the restored Creation to find that

---

20. Jer 29:11.
21. 2 Cor 12:9.
22. Spafford, "It Is Well With My Soul."
23. Nimoy, *Star Trek IV*.

these people are their new neighbors. God will save whom he will save[24] and no one—not even the Church—can bar their entry into his presence.

George and Gracie must now be tracked in the open sea of Alaska. When they are found, they are already targets for whale hunters. Sinful humans are making one last stab at Grace, unwittingly working toward their own demise. "If there is a heavy [a villain] in the picture," producer Harve Bennett says, "it's the actions of the world 300 years before, personified in the film . . . by the whale hunters . . . . And what's at stake here is salvation and redemption."[25] The harpoon is launched, ready to put an end to salvation, to truncate redemption—but the whale hunters are thwarted. One might even say that the de-cloaking bird of prey "put the fear of God into them." Hopefully, their whale hunting days are over. With the whales safely aboard, the crew makes way for the twenty-third century. "I hope you like our little aquarium," Scotty says to Gillian. She does. "A miracle, Mister Scott." "A miracle?" Scotty replies, "That's yet to come." Indeed it is.

As the ship rockets toward the sun to make its slingshot back to the future, things are not going smoothly. "Admiral," Spock says, "I need thruster control." Kirk gives it to him. Spock has control. He is the reason for the whole movie and is the agent of salvation. With Spock in control, the bird of prey makes the trip. Computers are nonfunctional, mains are down, and helm control is lost. The crew is no longer in control, but something, somehow, guides them to exactly where they need to be. Spock returns to Earth from above at the end of all things. He is coming on the clouds with his followers, returning from a heavenly place (Vulcan). The absence of the whales is the evidence and the effect of our sin. But the scar of sin will soon be covered by the return of the whales. Gracie is "very pregnant." Grace is about to give birth to salvation. Spock is repairing what was damaged and restoring the Earth, just as Christ ultimately restores all of creation. We had to cry out in humility, to admit our culpability and our powerlessness in a prayer for salvation. The clouds move in reverse, "the clouds be rolled back as a scroll."[26]

The grace of God is evident in this film series, and it wears pointed ears. Everything that happens in this film is made possible by Spock. His death has saved the crew. His resurrection has brought them together to be with him. His plan leads to salvation. His return restores creation. But Kirk

24. Rom 9:15.
25. Nimoy et al., "Future's Past: A Look Back."
26. Spafford, "It Is Well With My Soul."

releases the whales. Returning to the analogy of Kirk as the Church, this echoes the idea that Christ has chosen his Church—his people, all believers in him, not just institutions—to do the work of bringing his kingdom. Only when he returns will his ultimate rule and reign take hold, but until then, he entrusts his followers with the task of setting loose on the Earth that which he has earned. The whales are released. Kirk is puzzled. "Why don't they answer? Why don't they sing?" God's blessings don't always come when we'd like. We can become impatient for him to act. But, in his time—in the right time—his will is done. The whales sing, the probe is satisfied, and all is restored.

Rain falls. It is the first rain in Star Trek.[27] "O God," the psalmist writes, "you cause abundant showers to fall on your chosen people. When they are tired, you sustain them, for you live among them. You sustain the oppressed with your good blessings, O God."[28] The joy is unrestrained. Everyone jumps into the water—a kind of joyous, group baptism that recalls the opening scene of the film *Godspell*. Even Spock is smiling and laughing. Death is conquered. Destruction is averted. Creation is restored. The work of salvation is complete. Almost.

"Bring in the accused." The Federation president's voice is a harsh reminder that Kirk and company still have to answer for their wrongdoing. Without missing a beat, Spock rises with the rest of the crew and joins them before the seat of judgment. "Captain Spock," the president says, "You do not stand accused." "I stand," Spock replies, "with my shipmates." Spock does not stand accused. He stands with his friends. Christ comes also to stand with us before the seat of judgment. He comes, innocent and blameless, to advocate for us.[29] The charges are read: conspiracy, assault, theft, sabotage, willful destruction, and disobedience. "Admiral Kirk," the president continues, "How do you plead?" When we see Kirk, it's a two-shot—Kirk and Spock. Kirk does not stand alone. "On behalf of all of us, Mr. President," Kirk replies, "I am authorized to plead guilty." This is the resolution that was made at the beginning of the film—to accept guilt and punishment. When we stand before God, we are without excuse.[30] But, because of "mitigating circumstances," the president says, all charges but one are dropped. Indeed, those mitigating circumstances arise from the crew's

---

27. Okuda, "Text Commentary" for *Star Trek IV*.

28. Ps 68:9–10.

29. 1 John 2:1.

30. Rom 1:20.

faithfulness to pursue Spock, to respond to his sacrifice with abandon, and to help bring about the salvation of the world.

> PRESIDENT: The remaining charge, disobeying orders of a superior officer, is directed solely at Admiral Kirk. I'm sure the Admiral will recognize the necessity of keeping discipline in any chain of command.

> KIRK: I do, sir.

> PRESIDENT: James T. Kirk, it is the judgment of this council that you be reduced in rank to captain and that, as a consequence of your new rank, you be given the duties for which you have repeatedly demonstrated unswerving ability: the command of a starship. Silence. Captain Kirk, you and your crew have saved this planet from its own shortsightedness. And we are forever in your debt.[31]

Kirk's "punishment" becomes his reward. He is restored, to his "first, best destiny," to the destiny for which he was created. How often do we make ourselves admirals in our own lives? How often does our human arrogance seek to order our own destinies as if we were in command? Kirk has humbled himself, been willing to sacrifice his power, his position, his career, his very life, and because of his faithfulness, he has been restored—not to the position of highest rank and authority, but to his right place, his proper position, the destiny for which he was created. But now, while he has authority, he must submit to authority to be renewed to the calling he was given at the beginning. Finally, Kirk is fully renewed. Kirk's progress over these three films bears out the Christian saying "I have been saved, I am being saved, I will be saved."[32] In other words, salvation has been wrought by Christ[33] (regeneration, *Star Trek II*, life from death), is being worked out daily as we grow in faith[34] (sanctification, *Star Trek III*, a life lived in faith), and will be completed at the end of all things[35] (glorification, *Star Trek IV*, the restoration of Creation).

Spock then has a quiet but powerful exchange with his father. "It was most kind of you to make this effort," Spock says. "It was no effort," Sarek replies. "You are my son. And besides, I am most impressed with your

---

31. Nimoy, *Star Trek IV*.
32. Witherington, *Paul's Letter to the Romans*, 51.
33. Eph 2:8.
34. 2 Cor 4:6.
35. 1 Pet 1:5.

performance in this crisis." This is a very Vulcan way of saying, "You are my beloved son, in whom I am well pleased."[36] "As I recall," Sarek continues, "I opposed your enlistment in Starfleet. It is possible that judgment was incorrect. Your associates are people of good character." I don't like going too far with the idea of Sarek as God the Father, but here Spock's father reverses his judgment against Kirk and the other humans because of their devotion to Spock. Spock replies, "They are my friends." We, too, have God's judgment against us reversed because Christ calls us friends.

Finally, as the crew huddles in a shuttlecraft on their way to see their new commission, their conversation is telling. McCoy is as cranky as ever. "The bureaucratic mentality is the only constant in the universe," he gripes. "We'll get a freighter." Sulu is optimistic (and prescient!). "With all respect, Doctor," he counters, "I'm counting on *Excelsior*." Scotty is as passionate as ever about spacecraft. "*Excelsior*?" he exclaims, "Why in God's name would you want that bucket of bolts?" But Kirk, captain once again and as always, reins them all in. "A ship is a ship." Scotty relents. "Whatever ye say, sir. Thy will be done." Incidentally, this phrase recalls both the Lord's prayer[37] and Jesus' words in the garden of Gethsemane.[38] At this moment, their new ship comes into view—the *Enterprise*. Kirk and crew are returned to their Enterprise—they are given their original calling back again. They are restored to their first stewardship, but their *Enterprise* is renewed, restored, and made whole. God created us as humans to be human and not anything else. Our ultimate destiny is a human destiny. Our humanity is not abolished or obliterated; it is made whole, brought to its fullest, purest expression in the fullness of the glory of God. Our ultimate calling is our original calling. The fullness of our restored humanity is our *Enterprise*.

36. Mark 1:11.
37. Matt 6:10.
38. Luke 22:42.

5

Star Trek V: The Final Frontier

"Jim! You don't ask the Almighty for his ID!"

—Dr. Leonard "Bones" McCoy

"What does God need with a starship?" This simple question, posed by Kirk in the climactic scene of *Star Trek V*, pokes an obvious and rather gaping hole in the supposed deity of the being encountered by Sybok and the *Enterprise* crew on the planetoid beyond the Great Barrier. The being sits in a crater, surrounded by pillars—not unlike the place in which Kirk and company find V'Ger in *Star Trek: The Motion Picture*. If this being is in fact God, why is he confined here, and why does he need a starship to carry him and his message? Clearly, a God who can be confined to a physical space, unable to free himself without outside help from finite, mortal beings, is no God at all. Though this moment is often cited as an example of Star Trek asserting a strong atheist stance, it really is nothing of the kind. The god being could be interpreted as Yahweh God, but only if one assumes that the being is truthful when he claims to be the entity identified by the various names for God from across the galaxy. It is more likely, however, that this is a limited being claiming a breadth of influence that is beyond his reach. Spock says, "This is not the god of Sha-Ka-Ree, or any other god."[1] Spock does not assert, nor does anyone in the film, that God does not exist. He merely states that the being they have encountered is not God. There is every opportunity here for an assertion of atheism, but one is not given. In fact, in the film's penultimate scene, screenwriter David Loughery has a golden opportunity to have Kirk, Spock, and McCoy decide

1. Shatner, *Star Trek V.*

134

amongst themselves that God does not exist. Instead, they conclude that they have simply been looking for him in the wrong place. On the observation deck, Kirk approaches his two closest friends as they gaze out upon the stars and strikes up the ultimate metaphysical conversation.

KIRK: Cosmic thoughts, gentlemen?

McCOY: We were speculating. Is God really out there?

KIRK: Maybe He's not out there, Bones. Maybe he's right here . . . in the human heart.[2]

The first notable event in this scene is that Spock and McCoy are speculating together—together—with no argument, each of his own respective free will, quietly, and without judgment. This is a cosmic feat that should make even the most hardened naturalist begin to wonder about the possibility of miracles. Or perhaps this small moment of peace sub-textually points to the profoundly singular nature of the core idea in the scene: God is in the human heart.

Kirk, Spock, and McCoy comprise a triumvirate—a trinity—that is at the very heart of the series. In many instances, a discussion between the three is likened to three parts of the self, especially when discussing options in a given situation. The Freudian construct of id, ego, and superego is often cited, with Spock representing the ego (associated with reason and intellect), McCoy representing the id (associated with impulses and emotions), and Kirk representing the superego (associated with the conscience), who seeks a balance between the other two.[3] Indeed, Star Trek is at its best when intellect and emotions are in harmony and appealed to equally.

So, it is not insignificant that this moment represents a calm, a time of comfortable unity between these three friends who often find themselves somewhat at odds with one another. Having had their bonds of friendship tested, they have remained connected and are perhaps stronger friends than ever (as attested by their closing campfire song). This kind of closing unity occurs many times throughout the Original Series and in the first six Trek films. Particularly, this moment in *Star Trek V* recalls the conversation between Kirk and McCoy at the end of *Star Trek II*. As the two stand, gazing upon the birth of the Genesis planet with Carol Marcus and the rest of the crew, there is an easy familiarity between them that is mirrored in

2. Ibid.
3. Cf. Berger, *Media Research Techniques*, 133.

this discussion of "cosmic thoughts." Even though Spock is not physically present in *Star Trek II*, he is nonetheless an enormous presence in the conversation. The Kirk, Spock, McCoy triumvirate in unity is a Star Trek code for peace, wholeness, realization, and growth. When these three characters come together around an idea and stand in agreement with it, we as audience members know we are hearing the primary message of the episode or film we've just watched, and often an essential message of Star Trek itself.

Both conditions certainly hold true here. Kirk suggests, and McCoy and Spock seem to agree, that God exists somewhere, just not where they were looking. Specifically, it is profoundly important that Kirk locates God within the human heart, as this represents the closest thing to Gene Roddenberry's actual theology that had, to this point, found its way into Star Trek. While the films and series have often dealt with matters of religion, faith, and the supernatural, the characters rarely express their own views on these broader subjects and almost never discuss their beliefs about God. Specific false gods and false alien religions are certainly denounced, but characters almost never express their general views regarding religion, faith, or the supernatural, or express a specific faith or religion.

Here, the subject seems unavoidable. The crew has spent the entire film pursuing God and has found a pitiable, lonely, maleficent being instead. At the end of a film discussing such a weighty theme as the search for God, there is a clear need for some kind of conclusion, some moment of clarity in which to address the enormous implications of what has just taken place. Was the being they met really God? Clearly, it was not. It was far too limited and failed to pass the simplest test—a single question: "What does God need with a starship?" This is a test against which McCoy expresses strong opposition. "Jim!" the doctor protests, "You don't ask the Almighty for his ID!" The appropriate answer to McCoy's objection would appear to be, "Oh yes you do."

As Kirk and Spock challenge the being further, it soon shows itself to be no god at all and the faith of all those who might have believed, including McCoy and even Sybok, is shattered. The being fails the "God test." Intentionally or not, in this scene, Kirk, Spock, and McCoy lay out qualifications a being must meet in order to make a justified claim that he, she, or it is God. These qualifications are consistently not met by the god-being, demonstrating that it is not who it claims to be. The exchange is a very scientifically minded exploration of a larger question of existence: Who (or what) is God? It just so happens that each of the qualifications given by Kirk, Spock, and McCoy actually reflect important ideas in Christian theology.

The first qualification is that God is not limited in power.[4] As Kirk asks, "What does God need with a starship?" God should not depend on anyone to have power. He can use whatever means he chooses to work his will. This speaks to the Christian theological assertion of God's omnipotence. In his omnipotence, he is all-powerful and cannot be limited by any force outside himself. This all-powerful nature leads directly to the next qualification.

God is not limited in his presence.[5] Because he is omnipotent, he is also omnipresent because he cannot be limited by any force that could ask him to stay in one place. He could never be trapped on a planet, desperate for the use of something as miniscule as a starship. "An eternity I've been imprisoned in this place," the god-being says, "The ship! I must have the ship!" In his omnipresence, God is not confined to any space (like a planet), but is present everywhere, in all of Creation.

The third qualification for God that is laid out is that he must not be limited in knowledge.[6] When the god-being asks who Kirk is, the captain replies, "Who am I? Don't you know? Aren't you God?" Clearly, God should know all things—including the identity of random persons whom he may encounter. This comports with the Christian doctrine of God's omniscience. As an omniscient being, God, quite simply, knows all. Nothing is beyond him—neither the farthest reaches of the universe, nor the number of hairs on an individual's head.[7]

Fourthly, in Kirk, Spock, and McCoy's view, God must not be limited in his self-evidence.[8] "I seek proof," Kirk says, only to be knocked to the ground by an energy beam. In the Christian view, God has made himself known in all Creation[9] and seeks relationship with humankind. He has made himself known though Christ and by the Holy Spirit, through Scripture and revelation. He reveals himself in the order of the universe and in the human heart.

---

4. Rev 4:26, among others.
5. Jer 23:24, among others.
6. Heb 4:13, among others.
7. Matt 10:30.
8. Isa 45:5, among others.
9. Rom 1:20.

The triumvirate's fifth qualification is that God is not limited in his righteousness.[10] When Kirk asks, "Why is God angry?" he does so with a clear sarcasm which points to the fact that the god-being has no justifiable cause for anger. In the Christian view, God is slow to anger[11] and quick to forgive.[12] His anger is righteous and he does not lash out at humankind. What is more, his wrath has been borne by Christ and is no longer directed at those who trust in him.[13]

Finally, Kirk, Spock, and McCoy lay out the requirement that God must not be limited in his kindness and compassion.[14] As McCoy states, "I doubt any God who inflicts pain for his own pleasure." God's kindness and compassion are rooted in his love, which is the essence of his being.[15] In Christian theology, this characteristic of God permeates all the others and is the reason for his justice, his mercy, and his grace. "Truth in art," songwriter and musician Billy Crockett once said, "can be rendered by telling something honestly hopeful, or by telling something that's bleak that leaves the shape of what's clearly missing."[16] In a short scene, by pointing out why the god-being is not God, *Star Trek V* paints an excellent picture of who God truly is.

Returning to the observation deck scene, Kirk, Spock, and McCoy have once again exposed and dethroned a false god. In the popular conception of Star Trek, the three should stand in the pride of their human arrogance and declare that they have found yet more proof that no god exists. Instead, they seem to indicate that God is yet undiscovered, and somehow revealed in the human heart. This closely reflects Roddenberry's pantheistic vision of all humankind as a part of God. However, it is not out of keeping with a Christian view of God to say that he is in the human heart, for a number of reasons.

First, Christian theology holds to the concept of general revelation— that is, there are certain things about God that are available to all humans. There is a sense of the Divine that we have when we encounter creation, when we ponder our existence, and when we find incredible joy and

10. Ps 145:17, among others.
11. Joel 2:13.
12. 1 John 1:9.
13. Isa 53:5.
14. Ps 103:8, among others.
15. 1 John 4:7.
16. Harris, "Billy Crockett."

enlightenment through one another. After all, human beings are made in the image and likeness of God,[17] so it is not at all surprising that we should find something of who God is within ourselves.

Secondly, the Scriptures tell us that the law of God is written on the human heart.[18] In that universal human sense of morality and ethics upon which so much of Star Trek is based is another aspect of general revelation. There is a sense of right and wrong that all humans share. It is not in our nature to view life amorally; instead we have a strong need for justice and right action and the correcting of wrongs. At our best, these ideas guide our decisions and lead us to greater righteousness.

Thirdly, it is the heart where God speaks to us and the heart is where he seeks to live. The condition of the heart is the basic underpinning of all the teachings of Christ and the core of our relationship to him. Words and songs, rituals and religion, are not the way to God. The way to God is through a humble heart and a contrite spirit.[19] It is out of the heart that the mouth speaks.[20] The heart is the seat of human identity and it is the heart that seeks to know God. So, while the probable intention of Kirk's words about God in the human heart do not comport with Christian theology, the essential notion that we must know God—that we can only know God—in our hearts is absolutely essential to a Christian worldview.

The scene concludes with Kirk's hand drifting toward the plaque beside him, which we see in a close-up. The words on the plaque are those that fans of Star Trek and even those who have never seen an episode know so well: "Where No Man Has Gone Before." This moment links the great tag line of Star Trek with the preceding conversation about God. As I've stated before, the outward journey in Star Trek is really an inward journey. The real quest in Star Trek is for meaning and the fulfillment of the human heart. As Star Trek writer David Gerrold notes, "The final frontier is not space. The final frontier is the human soul."[21] In this context, the words "Where no man has gone before" in this scene could be seen as a reference to God, or perhaps to intimacy with God. What is going on in *Star Trek V* is a somewhat larger-scale version of what happens throughout Star Trek, especially the Original Series—the taking down of a false god. And one must

17. Gen 1:27.
18. Rom 2:15.
19. Ps 51:17.
20. Matt 15:18.
21. Gerrold, "Trials with Tribbles," 87.

admit that, even if attention is not directly being drawn to the one true God (Yahweh), the taking down of false gods is a noble pursuit. Of course, the Star Trek quest would lead us to a pantheistic God, but it is not insignificant that the human heart in Roddenberry's worldview and in Star Trek itself is the true location of God and the true aim of the Star Trek quest.

Whatever it is that is divine in the human soul, whatever it is that gives order and meaning to the universe, whatever it is that makes us human, that is what Star Trek seeks. In Roddenberry's view, this is the God that we are all a part of. In Star Trek in general, it is the depths of the human heart and soul and the betterment thereof. In *Star Trek V*, the human heart is where we find God. So, it could ultimately be said that the journey of Star Trek is a quest for God. Either implicitly or explicitly, this seems to hold true because everything Star Trek is seeking—peace, justice, unity, equality—can only be found in God and specifically through Christ. The idyllic future Gene Roddenberry longed for, the one that was even freer of conflict and pain than what was ultimately depicted on television and in films, reflects deep human longings that span continents, generations, and even millennia of human history. These longings are ultimately fulfilled in the narrative of Scripture, when the rule and reign of Christ brings order to all creation, to all humankind, and to the relationship between humankind and God. The future Gene Roddenberry longed for is the ultimate fulfillment of the gospel.

Star Trek VI:
The Undiscovered Country

"Don't let it end like this, Captain."

—Chancellor Gorkon

" B lessed are the peacemakers,"[1] Jesus says, and perhaps we don't hear him. Perhaps the images that come to mind when we hear the word "peacemakers" are of kind, gentle people who try not to stir up arguments or cause fights. They are of sweet old ladies who encourage warring siblings to "hug it out" and brave young boys and girls who step in and stop schoolyard fights. But, in the larger world of politics, diplomacy, and wars between nations—not to mention culture wars—peacemaking is very long, very hard work. It takes patience, sacrifice, compromise, and perhaps most challengingly, forgiveness. It is of this kind of peacemaking and of deep, personal forgiveness that *Star Trek VI* speaks—and powerfully so.

While Star Trek frequently deals in the metaphorical and even the metaphysical, it is often at its best when it discusses real-world issues. In *Star Trek VI*, much in the vein of classic episodes like "Let That Be Your Last Battlefield," it deals directly with then–present-day geopolitical realities, offering not only a commentary on events contemporary to its release, but on similar situations and issues that resonate even to the current cultural climate in the United States. As *The Undiscovered Country* explores the frightening portent inherent in the beginnings of peaceful negotiations with a bitter enemy in a geopolitical cold war, the implications for the

---

1. Matt 5:9.

equally volatile climate of a culture war are immediately potent to our current social and historical context. Klingon Chancellor Gorkon characterizes the "undiscovered country" of the film's title as the unknown possibilities of the future, but it is also indicative of an encounter with the unknown and deeply feared "other." That fear and distance is the first, most difficult hurdle to overcome in the journey toward peace. It requires letting down our guard and choosing to listen—really listen—to those with whom we are in conflict, and to seek to learn and understand. Co-story developer Leonard Nimoy expressed his vision for the film this way:

> My hope, my dearest dream was that, aside from this clever and useful plot, there would be an idea that would grow out of this film that would resonate even more deeply than the idea of trying to come to grips with our former enemies, and that would be to learn something about our former enemies that we had never known before. What made these people tick? Who are they? All we've seen is the blustering, angry, "we'll kill you" Klingons. We have never seen, never been inside the Klingon mind or the Klingon world, the Klingon lifestyle, the Klingon philosophy. How did they arrive at this? What has driven them to this?[2]

That first step of listening, of seeking understanding, is vitally important. In *Star Trek VI*, the first movements in this direction are painful. A supposedly diplomatic dinner devolves into a tense, barely civil evening, filled with too much alcohol and too little self-control. Barbs fly, emotions flare, and egos are wounded. Everyone is too raw, too defensive to build bridges. Every time someone tries, it goes up in flames. Even the peace-minded chancellor's own daughter, Azetbur, is not immune.

> CHEKOV: We do believe all planets have a sovereign claim to inalienable human rights.

> AZETBUR: Inalien. If only you could hear yourselves. "Human rights." Why, the very name is racist. The Federation is no more than a *homo sapiens*-only club.[3]

"If there is to be a brave new world," Gorkon admits to Kirk as he prepares to leave the *Enterprise*, "our generation is going to have the hardest time living in it."[4] This deep difficulty in communicating is capitalized upon

2. Kiselyak, "The Perils of Peacemaking."
3. Meyer, *Star Trek VI*.
4. Ibid.

when General Chang frames the *Enterprise* for firing on the chancellor's vessel, and blames Kirk and McCoy for the chancellor's assassination. In our present cultural conflicts, unlike the *Enterprise*, Christians have indeed fired—repeatedly and mercilessly. We were not framed. We are culpable. We therefore have upon us the greater burden of contrition and humility in the negotiations before us. Until we accept responsibility for our actions and their consequences, we can never move forward in the journey toward peace and reconciliation. In short, we must admit our wrongdoing and ask forgiveness. Certainly, the intention to create conflict and injure our neighbors may not have been present. But, just as Kirk and McCoy submit to the judgment the court makes against them, despite their innocence, so we too must accept the judgment due us, despite our best intentions. For we have caused harm, and we must make amends. We stand in judgment, having delivered injurious and even deadly blows against foes we should have recognized as our neighbors. Though wrongs are being righted without our participation, we have a responsibility to help repair the damage, just as McCoy tried desperately to save Gorkon. Now, as we assess the damage our actions have caused, we must hear and heed the dying words of Chancellor Gorkon: "Don't let it end like this."[5]

However, Gorkon's plea is made, it would almost seem, to the wrong man. Kirk had objected strenuously to Spock recommending him for the peace mission in the first place. "How could you vouch for me?" he angrily asks Spock. "That's . . . arrogant presumption . . . you know how I feel about this. They're animals!" "Jim," Spock calmly replies, "there is an historic opportunity here." Kirk's staccato response is almost knee jerk. "Don't believe them! Don't trust them!" "They're dying," Spock appeals. Kirk's response is quick. "Let them die!"[6] Such vitriol from the *Enterprise* captain who once scolded a helmsman with the words "Leave any bigotry in your quarters. There's no room for it on the bridge,"[7] may seem drastically out of character—and it is. William Shatner himself objected to the line and fought to either remove it or at least soften it with a gesture of immediate regret. Director Nicholas Meyer let him add the gesture, but cut it from the final film.[8] A racist Kirk may seem an impossible idea, but *Star Trek VI* potently

---

5. Ibid.
6. Ibid.
7. McEveety, "Balance of Terror."
8. Meyer, "Audio Commentary" for *Star Trek VI*.

shows how years of conflict and distrust can cause prejudice to sneak, unnoticed, into even the most vigilant of hearts.

In *Star Trek V*, when Sybok offers to take Kirk's pain, presumably the pain of losing his son at the hands of Klingons, Kirk flatly refuses, famously barking, "I need my pain!"[9] And he is right. Instead of running from our pain or seeking to have it removed, we must confront and struggle with it in order to move forward. By the time of *Star Trek VI*, though, it is clear that, rather than working through his pain, Kirk has allowed it to fester and slowly grow into unforgivingness, prejudice, and hatred. "I've never trusted Klingons," Kirk says in his personal log, "and I never will. I can never forgive them for the death of my boy."[10] Kirk feels justified in his distrust and animosity toward Klingons, but he is wrong. He is wounded and is too distracted by the pain of his wound to see Klingons as anything other than the ones who hurt him.

But Kirk grows in this film and learns to forgive. The injustice of the kangaroo Klingon court that sends him and McCoy to the penal colony on Rura Penthe, the depth of deception and disregard for life to which Valeris and her coconspirators are led, and the cruel obsession with conflict that drives General Chang all help him to see that he is on the side of injustice. The assassination plot against Gorkon itself shows him that holding on to past disagreements and hostility only begets more death. "Gorkon had to die," he tells Spock, "before I understood how prejudiced I was."[11] But, in his conciliatory exchange with Azetbur, after thwarting the assassination of the President of the Federation, he is finally able to let go of his hatred and to forgive the death of his son. This completes a long arc of transition for Kirk that is not unlike the one followers of Christ go through. If he was freed from his sin in *Star Trek II*, then he has now learned to share that freedom with others through forgiveness. In Christ, we are forgiven. And we often stop there. Yet we are not forgiven just for our own sake, but so that we might forgive others as well. As Jesus told his disciples, "If you forgive anyone's sins, they are forgiven."[12] But he also said, "If you retain anyone's sins, they are retained."[13] When we harbor a lack of forgiveness

9. Shatner, *Star Trek V*.

10. Meyer, *Star Trek VI*.

11. Ibid.

12. John 20:23a.

13. John 20:23b.

in our hearts, the results are just as efficacious. At the end of the film, the members of the *Enterprise* crew reflect on their own prejudices.

KIRK: Once again we've saved civilization, as we know it.

McCOY: And the good news is they're not going to prosecute.

UHURA: They might as well have prosecuted me. I felt like Lieutenant Valeris.

McCOY: Well, they don't arrest people for having feelings.

CHEKOV: And it's a good thing too. If they did, we'd all have to turn ourselves in.[14]

You can't be arrested for a feeling. Many of the *Enterprise* crew may have felt like Valeris did, but they did not conspire to assassinate Chancellor Gorkon and the UFP President. When we feel justified in our beliefs, however, we may take actions that, while they may be less nefarious than plotting assassinations, may still be damaging and unloving to our neighbors, even as they seem to logically follow from our beliefs. We may have a feeling or hold a belief, but that does not mean that we are justified in any action we take that is based on that belief. There are often larger issues at play. Valeris was motivated by prejudice and, many times—whether we admit it to ourselves or not—so are we. But, like Kirk, we may be blind to the hardness of our hearts. We must therefore be vigilant, questioning both our actions (which can be wrong, even when motivated by deeply held beliefs) and the motivations behind our actions, which can sometimes reveal feelings, biases, and prejudices we did not know we had. Human beings, even when motivated by good intentions, are fallible. We may not be planning any assassination conspiracies, but if our ideas of living out our beliefs lead us to privilege ourselves over others or to work for injustice for our neighbors, then there is an essential imbalance between our actions and what should be the core ethic of our lives as Christians: "Love your neighbor as yourself."[15] Often, our inability to love our neighbors is rooted in an essential distrust that God is in control. As Spock told Valeris during their conversation in his quarters, it is a matter of faith.

VALERIS: (referring to a painting on the wall) I do not understand this representation.

14. Meyer, *Star Trek VI*.
15. Matt 22:39.

SPOCK: It's a depiction from ancient Earth mythology. "The Expulsion from Paradise."

VALERIS: Why keep it in your quarters?

SPOCK: To be a reminder to me that all things end.

VALERIS: It is of endings that I wish to speak. Sir, I address you as a kindred intellect. Do you not recognize that a turning point has been reached in the affairs of the Federation?

SPOCK: History is replete with turning points, Lieutenant. You must have faith.

VALERIS: Faith?

SPOCK: That the universe will unfold as it should.

VALERIS: But is this logical? Surely we must . . .

SPOCK: Logic? Logic is the beginning of wisdom, Valeris, not the end.[16]

But Valeris lacks the faith of which Spock speaks. She feels, along with some Klingons and others in the Federation, that action must be taken to perpetuate conflict, to avoid reconciliation, to avoid the fearful "undiscovered country" of forging peace. Many Christians today seem to also feel that there can be, in Chang's words, "no peace in our time," that they must take up arms against their neighbors in a culture war that seeks, not conviviality, but social and political dominance. The future is frightening. As Kirk observes, "People can be very frightened of change."[17] But Christians need not fear change, whatever it may look like, whatever cultural influence they may feel they are losing in the process. God is still sovereign. Instead of trying to force our culture to resist change so that we feel more comfortable, we must instead ask ourselves how best to love our neighbors in a changing cultural landscape. If we ask that question deeply and openly enough, we may find the very change we fear is the best way for us to show love and compassion, that change is an opportunity to seek understanding, to overcome our own prejudices, to forgive, to seek forgiveness, and to truly become peacemakers in our world.

16. Meyer, *Star Trek VI*.
17. Ibid.

The Gospel According to The Kelvin Timeline

1

Star Trek (2009)

"Our destinies have changed."

—SPOCK

Destiny is a long-standing theme in Star Trek, as are time travel and the idea of alternate timelines. In the 2009 film *Star Trek*, the first to recast the roles from the Original Series and reimagine the world of the twenty-third century, these ideas are taken in new, exciting directions. The film is off-putting to many fans of the Original Series and the original cast, simply for taking stylistic license with the Star Trek aesthetic. It is a much heavier action story than previous Star Trek films and television series have been, and therefore also has the reputation of being all explosions and visual effects, ignoring character development, and lacking any Star Trek themes. While this assessment is certainly understandable—the action and visual effects sequences are startling and overwhelming to those more accustomed to the pace and scale of previous Star Trek—it is shortsighted. In reality, the film is rooted in its characters and puts a great deal of effort into telling a story that posits important and fascinating ideas about destiny, calling, and purpose. While they may be distracting to some, the action sequences are in support of this story.

There are many stories throughout Star Trek of time travel causing changes in the space-time continuum. In these stories, the crew is tasked with restoring "right time," with returning the time stream to its "correct" order, so that events will flow as they should. In *Star Trek VI*, Spock tells Valeris, "You must have faith that the universe will unfold as it should,"[1] suggesting both

1. Meyer, *Star Trek VI*.

a plan to the order of the universe and the necessity of a faith that the plan will not be disrupted. This film again appeals to Spock's dependence upon faith, but it also takes an unprecedented step in Star Trek history by asking a simple question: "What if the timeline were altered and we couldn't change it back?" For the first time in Star Trek history, our characters are completely unable to affect a restoration of the time stream, in part because they are totally unaware that a change has taken place. Only later in the film do they realize they are living in an "alternate reality," but no discussion takes place as to how they will return reality to "normal." This is absolutely revolutionary and posits the idea that destiny is not bound by the events that take place. Rather, destiny is the driving force that causes our characters' lives to fall into the right place, even as they exist in "wrong" time.

The opening scene quickly sets the tone for the film. We are immediately immersed in a tense, dangerous situation. A giant ship looms and attacks. We are not used to ship battles this early in a Star Trek film, nor to action at this level of intensity. But attentive ears will notice in Ben Burtt's sound design callbacks to the familiar beeps and chirps of the Original Series *Enterprise's* bridge. As quickly as the film dives into an intense action story, it also plunges into a heartrending character story. A young mother, pushed into early labor by a panic-inducing crisis, and a young father who chooses to give his life to provide his wife and newborn child the chance to escape and live share their final, tear-filled conversation over a communicator. Sorrow and joy meld and merge as the young mother grieves the loss of her husband, even as she holds her newborn baby boy. Once again, new life springs from sacrificial death. This is the birth of James T. Kirk. This is the beginning of *Star Trek*.

In both a recapitulation of events in earlier films and a prefiguring of events that will later color the life of the bold Starfleet captain, James Kirk is alive because of a sacrificial death. He lives because someone dies for him, but it takes him his whole young life before he learns how to respond. Raised with a father figure who (as is more fully demonstrated in deleted scenes) is long on rules and short on love, young Jim Kirk chooses rebellion and covers his anger and hurt with cocky arrogance and a proclivity for breaking the rules. That is, until he meets Christopher Pike. After stopping a barroom brawl with Starfleet cadets that leaves Kirk disoriented and bleeding, lying on top of a table, Pike stands over the smashed face of the humiliated young man and asks, "You alright, son?" It's a fitting way for Pike to address Kirk, as he will soon become a father figure to him—someone who believes in him, but is not afraid to tell him the truth, who challenges him to be something more than what he is.

"I couldn't believe it," Pike says, "when the bartender told me who you are." "Who am I, Captain Pike?" Kirk replies, perhaps really wanting to know. Pike is direct. "Your father's son." Kirk evades, calling over his shoulder to the bartender, "Can I get another one?" Kirk doesn't want to talk about his father. He wants to hide from the pain, from his past, and perhaps also from the future he knows his father would have wanted for him—a future in Starfleet. Being a Starfleet officer killed his father, and Kirk wants no part of it. "Something I admired about your dad," Pike says, "he didn't believe in no-win scenarios." This is the film's first callback to _Star Trek II_, a major influence on both of Abrams' Trek films. It also reveals something about how Kirk views his father's death. "Sure learned his lesson," Kirk retorts. Pike counters, "Well, it depends on how you define winning. You're here, aren't you?"[2] An apparent defeat is actually a victory. This is a very Christian idea. Christ on the cross may seem a symbol of defeat, but the cross is where Christians see the victory of Christ. As Paul writes, "[Jesus] has destroyed what was against us . . . . He has taken it away by nailing it to the cross." He writes that Christ has disarmed and "made a public disgrace" of rulers and authorities, "triumphing over them on the cross."[3] The cross was invented as a tool of public disgrace and shame, yet Paul says that, in being crucified, Christ has disgraced those who were against him. In the same way, George Kirk may have died, but he won a great victory. "No one has greater love than this," Jesus said, "that one lays down his life for his friends."[4] Certainly, George Kirk would have had many friends aboard the _Kelvin_, but no greater friend than his wife and no greater act of love than his sacrifice for her and his son.

"Your aptitude tests are off the charts," Pike tells Kirk, "so what is it? You like being the only genius-level repeat offender in the Midwest?" Kirk's indignation is instant. "Maybe I love it." Pike won't be thrown off course. "Look, so your dad dies. You can settle for less than an ordinary life. Or do you feel like you were meant for something better? Something special?" Pike is acting on faith that there is something inside of Jim Kirk that does feel destined for something more. This echoes the fact that Star Trek is not science-based, but faith-based. He doesn't appeal to practical concerns or

2. Abrams, _Star Trek_.
3. Col 2:14–15.
4. John 15:13.

career considerations. He doesn't beat Kirk up with what the consequences of his present actions will one day bring him. He doesn't guilt him or shame him. He tells him he was meant for something more—an idea he has probably heard from no one in his life, with the possible exception of his mother. And he encourages Kirk to enlist in Starfleet. At first, Kirk laughs it off, but as Pike presses, "You could be an officer in four years. You could have your own ship in eight," Kirk shuts down. "We done?" Kirk interrupts. Pike takes the cue. "I'm done," he says, but he leaves the door open. "Riverside Shipyard. The shuttle for new recruits leaves tomorrow, oh-eight hundred." And then, with words he might have considered holding back, Pike speaks both to the nagging tug of destiny he senses Kirk might feel and the young man's ability to defiantly rise to a challenge he knows is there. "You know, your father was captain of a starship for twelve minutes," he says. "He saved eight hundred lives, including your mother's. And yours. I dare you to do better."[5] It is a powerful moment—the potent end to one of the finest scenes in Star Trek history. It puts Kirk at a crossroads, a point of life-changing decision brought on by a little flirtation and a bar fight. Like so many destiny-altering moments in this film, it arises from an apparent fluke. But the message of this film is continually that there are no flukes, even when the timeline is skewed.

When Kirk shows up to Riverside Shipyards the next morning, still in his bloody T-shirt from the previous night's altercation, he gives away his motorcycle to a man who compliments him on it—like a disciple selling his possessions to follow after his master. He has come to submit to Pike's authority, to rise to his challenge, but not without his trademark rebellious flare. "Four years?" he remarks to Pike as he enters the transport vessel, "I'll do it in three." This moment merges the new, rebellious Kirk of this timeline with the Kirk we knew before. In the Original Series, Kirk was an ace cadet—responsible, high achieving, always excelling academically. Indeed, Pike calls Kirk a "genius-level repeat offender."[6] Here, Kirk defiantly resolves to be an excellent, even exceptional cadet at Starfleet Academy. He rebels by being a good student. Sometimes, all it takes for us to do the right thing is the right kind of encouragement from the right person, the right motivation and perspective to make the challenge before us enticing instead of daunting. This kind of change in attitude and vision is not just beneficial;

5. Abrams, *Star Trek*.
6. Ibid.

it can be a Divine intervention. But Kirk's journey toward his destiny is only one in this film. The other primary story is, of course, Spock's.

We first see Spock as a young boy on Vulcan, one of many students in what may be described as "computer bowls," half-sphere holes in the floor of a training room, where students are rapidly responding to questions posed in audio and in visual displays projected around them, recalling Spock's computer tests on Vulcan in *Star Trek IV*. The questions and answers come in an indecipherable barrage, but the last answer we hear Spock give is, "When it is morally praiseworthy, but not morally obligatory." Though we do not hear the question, working backwards from this answer, we can deduce that the question was, "When is an action a supererogation?" The essential idea here is that to supererogate is to go beyond what duty requires. In Vulcan terms, it might mean to do more than what is simply logical. This prefigures Spock's actions in *Star Trek II*, surely going above and beyond the call of duty to do what was necessary to save the ship, his crewmates, and especially Kirk.

This scene also highlights Spock's nature as an outcast among his Vulcan peers, as several other Vulcan boys taunt Spock, attempting to elicit an emotional response. Spock remarks that this is their thirty-fifth such attempt, but it is the first that is successful. "You're neither human nor Vulcan," one boy says, "and therefore have no place in this universe." Another chimes in, "Look at his human eyes. They look sad, don't they?" The boys shove Spock, who is becoming visibly upset, but it is an insult against his parents for which young Spock will not stand. "He's a traitor you know, your father," says the first boy, "for marrying her—that human whore." At this, Spock flies into a rage, throws the other boy into one of the computer pits, slides down the side after him and, taking a single hit to the mouth, overpowers the bully and straddles him, pounding away at the boy's face with his fists. The shocked expressions on the faces of the other two bullies seem to indicate that they will not be taunting Spock anymore. The fight, however, leads to an inevitable talk with Sarek, Spock's father. He tells Spock that Vulcans are an emotional race.

> SAREK: Emotions run deep within our race. In many ways, more deeply than in humans. Logic offers a serenity humans seldom experience. The control of feelings, so that they do not control you.
>
> SPOCK: You suggest that I should be completely Vulcan, and yet you married a human.

> SAREK: As ambassador to Earth, it is my duty to observe and understand human behavior. Marrying your mother was . . . logical. Spock, you are fully capable of deciding your own destiny. The question you face is: which path will you choose? This is something only you can decide.[7]

This scene exposes both the conflict within Spock and Sarek's preference that Spock choose the Vulcan way, even as he leaves the choice open to Spock. "Which path will you choose?" Sarek asks. As Spock grows, however, he learns that, rather than choosing one half of his nature over the other, he must honor both and find a balance between them. This scene also gives us a logical perspective on the central idea of the film: destiny. "You are fully capable," Sarek tells Spock, "of choosing your own destiny." In Sarek's view, it is Spock's active choice that will determine the course of his life. And he is right. Spock does determine his own destiny as a young man, when he is accepted into the Vulcan Science Academy.

There is a cathedral-like feel to the Vulcan Science Academy. High windows and angular architecture abound. There is good reason for this. The scenes inside the academy were filmed at SkyRose Chapel at Rose Hill Memorial Park & Mortuary in Southern California.[8] [9] The filmmakers seem keenly aware that the scientific establishment of Vulcan culture is also its religious establishment. As Spock speaks with his mother prior to appearing before the council, Gregorian-like chanting can even be heard in the background. Again, as in previous films, Spock is monk-like and involved in a deeply religious culture. Appearing before the council, who sit in a highly elevated position in front of him, Spock stands at the feet of the gatekeepers of his religious culture. He has the ability to be successful here and is readily accepted. But the Minister of the Vulcan Council exposes his view of Spock's heritage. "It is truly remarkable, Spock," he says, "that you have achieved so much, despite your disadvantage."

> SPOCK: If you would clarify, Minister. To what disadvantage are you referring?

> MINISTER: Your human mother.

> SPOCK: Council, ministers, I must decline.

7. Ibid.
8. "Star Trek Filming Locations."
9. Abrams et al., "Audio Commentary," *Star Trek*.

MINISTER: No Vulcan has ever declined admission to this academy.

SPOCK: Then, as I am half-human, your record remains untarnished.

SAREK: Spock. You have made a commitment to honor the Vulcan way.

MINISTER: Why did you come before this council today? Was it to satisfy your emotional need to rebel?

SPOCK: The only emotion I wish to convey is gratitude. Thank you, Ministers, for your consideration. Live long and prosper.[10]

In this moment, the minister exposes his prejudice against Spock. He has been insulted for his human heritage for the last time. It is clear to Spock that, however much a part of the Vulcan Science Academy he may have become, he would do so only insofar as he was willing to functionally accept the council's assessment that his human heritage is a disadvantage. He could never be fully himself; he could never be truly accepted. This mirrors Jesus' own experience, as he found himself at odds with religious leaders and cast out of his home synagogue. "I tell you the truth," he says in Luke's gospel, "no prophet is acceptable in his hometown."[11] It is this lack of acceptance that sends Spock to Starfleet.

Like Kirk's life-altering bar fight, this event is part of a series of apparent flukes, accidents, and incidental events that bring each future member of the *Enterprise* crew closer to his or her destiny. Uhura demands that Spock assign her to the *Enterprise*. McCoy pretends Kirk is ill and pulls rank on a duty officer to get Kirk aboard the transport shuttle going to the *Enterprise*. Sulu is at the helm because Helmsman McKenna has lung worm. Uhura becomes Communications Officer because she happens to be on the bridge (thanks to Kirk and an overheard conversation) when Pike needs someone who speaks Romulan. McCoy becomes Chief Medical Officer because Dr. Puri is killed. Chekov is on the bridge, despite his youth, because he is, in Pike's words, a "whiz kid." Spock is made acting captain because Nero demands that Pike go to the *Narada*. Kirk is made acting First Officer because he happens to be present, even though he is, as Pike says, "not even supposed to be here." And Engineer Olson dies during the space

10. Abrams, *Star Trek*.
11. Luke 4:24.

jump to stop the *Narada*'s drill, leaving room for Scotty to fill the role. Of course, first Scotty must get on the *Enterprise*—a difficult task indeed, as he is assigned to a post on the ice planet Delta Vega. Fortunately, this is exactly the planet on which Spock maroons Kirk after Kirk vehemently disagrees with his decision to regroup with the fleet in the Laurentian system. It also happens to be the same planet on which Nero marooned the elder, prime timeline Spock, so he could watch the destruction of Vulcan. Of all the gymnastics that take place to pull the *Enterprise* crew together, this was where even director J.J. Abrams became incredulous. "I remember, when it was first pitched, [saying], 'How are you guys ever gonna make running into Spock in the cave work?'" The answer that convinced him it would work, though, came from writers Roberto Orci and Alex Kurtzman. "But what you guys did so brilliantly," Abrams says, "was . . . saying, 'It's fate.' That . . . it's destiny. These characters must be together . . . . It literally, for some reason just made [sense]."[12]

This idea illustrates the survival of the concept of destiny in the absence of a predetermined narrative. The age-old theological debate regarding the sovereignty of God over events that occur in time is the debate between "free will" and "determinism," or "predestination." In short, the debate is over whether every second of time is predetermined by God and unfolds exactly according to plan or humans have free will to determine their own destinies. The idea posited in this film is that events can change wildly, but there is a constant destiny that operates through and in cooperation with the chaos of free will. In theological terms, this would mean that God's will cannot be thwarted, not because there is no such thing as free will or chaos, but because the will of God is able to absorb chaos into its matrix. This film exists in an alternate reality—an entirely new set of circumstances and conditions, created by a disruption in the flow of space-time. This relates to an idea known as the "many-worlds interpretation" of quantum mechanics.[13] It is one of many theories of a multiverse, the controversial idea that multiple, perhaps infinite, universes exist simultaneously. In the many-worlds interpretation, all possible outcomes exist as realities in parallel universes. These ideas are not supported by all physicists and are hotly debated in many circles. This film proposes, however, a reality in which, it would seem, such things can and do exist. This idea raises an interesting understanding of God's sovereignty. If God is the creator and sustainer of the universe,

12. Abrams et al., "Audio Commentary," *Star Trek*.
13. Vaidman, "Many Worlds Interpretation of Quantum Mechanics."

who exists eternally, outside space-time, and if all these parallel universes really do exist, then it would follow that, in every universe, in every possible expression of every possible outcome, God is sovereign. His will and plan for the universe and for the human race includes literally every possibility and, in every eventuality, his will is accomplished. In this vision of reality, our destinies have less to do with what events take place in our lives and more to do with who and what we become. In Abrams' _Star Trek_, every character finds his or her destiny, regardless of the circumstances of their lives and also exactly because of the circumstances of their lives. Chaos comes to rock their existence and throw them far away from their destinies. And chaos also comes to push them right back to their destinies again.

"Nero's very presence," Spock says, "has altered the flow of history, beginning with the attack on the USS _Kelvin_, culminating in the events of today, thereby creating an entire new chain of incidents that cannot be anticipated by either party." "An alternate reality?" Uhura asks. "Precisely," Spock confirms. "Whatever our lives might have been, if the time continuum was disrupted, our destinies have changed."[14] But Spock is wrong. The point and purpose of the entire film is to show how the crew of the _Enterprise_ is assembled together, each in his or her right place, each fulfilling his or her destiny, regardless of the events that have taken place. The audience is well aware that these people all ended up on the same ship, doing the same jobs, in their original reality. We can see the mirroring, the echo of events from the previous timeline. The characters in the film cannot. To them, the events of the story are absolutely chaotic, totally random—exactly the kinds of flukes and unplanned events that pave the way for us to find our own destinies in real life. And perhaps, when we make major decisions, we engage in interdimensional travel, punching through from one universe to another, creating new realities in our wake. Whatever the case, we will reach our destinies whether we want to or not, in spite of ourselves. This is the interplay with free will and determinism. Like the time-honored psychological debate of nature vs. nurture, free will and determinism is a both/and proposition.

When Kirk asks if Spock Prime is accompanying him and Scotty to the _Enterprise_, Spock Prime replies, "No, Jim. That is not my destiny." Here, Spock seems to espouse a belief in a destiny that he does not control, a fate that is outside him. This is the opposite of what Sarek taught him as a boy. In the film, neither perspective is said to be untrue. Rather, they play off

14. Abrams, _Star Trek_.

one another, as we see both conscious choice and random chance affect our characters' destinies. Spock has faith. He is acting on faith in this film by not accompanying Kirk. He has faith that if Kirk is captain and Spock is in his right place as First Officer, everything will turn out as it should. "Under no circumstances," Spock Prime says, "can he [young Spock] be aware of my existence. You must promise me this." He then speaks to Kirk's proclivity for rebellion. "Jim, this is one rule you cannot break. To stop Nero, you alone must take command of your ship." At the end of the film, young Spock is puzzled by his elder self's risky actions. "Why did you send Kirk aboard," he asks, "when you alone could have explained the truth?" "Because," Spock Prime replies, "you needed each other. I could not deprive you of the revelation of all that you could accomplish together. Of a friendship, that would define you both, in ways you cannot yet realize."[15]

In this, Spock reflects the answer God might give, were we to ask him why he chooses to work through frail, limited humans, why he chooses to allow such chaos and uncertainty in the universe, or why there is such mystery to our existence when he could simply explain everything. We need the experience. The information alone would deprive us of the benefit of everything we learn by going through the process. Experiential knowledge, understanding that produces gradual, difficult growth and change, is essential to our humanity. Without it, we cease to be learning beings. Our souls wither and die. We function on the fuel of failure, frailty, and faith. Young Spock calls Spock Prime's plan "a gamble." Spock Prime recasts it as "an act of faith" and advises his younger self to stay in Starfleet, encouraging him to "put aside logic" and "do what feels right."[16] Once again, this moment demonstrates that faith is at the heart of Star Trek. Like Pike in his conversation with Kirk, Spock Prime appeals to young Spock's inner sense of his own destiny. And perhaps it is ultimately that internal compass in our souls—what Christians would call the movement of the Holy Spirit—that keeps us bending toward our destinies in all our (theoretically possible) alternate realities.

At the end of the adventure, the *Enterprise* crew is on the bridge and in engineering—each of them in their proper places. They are setting out on their destiny. Incredible things have happened to tear them away from their destinies, but incredible things have also happened to bring them right where they belong. This also demonstrates the relationship between

15. Abrams, *Star Trek*.
16. Ibid.

the individual and the community. This is about their individual destinies, but also about their combined destinies. In Star Trek, individual characters are important, but so is the human community. This is true in the will and plan of God as well. His focus is macrocosmic and microcosmic, including the small and the great. And, in Abrams' _Star Trek_, all the small things work together for the greater good of the galaxy.[17]

17. Rom 8:28.

2

Star Trek Into Darkness

"Our first instinct is to seek revenge when those we love are taken from us. But that's not who we are."

—Captain James T. Kirk

In the opening scene of *Star Trek Into Darkness,* on the planet Nibiru, we see the first depiction of religion (apart from Vulcan religion) in this iteration of Star Trek. In this scene, the religious people of Nibiru are stopped in their tracks by a sacred scroll, before which they bow. While this seems to demonstrate a long-held and specific belief system, when they see the *Enterprise* rising from their ocean, they appear to immediately ascribe divine attributes to the ship. Within seconds, they are drawing a representation of the ship on the ground and bowing down to it. This moment reinforces the idea that religion is something people use to explain things they don't understand. While this is certainly true to some degree, limiting religion merely to this idea does not explain the religious impulse. Why do we worship? If there is to be an explanation for things we don't understand, why should we prostrate ourselves before it? Why do we seek to connect with something that is greater than ourselves, and even greater than our human community? If there is an instinct, there tends to be a satiation. If we have an impulse to worship, there must be a reason, and it's not merely to explain what happens when we die (or to ascribe supernatural significance to starships hidden in incredibly foolish places). The idea that religious people will immediately worship anything big and beyond their understanding is insulting to the intelligence of religious people. Of course, like all Star Trek representations of religion, this should not be taken as a blanket statement regarding all religion. And, in context, it seems to be more a quick and seemingly clever way to illustrate the dangers of violating the Prime Directive than a comment on religion itself.

Speaking of the Prime Directive, Kirk's decision to neutralize Nibiru's potentially planet-destroying volcano breaks that directive in a big way. As Pike explains to Kirk, interfering in the natural course of a planet's development is not the business of Starfleet. "Starfleet's mandate," he tells Kirk and Spock, during a scathing dressing down, "is to explore and observe, not to interfere," and later, "You were supposed to survey a planet, not alter its destiny." This single use of the word "destiny" harkens back to the theme of the first film, which does come somewhat into play here. Kirk and company found their destinies in the first Abrams film, but they have made some mistakes. Finding one's destiny must be followed through with wisdom. Kirk took a huge risk with his plan on Nibiru and, in Pike's words, "violated a dozen Starfleet regulations and almost got everyone under your command killed."[18] The problem here is that Kirk sees the fact that he made it through by the skin of his teeth as justification for taking that risk. "Although there is greatness in Kirk," Pike actor Bruce Greenwood explains in the DVD commentary, "he is arrogant and he feels he's invincible. And that's really dangerous." Kirk actor Chris Pine calls this a "self-serving quality" that is rooted in Kirk's desire "to prove that he's the best, that he can get away with all this, that he can win."[19]

"What's worse," Pike tells Kirk, "is you're using blind luck to justify your playing God." There is a long history in Star Trek of characters playing God, going back to Gary Mitchell in the 1966 Original Series pilot.[20] It never ends well. In fact, playing God seems to be one of the worst things a character can do in Star Trek. One may ask, though, whether Kirk and company's actions on Nibiru hold to a higher law. Saving an intelligent race from destruction would seem to be the compassionate thing to do. However, the Prime Directive exists precisely because the consequences of interference cannot be known and can often be worse than the consequences of noninterference, not to mention the wider implications of actions taken. For example, what will the effect of stopping the volcano be on the planet? Certainly, it is saved for now, but volcanoes are an important part of a planet's ecosystem. The pressure of the magma from within the planet must

18. Abrams, *Star Trek Into Darkness*.
19. Abrams et al., "Kirk and Spock."
20. Goldstone, "Where No Man Has Gone Before."

be released somewhere. Have the *Enterprise* crewmembers merely delayed an inevitable disaster? It's hard to believe they could create a worse one, but might they have? Christians often wish to help and be compassionate to others and engage in philanthropic and charitable efforts. This is a good impulse. But it is very important to take stock of the larger impact of charitable efforts. Is the organization using its resources wisely or wastefully? Is it providing true benefit or causing more problems? It may seem a wonderful idea to give shoes to a woman who walks five miles barefoot every day to get water, but is the problem that she is barefoot (as many indigenous peoples have been for thousands of years) or is it that she has to walk five miles to get water? Seeking solutions that provide sustainable help and address root problems instead of offering temporary fixes or imposing Western cultural norms is an important part of charitable efforts. We cannot refrain from interfering when fellow humans need help, but sometimes the help we offer may just be stopping up a volcano—delaying, ignoring, or exacerbating the real problem. Kirk's intentions may be noble, but his brashness and arrogance may cause more problems than they solve.

"Is there anything," Khan asks Kirk, "you would not do for your family?" This line is the final punctuation in a speech from Khan that is supposed to make the character sympathetic, to show the audience that he has understandable motives and cause them to question how evil he really is. But the scene falls well short of achieving this goal. "I had every reason to suspect," Khan says, "that Marcus had killed every single one of the people I hold most dear. So I responded in kind." Khan acted, then, on a suspicion. He had no actual evidence that Marcus had killed his crew—and, in fact, Marcus hadn't killed them. He then struck out in vengeance, not responding "in kind," but committing acts of terrorism, destroying buildings and killing innocent people who had nothing to do with the actions Khan incorrectly assumed Marcus had taken. Somehow, that fails to hit the sympathy button. Khan's situation is apparently meant to be mirrored by that of the Starfleet officer Khan recruits to carry out the first strike. His daughter is terminally ill and he is desperate for a solution. Khan offers him one: the miraculous powers of Khan's blood, the saving of the little girl's life, in exchange for an act of terrible violence that will result in the officer's death and, ultimately, that of forty-two other innocent people. Is there anything I would not do for my family? Yes. I would not blow up a building and kill myself and an unknown number of innocent people. How is this officer's daughter supposed to feel, growing up knowing that her father committed an act of terrorism to save her life? Is that the kind of legacy anyone would want to leave for his or her child? The cost seems far too high. While both of these characters are portrayed as being motivated by grief, only the Starfleet officer is motivated by a desire to save someone he loves. Khan is motivated by blind, careless vengeance—notably the name of Marcus' ship, the USS *Vengeance*, which Khan eventually runs into the ground.

Vengeance is a recurring theme in the film. In Kirk's initial confrontation with Khan, his immediate instinct is to have his revenge for the death of Pike. Khan has surrendered and Kirk takes the opportunity to pound his desire for vengeance into the genetically engineered superhuman. Kirk lands punch after punch, slamming away at Khan's face, leaving not a mark on his foe, but nearly exhausting himself in the process. Khan is completely unharmed by the attack; it is Kirk alone who suffers. This symbolically and beautifully demonstrates the utter futility of revenge. When Kirk threatens Khan in the *Enterprise* brig, Khan taunts, "Oh, Captain, are you going to punch me again, over and over, till your arm weakens?"

The USS *Vengeance* itself is an illustration of the pursuit for which it is named. Built at a hidden facility, it grows in secret, fueled by anger—the anger of Admiral Marcus. It is large and menacing, but, as it is designed for a skeleton crew, internally empty and vacuous. And, as Khan, overcome with rage, plows the ship into San Francisco, it illustrates the destructive cycle of vengeance as it causes incredible collateral damage. Finally, as Spock—the only character who poses any physical threat to Khan—pummels the warlord within an inch of his life, it is clear that he will accomplish nothing, as Uhura halts him with the words, "Stop! He's our only chance to save Kirk!" Only mercy will accomplish true salvation and, in seeking vengeance, we once again play God. "Do not avenge yourselves, dear friends," Paul writes "but give place to God's wrath, for it is written, 'Vengeance is mine, I will repay,'[1] says the Lord."[2] God claims ownership over the very idea of giving people what they deserve. This is a mercy, because he knows how destructive revenge is to the human heart, how easily we become what we lash out against. "Do not be overcome with evil," Paul continues, "but overcome evil with good."[3] As James, the brother of Jesus, writes, "Human anger does not accomplish God's righteousness."[4] At the end of the film, Kirk puts it this

1. Deut 32:35.
2. Rom 12:19.
3. Rom 12:21.
4. James 1:20.

way: "There will always be those who mean to do us harm. To stop them, we risk awakening the same evil within ourselves. Our first instinct is to seek revenge when those we love are taken from us. But that's not who we are."[5] We are not those who repay evil for evil, nor are we those who play God. We seek to overcome evil with good. This idea comes to a sense of both destiny and identity and might call to mind Kirk's line from the previous film: "Who am I, Captain Pike?"[6]

Firstly, in this film, Kirk is a man who learns humility. When Admiral Marcus stands ready to destroy the *Enterprise*, Kirk humbles himself and acts like a captain. "Sir," he pleads, "my crew was just, was just following my orders . . . I take full responsibility for my actions. But they were mine and they were mine alone. If I transmit Khan's location to you now, all that I ask is that you spare them. Please, sir. I'll do anything you want. Just let them live." Marcus almost seems impressed. "That's a hell of an apology," he replies. "But if it's any consolation, I was never going to spare your crew." As Marcus gives the order to fire, Kirk says to his crew, "I'm sorry." In his moment of true humility, the weapons on the USS *Vengeance* are disabled. Vengeance cannot destroy him. He has let go of it.

Later, as Kirk plans to execute a space jump over to Marcus' ship, Spock objects. "I cannot allow you to do this," the First Officer says. "It is my function aboard this ship to advise you on making the wisest decisions possible, something I firmly believe you are incapable of doing in this moment." Kirk doesn't defend himself. "You're right!" he replies. "What I'm about to do, it doesn't make any sense, it's not logical. It is a gut feeling. I have no idea what I'm supposed to do. I only know what I *can* do. The *Enterprise* and her crew need someone in that chair that knows what he's doing. And it's not me. It's you, Spock." As in the first film, this moment touches on the interplay between free will and determinism. Many of us spend a great deal of time and energy asking "What does God want me to do?" We are seeking to be in that "right time," doing the "right thing" so God will bless us. But, as we worry about what we're "supposed" to be doing, our fretting is keeping us from doing *something*. In the end, God has given us brains and hearts, minds and souls, and the ability to make decisions. Sometimes, all we can do is what we *can* do. It may or may not be wise, but if we don't try, we'll never learn. Finally, Kirk puts Spock in command. He steps aside and relinquishes control to Star Trek's preeminent

5. Abrams, *Star Trek Into Darkness*.
6. Abrams, *Star Trek*.

Christ figure. In the same way, we must recognize that it is God who is in the captain's chair. Our decisions may go wrong, our best attempts may fail, but we must always recognize who holds it all in his hands and trust that he is working to bring about good.

Once again, then, we can see glimmers of Spock as a Christ figure in this film—and of Kirk as the Church. One small moment comes in the viewscreen conversation between young Spock and Spock Prime. Young Spock asks Spock Prime about Khan, whom Spock Prime describes as "the most dangerous adversary the *Enterprise* ever faced." When young Spock asks, "Did you defeat him?" Spock replies, "At great cost. Yes." Sadly, these are Leonard Nimoy's final spoken words as Spock on film. In them, he refers to Spock's sacrifice in *Star Trek II*, a reference to the event that solidified Spock's place as a Christ figure. An earlier reference to this event comes when Spock is trapped in the volcano. When Kirk expresses his intent to mount a rescue, Spock protests with his famous words from *The Wrath of Khan*, "The needs of the many outweigh the needs of the few."[7] As he accepts the impending reality of his death, Spock closes his eyes and stretches out his arms, as far as his protective suit will allow, in a nearly crucifix-like pose. But it is not Spock who will sacrifice his life in this film.

As Kirk climbs the internal structure of the warp core, it is as though he is climbing his Golgotha. He reaches up, again in an almost crucifix-like pose, and kicks the warp drive housing back into place. At the beginning of the film, when Spock is in the volcano, Kirk asks McCoy, "If Spock were here and I were there, what would he do?" McCoy, perhaps not the most objective source of opinions about Spock, coldly replies, "He'd let you die." At this point in Spock's development as a character, that may be true. But Kirk knows that is not the better part of Spock. He has faith in Spock's humanity. Spock, indeed, has done the human thing, using what Khan wanted against him. As Kirk dies inside the radiation chamber, in a clear mirroring of the events of *Star Trek II*, he compliments Spock on this. Spock replies, "It is what you would have done." "And this," Kirk tells Spock, referring to his own self-sacrifice, "is what you would have done. It was only logical." In this scene, then, we have a picture of Kirk (the Church) doing what Spock (Christ) would do. Indeed, Christians are called to embody Christ,[8] to take to heart both his words and his deeds and to live as he taught us to live. As Kirk places his hand on the glass, Spock places his there as well, making the

7. Abrams, *Star Trek Into Darkness*.

8. 1 Cor 12:27.

Vulcan salute. In a deviation from the 1982 film, Kirk moves his fingers to line up with Spock's, returning the sign. This may be seen as a symbol of the Church being conformed to Christ's image, a tiny visual representation of the process of sanctification. Kirk has humbled himself, as we must humble ourselves before God.[9] He has put Spock in charge, as we must put Christ in charge—the path to true freedom.[10] He has done what Spock would do, as we are called to follow Christ's example, even to the point of sacrifice.[11] Spock has humbled himself to become like Kirk, as Christ came to be like us.[12] And, ultimately, Kirk has come to reflect Spock, as we are conformed to the image of Christ[13]—the true image of our best, fullest humanity. As James, brother of Jesus, writes, "Humble yourselves before the Lord and he will exalt you."[14] This reflects the constant balancing act in Star Trek between humility and pride—in humility, we have the chance to discover greatness within ourselves, even as we recognize the greatness that is beyond us.

"What makes a great story," J.J. Abrams says, is that it is "always about selflessness . . . . A myth teaches people to look outside of themselves."[15] Star Trek is indeed a myth. Its characters are the stuff of legend, iconic and widely recognized. At its best—even within some of its weakest iterations—Star Trek is able to help us see beyond ourselves, to seek out new ideas as though they were "new life forms and new civilizations." Even as it goes *Into Darkness*, Star Trek has the ability, like the stars themselves, to cause us to look up.[16]

9. Mic 6:8.

10. 1 Cor 7:22.

11. Eph 5:2.

12. Phil 2:5–8.

13. Rom 8:29.

14. James 4:10.

15. Abrams et al., "Kirk and Spock."

16. Ps 123:1.

3

Star Trek Beyond

"Ye cannae break a stick in a bundle."

—Chief Engineer Montgomery Scott

C aptain James T. Kirk is bored with adventure. In the opening scene of *Star Trek Beyond*, we encounter the man who was once our brash, rebellious young hero, looking a good deal more grown-up, performing the noble duty of a Starfleet captain: brokering a peace treaty—in this case, between the Teenaxi and the Fabonans. Standing before the Teenaxi delegation in a cave-like meeting hall, hewn in rock and resembling a high-rise stadium, he hits the points of his carefully scripted speech like a professional diplomat—with both the poise of confidence and a hint of the weariness of perhaps too much experience for his taste. "I bring you a message of goodwill," he says, "and present to you, esteemed members of the Teenaxi delegation, a gift from the Fabonan High Council, with the highest regard." At this point, what should be a perfunctory moment of ceremonial acceptance turns frustratingly uncomfortable. "What's wrong with it?" barks the lead Teenaxi delegate, an imposing figure with giant eyes and a build like a bipedal ox. Kirk is confused. "Excuse me?" "Why don't they want it anymore?" the delegate continues. As Kirk tries to reassure the delegate, the exchange only escalates, as the vocally suspicious Teenaxi spirals into a blusterous, paranoid rage.

> KIRK: Well, this was once a piece of an ancient weapon, and now they offer it as a symbol . . . of, of peace. In the Fabonan culture, to surrender a weapon is an offer of truce.
>
> TEENAXI: How did they come by it?

KIRK: They told me the acquired it a long time ago.

TEENAXI: So they stole it, then!

KIRK: No. They, um, well . . .

TEENAXI: You do not know the Fabonans like we do!

KIRK: Yeah, that . . . that's very true. Your Excellency, this gift is a
. . .

TEENAXI: They are a tribe of untrustworthy thieves, who want to
see us murdered in our own beds!

KIRK: This beloved artifact is a symbol of trust and peace.

TEENAXI: They want to chop us into pieces, and roast us over a
fire . . .

KIRK: No, no. I don't think that's true . . .

TEENAXI: . . . and eat us!

KIRK: What?[1]

Bounding from his high perch, the Teenaxi delegate's heretofore apparently imposing frame is quickly exposed as diminutive, as his roar of anger shifts upward into a high-pitched ululation, exposing that he is, indeed, small enough to be eaten. Kirk looks quizzically down at the Teenaxi, much like Captain Pike looked down at a pre-Starfleet Academy Kirk as he lay, bloodied and battered, atop a table after an unsuccessful bar fight a few years prior. The look provides a pause just long enough to allow Kirk to be assaulted on all sides by angry, jumping, clawing, and biting Teenaxi. He is only just able to beam out in time. As two Teenaxi hangers-on are chased about the transporter room by red-shirted crewmembers, Kirk sighs. "I ripped my shirt again."

Fifty years on, this line is one of the film's earliest callbacks to the Original Series (wherein Kirk's shirt was ripped or removed a total of twenty times[2]) and also serves as an expression of Kirk's weariness with the less glamorous duties of command. As Kirk joins Spock and McCoy in the *Enterprise* corridor, Dr. McCoy offers his professional medical assessment of Kirk: "Jim, you look like crap." "Thank you, Bones," Kirk replies, clearly feeling much akin to Bones' description. "You got that little vein poppin'

1. Lin, *Star Trek Beyond*.
2. "Kirk's Ripped or Removed Shirts," Ex Astris Scientia.

outta your temple again," McCoy observes. "You okay?" "Never better!" Kirk responds, dripping with sarcasm, "Just another day in the fleet."[3]

To be precise, according to Kirk's Captain's Log, it is the 966th day of the _Enterprise_'s five-year mission, just around the halfway point. (The day is also a reference to September, 1966, the month and year of _Star Trek_'s television premier.[4]) Halfway can be a depressing place to be. If the time and effort heretofore have worn you down, you can look forward to having to go through it all again. The opening scene and the Captain's Log scene that follows not only provide context for the film; they establish its major themes as well. The first film in the Kelvin Timeline deftly explored the subject of calling and destiny—of finding one's place in life, and in the universe. In these opening scenes especially, _Beyond_ notes that the carrying out of one's calling can lead to its own particular sense of lostness. Being who we are called to be—even being a starship captain—often requires hard work that, at times, can become monotonous. "The more time we spend out here," Kirk says, "the harder it is to tell where one day ends and the next one begins. It can be a challenge to feel grounded, when even gravity is artificial." Sometimes, the bright-eyed enthusiasm of finding a sense of purpose is dulled as that purpose begins to seem a greater and greater distance away from where we are. "The farther out we go," Kirk continues, "the more I find myself wondering what it is we're trying to accomplish. If the universe is truly endless, then are we not striving for something forever out of reach?"[5]

As Kirk contemplates the question of whether the goals of the _Enterprise_'s mission are truly unreachable, he begins to wonder if the quest itself is futile. This sense of futility is not only the domain of starship personnel, hurtling ever outward into the vast unknown. It is often true of the human experience, as we seek meaning in our lives, personal advancement, and indeed, God. Here the "Beyond" of the film's title might take on further meaning. Certainly, this adventure is taking the _Enterprise_ crew "beyond" Earth and the Federation worlds they have heretofore explored, venturing deeper into space than ever before. But the themes of the film also have to do both with that which is beyond our previous experience and that which is seemingly beyond our capabilities. If we spend the whole of our lives striving for these things, if we never reach a point when we feel we have "arrived," aren't all our efforts pointless? God, after all, is incomprehensible.

3. Lin, _Star Trek Beyond_.
4. Eisenberg, "Star Trek Easter Egg."
5. Lin, _Star Trek Beyond_.

If we can never fully reach or comprehend God, never even truly be certain of the answer to the question of God's existence, why keep striving?

Two days before Kirk's birthday, McCoy engages him in a quiet, near grudging recognition of the occasion with a brief indulgence in some fine Scotch. "I know you don't like celebrating it on the day," McCoy says, "'cause it's also the day your pa bit the dust. Just being sensitive." Kirk responds to McCoy's dubious brand of sensitivity by questioning his understanding of bedside manner, before reflecting on the particular significance of his thirtieth birthday.

> KIRK: One year older.
>
> BONES: Yep, that's usually how it works.
>
> KIRK: A year older than he ever got to be. He joined Starfleet 'cause he . . . he believed in it. I joined on a dare.
>
> BONES: You joined to see if you could live up to him. You've spent all this time trying to be George Kirk, and now you're wondering just what it means to be Jim—why you're out here.[6]

Like many of us, inheriting the faith and life contexts of our parents, Kirk is reconciling his identity in relationship to his father's. At a time in his life when he is doubting his purpose and calling, Kirk is going through a transition most young adults face—that of owning his existence. For those of us raised in a familial context of Christianity, such a process can be particularly pivotal as we ask whether our faith is our own or simply a set of habits and attitudes passed down from our parents, with which we are not truly engaged. While we often wish to honor where we come from, we have to feel we have faith on our own terms, for our own reasons, before it is our faith at all. Just as Kirk does, we must encounter the question of what truly matters to us and whether the things that have shaped us thus far can continue to do so in a way that allows us to fully become our own selves.

Star Trek consistently recognizes the potential for greatness in those selves we create—both individually and in community—and its vision of hope and unity for humankind has rarely, if ever, been expressed in such a compelling and visually stunning fashion as in the starbase *Yorktown*. The intersecting rings of its atom-like structure are massive arcs of civilization, populated on both sides with countless city structures and shot through with green fields, bodies of water, and a giant, super-fast monorail system.

6. Ibid.

The most technologically advanced vision of human civilization we've seen in Star Trek, *Yorktown* also represents a kind of ideal society, where peace, harmony, and diversity abound. The station is home to millions from across the Federation, all living together in peace. In both its vision for human-kind and its enormous, opulent physical structure afloat in space, it echoes the biblical image of the New Jerusalem, the beautiful city of God.[7] It's an impressive and beautiful sight. But, like all declarations of the greatness of humanity in Star Trek, it is tempered with an acknowledgement of poten-tial failure. Upon seeing *Yorktown* on the *Enterprise* viewscreen, Dr. McCoy immediately counters the general sense of awe and wonder on the bridge with some trademark pessimism. "What a damn monstrosity," he barks. "Couldn't we just rent some space on a planet?" Spock replies, "Showing geographical favoritism among inducted Federation worlds could cause diplomatic tension." McCoy retorts, "Oh, you don't think that looks tense? Looks like a damn snow globe in space, just waitin' to break."[8]

The scene illustrates a few ideas. Firstly, it acknowledges that, however harmonious life on *Yorktown* may be, that harmony is carefully cultivated and maintained. Mismanagement of the base could cause conflict between Federation worlds. The paradise we see is the result of years of diplomacy and hard work, not just interstellar warm fuzzies. This scene also recog-nizes, as Star Trek always has, the fragility of peace and, indeed, of human-ity itself. McCoy's description of the starbase as a "snow globe in space" recalls in theme the speech Kirk gives in the Original Series episode "Who Mourns for Adonais?," when he describes humans as "a bit of flesh and blood, afloat, in a universe without end." Kirk concludes, however, that this frangible humanity finds strength and purpose in a sense of unity. "And the only thing that's truly yours," he continues, "is the rest of humanity. That's where our duty lies."[9] This scene also foreshadows the worldview of the film's villain (who has yet to emerge at this point). It is at that very fragility that Krall intends to strike and that very unity he intends to use against the Federation in an attempt to shatter its structure like McCoy's "snow globe." But the tension McCoy sees in *Yorktown* is first reflected in Kirk's own conflicted heart and mind.

Initially, Kirk's uncertainty about his calling leads him to seek an es-cape from the captain's chair. On the starbase *Yorktown*, he discusses a career

---

7. Rev 21:10–21.

8. Ibid.

9. Daniels, "Who Mourns for Adonais?"

change with Commodore Paris—specifically, his application to become Vice Admiral at *Yorktown*. Paris recognizes the motivation behind Kirk's actions better than he anticipates and her insight catches him off guard. "It isn't uncommon, you know—even for a captain—to want to leave," she says. "There's no relative direction in the vastness of space. There's only yourself, your ship, your crew. It's easier than you think to get lost."[10] Kirk begins to object to her characterization of his reasons for applying for the position, but she quickly changes the subject, promising to follow through on his application. In this, Paris seems to both acknowledge that Kirk is not ready to admit the state of his heart and to reassure him that she will not stand in the way of whatever decision he makes. But her analysis is spot-on. Paris has likely seen this kind of burnout before. Perhaps she has even experienced it herself. But, like so many characters in Star Trek, Paris makes an act of faith in this moment. Certainly, she has faith that Kirk and the crew of the *Enterprise* are up to the task of rescuing a crew stranded on a planet inside an uncharted nebula. But she also has faith that Kirk will find his way—that, in Spock's words from *Star Trek VI*, "the universe will unfold as it should."[11] This kind of faith is especially important in the Kelvin Timeline, a timeline in which our main characters are well aware that they are living in an "alternate" reality. As seen in the first film in this series, Star Trek's constant faith is that we humans will find our destinies (or they will find us), no matter the events that occur.

Spock is also questioning his destiny, largely in light of his knowledge of the shift that has taken place in his reality. Firstly, he is considering ending his romance with Uhura in order to help repopulate his species by marrying a Vulcan. But then his reality shifts once more as he receives the news that Ambassador Spock has died. Of course, this reflects the death of Leonard Nimoy on February 27, 2015—a loss felt even by those outside the Star Trek community. For most people, there was really no one alive who embodied Star Trek more than Nimoy and, in the wake of his death, it seemed it might be difficult for Star Trek to carry on. He was a beacon on a hill for the Trek community, much the way Gene Roddenberry and Majel Barrett-Roddenberry had been. He may not have made it to the official fiftieth anniversary of Star Trek, but Nimoy had been present even further back than the first broadcast of "The Man Trap" on September 8, 1966—all the way back to 1964's rejected pilot episode, "The Cage." As lost as Star

10. Lin, *Star Trek Beyond*.

11. Meyer, *Star Trek VI*.

Trek fans may have felt after Nimoy's death, so too must Spock feel after losing his older self.

Similarly, current Spock actor Zachary Quinto had become close with Nimoy and his character's sense of loss in the film surely also reflects his own personal loss. "When you have lived as many lives as he," Spock says of his counterpart, "fear of death is illogical." The character of Spock has certainly lived many lives, shifting careers, dying and resurrecting, starting a new life in a new timeline, and more. Nimoy also lived "many lives" as an actor alone, not to mention his lives as a poet, photographer, and family man. "I want to live as he did," Spock tells McCoy in a candid moment of openness between the two men. Certainly, there are those who aspire to be like Nimoy,[12] but the statement also reflects the desire of a Christian life—to live as Christ did. The Evangelical world especially focuses a great deal of energy on the salvation accomplished by the death and resurrection of Christ, but this focus often comes at the expense of considering the importance of the life of Christ—not only of the life he lived, but the life he is going to live through us. To what kind of life—here and now—does Christ's life and example call us?

For Spock, asking this question regarding his predecessor at first leads him to a logical conclusion: leave Starfleet and continue the elder Spock's work on New Vulcan. Ultimately, though, the Ambassador has the final word. When Spock is going through a box of his alternate self's belongings (with which he has been rightfully entrusted), he discovers, in a small, rectangular case, a photograph of the Prime Timeline Spock with his *Enterprise* crewmates. This is what was most important to Ambassador Spock—the time he spent with his closest friends. Seeing the entire crew, all having grown old together on the starship they have, in the Kelvin Timeline, called home for a mere two and a half years, the younger Vulcan surely recalled the advice given to him when he first met a grey-haired man he initially mistook for his father: "Put aside logic. Do what feels right."[13] This may be seen as reflecting how we consider the call of the Christian life. When we ask the question of how to follow after Christ in our own lives, there may be easy answers we might consider—either ones with which we are most comfortable, or ones we think are especially "radical" or religious. But the ultimate arbiter of what we do with our lives is Christ. It is first and last his heart and example we should seek. Though the specific circumstances

12. Kelensa, "How Leonard Nimoy Saved My Life."

13. Abrams, *Star Trek*.

we experience and choices we make as a result of that reflection will all be different, the call on each of our lives will be guided by the same Spirit. In at least one important way, Spock's calling reflects something that every Christian (and human) life has in common: Spock, like so many other characters in this film, realizes he is stronger with a community around him—that he is called to be in community, and that he is not alone.

Kirk is also seeing the importance of human community. As the *Enterprise* sets out on its rescue mission, her captain seems to recall Commodore Paris' words that, while she has faith that the *Enterprise* is up to the task at hand, her trust is in more than its advanced technology. "The only ship here with more advanced technology is still under construction," she says. "But it's not just the ship that I'm sending." In his address to the crew, Kirk acknowledges that the *Enterprise* will be unable to communicate with Starfleet while inside the nebula. "We're gonna be on our own," he admits. "But the *Enterprise* has something no other ship in the fleet has: you." Having located the strength of the ship first and foremost in the crew, he recognizes that this same crew is probably experiencing some trepidation at entering an area of uncharted, isolating space. He offers this reassurance: "As we've come to understand, there is no such thing as the unknown— only the temporarily hidden."[14] This is again a statement of faith that echoes the words of Jesus: "Seek and you will find."[15] With these words, Kirk describes not only the voyage into an uncharted nebula, but his own quest of self-discovery. That kind of faith can be hard to maintain, especially when all the structures we trust in begin to crumble around us. Of course, the stranded crew does not exist. The mission into the nebula is a trap, and Krall unleashes his swarm on the *Enterprise*, destroying the vessel in unprecedented and spectacular fashion, and kidnapping or scattering its crew.

"There's only yourself, your ship, your crew," Commodore Paris told Kirk. In short order, he has lost the latter two. As pointed out by Geoffrey Reiter of the online magazine Christ and Pop Culture, *Star Trek Beyond* "is especially concerned about how its characters form meaning and identity when seemingly fixed points of reference have been removed."[16] Its exploration of what Reiter calls "the cosmography of relationship" seeks a locus of meaning for its characters as they strive for unity and purpose in unfamiliar and hostile territory.

14. Lin, *Star Trek Beyond*.
15. Luke 11:9.
16. Reiter, "Cosmography of Relationship."

Reiter points out that director Justin Lin's cinematic style—in terms of both its visual and auditory elements—is often disorienting, reflecting the disorientation experienced by the *Enterprise* crew as they are separated from Starfleet, their ship, and one another. Christians, he says, are grounded in Christ and in community with one another.[17] Similarly, I would contend that *Star Trek Beyond* locates the only truly fixed point of orientation where it always has—within the human heart and in human community. This has always been the anchor point for Star Trek's core ideals of faith and hope. But this faith reaches beyond just a faith in humanity to faith in an undergirding order in the universe that will carry us through adversity. When Kirk is finally reunited with Spock, his First Officer and best friend has received an injury that threatens his life. A spearhead-like shard of metal has pierced his side—a symbolically appropriate wound for Star Trek's Christ figure. As Spock lies in the USS *Franklin*, awaiting medical attention from Dr. McCoy, Kirk looks to his injured friend for wisdom. "How're we gonna get out of this one, Spock?" he asks. "We got . . . no ship, no crew. Not the best odds." Spock then shows that his time in Starfleet has served to make him more the person of faith his elder self was. He replies, "We will do what we have always done, Jim. We will find hope in the impossible."[18]

Hope in the impossible becomes another running theme in this film, albeit a bit less obvious. Over and over, various things are said to be "impossible," yet are ultimately accomplished. When Spock, Kirk, and McCoy are chasing the remaining swarm ships through *Yorktown*, Spock declares, "Captain, intercepting all three ships is an impossibility." All the same, Kirk is able to use the *Franklin* itself to stop all three ships at once. Similarly, as Scotty and Jaylah begin to attempt shutting down *Yorktown*'s environmental systems, Commander Finnegan insists, "Look, this main is impossible to shut down."[19] Still, Scotty, Jaylah, and Kirk are able to do just that, venting Krall and his bio-weapon, the Abronath, into space. Throughout the film, Kirk and company trust in things that probably won't—and really shouldn't—work. They act on faith time and again, and time and again, they prevail. "All things are possible," Jesus said, "for the one who believes."[20]

The theme of faith and hope in the impossible merges with the film's primary theme of strength in unity when Scotty asks Jaylah to join him,

17. Ibid.
18. Lin, *Star Trek Beyond*.
19. Ibid.
20. Mark 9:23.

Spock, McCoy, and Kirk in attempting to rescue the rest of the crew. Jaylah recounts the loss of her father and how she barely made it out of Krall's base of operations alive, as examples of the scars on her heart she believes are too deep to allow her to return. "What you want," she concludes, "is impossible." Scotty replies, "Maybe it's not. Ma wee Granny used to say, 'ye cannae break a stick in a bundle.' You're a part of something bigger now, lassie, all right? Now, dinnae give up on that, 'cause we'll sure as hell never give up on you. That is what being part of a crew is all about."[21] Jaylah will be able to accomplish what she thinks she cannot and overcome her deepest fears because she has a community of people surrounding her who will not give up on her. It is a sense of community she desperately needs. Even though she is the film's greatest loner, Jaylah demonstrates her need for others by using her holographic weapon to create copies of herself, her own virtual support system.[22] She knows that, however much she has been able to do on her own, she can do more as part of a group. In her final confrontation with Krall's second in command, Manas, it is the faith that she is no longer alone from which Jaylah draws her strength—a faith Kirk proves well-placed when he ensures her escape, refusing to leave her behind. Jaylah's newfound "bundle" will keep her from breaking.

Scotty's Granny's saying about a bundle of sticks seems to be a colloquial rendition of a verse from the book of Ecclesiastes that illustrates the power of human unity. "Although an assailant may overpower one person," the author writes, "two can withstand him. Moreover, a three-stranded cord is not quickly broken."[23] This piece of wisdom is something Krall believes to be a lie of the Federation. As he tells Uhura, "Lieutenant, unity is not your strength. It is your weakness." And later, he expounds, "The world that I was born into was very different from yours, Lieutenant. We knew pain; we knew terror. Struggle made us strong—not peace, not unity. These are myths the Federation would have you believe."[24] But the strength of unity is inescapable—even in the very event to which Krall refers when he calls unity a weakness. Entering the area of his base wherein the *Enterprise* crewmembers are held, he threatens to kill Sulu unless someone reveals the location of the Abronath. Ensign Syl cannot stand by and let Sulu die, so she reveals that the weapon is concealed within her cranial appendages,

21. Lin, *Star Trek Beyond*.
22. Avery and David, "SA195."
23. Eccl 4:12.
24. Lin, *Star Trek Beyond*.

interlaced like crab-like fingers over the back of her head. This is the moment to which Krall refers as an example of the weakness of unity—because of Syl's commitment to her crewmate, Krall now has what he wants. And he uses it to make an example of Syl, violating the very unity of her being as the Abronath breaks her into tiny particles.

This moment highlights a unity within the *Enterprise* crew, not just of mutual support, but also around the value of self-sacrifice. Uhura herself had exercised her belief in this value by putting Kirk's safety above her own, executing the final saucer separation once Kirk was safely in the saucer section, and locking herself in with Krall. "Your captain," Krall asks Uhura, once she has become his captive, "why did you sacrifice yourself for him?" "He would've done the same," she replies, with a conviction we know is sound after the events of the previous film. "And if he made it off that ship," she continues, "he will come for us." Krall comes in close. "I am counting on it, Lieutenant Uhura," he whispers, again undercutting the strength of unity by showing that he has used it to set a trap. Again, it appears that the closeness and commitment of the *Enterprise* crew have only served to give Krall the upper hand. As the theme of unity continues and repeats throughout the film, though, we see that no character can truly function without it. Contrary to the narrative Krall presents, as the crew gather themselves back together, their ability to succeed against Krall only grows.

Krall himself relies on unity, though his ultra-Darwinian focus on struggle as the only source of strength will not allow him to see that his own drone army relies on unity to function. They are overcome when they are brought to disunity. The *Franklin* and the *Yorktown* overwhelm the drones with their own unity, broadcasting the same song on the same frequency, working together to give Krall's army a taste of the disorientation they have felt for much of the film. Krall's focus on bringing discord and disunity has become a life mission and he is blind to the value of any other way of life. Kirk, having discovered that Krall is actually Balthazar Edison, the captain of the *Franklin* and a former soldier, seeks answers from Edison about how he became so distorted.

KIRK: What happened to you out there, Edison?

KRALL/EDISON: Edison. I have to say, Kirk, I've missed being me. We lost ourselves, but gained a purpose! A means to bring the galaxy back to the struggle that made humanity strong.

KIRK: I think you underestimate humanity.

> KRALL/EDISON: I fought for humanity! Lost millions to the Xindi and Romulan wars. And for what? For the Federation to sit me in a captain's chair and break bread with the enemy!
>
> KIRK: We change. We have to. Or we spend the rest of our lives fighting the same battles.[25]

In this scene, Kirk is fighting the same battle he fought at the beginning of the film—arguing for the reality of peace against the protestations of a mind overcome with thoughts of war. Edison cannot bear the thought of being asked to "break bread with the enemy" any more than the Teenaxi can see the Fabonans as anything but a (literally) all-consuming threat. The Teenaxi are afraid of being eaten, but they are themselves consumed by fear and hatred, much as Edison has also been consumed by revenge and subsumed into the identity he has created for himself. He has lost himself, no longer relying on others for support, community, or companionship, but only as part of a vampiric quest to extend his own life—a life he has forgotten how to truly live.

Breaking bread with the enemy is a central call of the Christian life, as Jesus tells his followers to "love your enemies, do good to those who hate you, bless those who curse you," and "pray for those who mistreat you."[26] Christ's call to love and forgiveness is often the hardest for us to accept, especially in a Christian culture that teaches us to fear enemies in nearly every part of public life—from media to politics to other Christians with differing doctrines. But, if we're honest, Christ wants those very people to come into community with us, to become a part of his family. In that reality, we would literally break the bread of communion with those who were once our enemies. If the gospel will eventually lead to true human unity, no one—especially our enemies—can be turned away from the table.

But Edison can't see this kind of future for humanity. To him, an enemy is always an enemy. A fight ensues between Kirk and Edison as Edison tries to release the Abronath into *Yorktown's* ventilation system, but the pair crash out of the glass enclosure and land, in the unpredictable gravity of the center of the base, on the side of a building, not sure exactly where they are or how to get back.

> KIRK: You lost! There's no way you can make it back now. Give up!

---

25. Lin, *Star Trek Beyond*.
26. Luke 6: 27–28.

KRALL: What, like you did? I read your ship's log, Captain James T. Kirk! At least I know what I am! I'm a soldier!

KIRK: You won the war! Edison. You gave us peace!

KRALL: Peace . . . is not what I was born into.[27]

Here, Kirk is confronted with his own sense of lost purpose. This time, however, he is able to find himself. Edison uses the bizarre gravitational slipstream near the core of *Yorktown* to guide him back to the enclosure and Kirk follows, literally taking a leap of faith. Back in the enclosure and finally able to immobilize Edison, Kirk prepares to complete the process that will vent the Abronath into space. It is here that Kirk claims his victory over the lostness with which he contended in those logs. "You can't stop it," Edison insists. "You will die." "Better to die saving lives than to live with taking them," Kirk replies. "That's what I was born into."[28] The strength of his father's sacrifice and the nobility of his example carry Kirk to become the man he's meant to be. In this moment, he crystallizes what it means to be both his father's son and his own man.

In the previous two films in this series, Kirk is still young and inexperienced, maintaining a youthful quality that shows up in both boyish charm and lack of maturity. Even as he angrily confronts Khan in the brig in *Into Darkness*, loudly asserting his authority, his voice shakes with a clear loss of control as he desperately tries to intimidate his prisoner. Khan replies coolly, evenly, presenting a deep calm that consistently makes a spectacle of Kirk's thin attempts at gravitas. In *Star Trek Beyond*, Kirk is older, less erratic, and more stable. His voice tends to stay in his lower register, expressing a maturity that we have not heretofore seen in him. In the first film in this series, after defiantly driving his stepfather's car off a cliff and narrowly missing going over the edge himself, a young Kirk is confronted by a police officer who has been pursuing him. "Citizen," the officer demands, "what is your name?" Kirk boldly replies, "My name is James Tiberius Kirk!"[29] In the original script for this scene, the writers note, " . . . damn if that kid doesn't have a swagger. It's like the first time he's ever stood in his life."[30] Though he floats weightlessly during his exchange with Edison, it is once again like the first time Kirk has ever stood, not just as a defiant young man,

27. Lin, *Star Trek Beyond*.
28. Ibid.
29. Abrams, *Star Trek*.
30. Orci and Kurtzman, *Star Trek* draft.

179

not just as his father's son, but also as the man he becomes because of both his father's legacy and his own choices.

But the test is not over. While Kirk struggles with the final lever to stop the air—and thus, the now released Abronath—from circulating, Edison finds his strength and floats upward. As he makes his ascent toward Kirk, we are uncertain of his intentions. He could be going to stop Kirk, or to help him. It seems for a moment as though the villain of this film might be redeemed and the expression on his face seems to suggest that he considers it. But when he sees his reflection in a floating shard of glass, Edison determines who he will be. He grasps the shard as a weapon and strikes out at Kirk. Symbolically, though, it is himself with which Edison is at war. It is his own rage, his own hurt, against which he truly struggles. And, contrary to the message he preaches throughout the film, it does not make him strong. His reliance upon himself, his cheating of death, his single-minded focus on bringing chaos, have made his humanity weaker than he ever realized. Whatever he may have believed about the power of his purpose, he has indeed lost himself. And, ultimately, that tragic loss is what brings him to his demise, devoured by the weapon of his own vengeance.

> COMMODORE PARIS: For decades, the Federation taught that he was a hero. I guess time will judge us all.
>
> KIRK: He just got lost.
>
> COMMODORE PARIS: You saved this entire base, Kirk. Millions of souls. Thank you.
>
> KIRK: It wasn't just me. It never is.[31]

Kirk has overcome his youthful arrogance, for which Pike had so bitterly criticized him. He has found his greatest strength in standing together with his crew and his confidence in himself and his mission is restored because he realizes he never has to be alone. Earlier in the film, indicating the *Franklin*'s captain's chair, in which Jaylah was casually lounging, Scotty whispered of Kirk, "He likes that seat!" He does like it, indeed. It's where he belongs.

> COMMODORE PARIS: Needless to say, the position of Vice Admiral is yours. No one deserves it more.
>
> KIRK: Vice Admirals don't fly, do they?

31. Lin, *Star Trek Beyond*.

COMMODORE PARIS: No. They don't.

KIRK: Well, no offense, Ma'am, but . . . Where's the fun in that?[32]

Kirk has once again accepted his destiny, this time knowing the struggles he will face in the second half of the _Enterprise_'s mission. He is no longer just taking a dare. He is doing something he truly believes in. Now, as McCoy ushers Kirk into a room full of _Enterprise_ crewmembers, all gathered to celebrate his birthday, Kirk can raise a glass with the rest of them.

SCOTTY: Everybody raise a glass to Captain James T. Kirk!

ALL: Captain Kirk!

KIRK: Aw, thanks, everybody. To the _Enterprise_.

ALL: The _Enterprise_.

KIRK: And . . . to absent friends.[33]

Kirk accepts the praise, but redirects it away from himself as well. It's not an act of self-deprecation, but of humility, of acknowledging that he did not get here on his own. The reference to "absent friends" recalls Kirk's words in _Star Trek III_ in honor of Spock and is a nod to the death of Leonard Nimoy. Though not intended at the time, of course, it can also be seen as retroactively acknowledging the tragic loss of Anton Yelchin, the Kelvin Timeline's brilliant young Chekov actor. But, in the context of the story, it likely also refers to Kirk's father and _Enterprise_ crewmembers who were lost during their mission, not to mention Christopher Pike and Ambassador Spock. Kirk has come to the realization that it's alright to talk about death, that honoring those who have gone before us can be a part of a celebration of life. Sorrow and joy, birth and death, can and do coexist. The gospel narrative beautifully captures this human truth, as new life is brought forth by the death of Christ, evidenced in his resurrection.

It's easy to get lost. And, even when we feel we're headed in the right direction, we can lose faith that we will ever become the best version of ourselves we can be. But when we realize that we don't have to be alone, we find that true strength lies in admitting that we need others. The sense of community to which this film continually appeals is one that reflects the words of Jesus, praying for his followers, "that they will all be one, just

32. Ibid.
33. Ibid.

as you, Father, are in me and I am in you."[34] Living in and striving for this unity is essential to Christian faith; as Geoffrey Reiter again notes, "Salvation is both personal and communal."[35] This is a Christian truth because it is a human truth. We are social beings, created to live in community, in an ongoing process of growth and change. It is therefore no surprise that Star Trek continually finds its characters' identities both as individuals and as a group, and that it emphasizes the journey far more than any destination.

Life is not about whether we've become all we're going to be or achieved a goal of self-actualization. Perhaps we can't explore the whole universe of possibilities, but we undertake the task of exploring as much of it as we can because the interior journey we take in the process is what is most important. Kirk realizes this at the end of the film when he returns to his "first, best destiny,"[36] not for the unreachable goal of finding the ends of the universe, but for the quest itself. This is the essence of humanity. Who we become along the way is just as much our calling as any major goal we may try to accomplish. We will be learning, changing, and growing until the day we die. We fail, we struggle, and we lose our way. That's human. But we also rise above those things and learn to be the best version of ourselves we can be. That's human too. And since no one is without both sides of that experience, we are uniquely equipped to share that journey with others. As *Star Trek Beyond* points out, we sometimes have little left but faith, hope, and love,[37] and even they can be hard to hold on to. But, ultimately, they are all we really have. And if God truly is love, then they are all we really need.

34. John 17:20-21.

35. Reiter, "Cosmography of Relationship."

36. Meyer, *Star Trek II*.

37. 1 Cor 13:13.

What Does God Need with a Starship?

" What does God need with a starship?" Like Kirk's famous question from *Star Trek V*, we may ask, "What does God need with Star Trek?" Why go through this process of putting Star Trek into conversation with Christian theology and a Christian worldview? Star Trek is just entertainment. Why bring such a trivial thing into a conversation about God? And, further, why bring God into Star Trek? Doesn't he have enough press all on his own? In this book, I hope I have shown that it is God who has always been a part of Star Trek, from Gene Roddenberry's Christian background to his continuing journey to understand the Divine; from Star Trek's earliest biblical references to its unintended but well articulated Christ figure; from the human journey out into the stars to the journey of the human soul. Our human quest for an identity as part of something larger than ourselves is the central narrative of the Star Trek universe. It is a narrative based not on science, but on faith.

Without faith in human potential, in the idea that, by exploring the farthest reaches of space, we can better understand ourselves and our place in the universe, Star Trek would just be another science fiction adventure show. Instead, it is something that has affected the lives of millions of people around the world. For fifty years, Star Trek has endured—far beyond any expectations for a television series that struggled to make it through just three seasons. It is not so widely loved because of spectacular starships, bombastic space battles, and sexy green girls in bikinis, though all of those are certainly attractions. It endures because of its beliefs about humankind—who we are, why we are here, and what we are meant to do. It shows us ways to overcome our faults and failings, to push past the worst parts of ourselves and accomplish truly remarkable things. It reminds us that our humanity, broken as it often is, is also good, noble, admirable, and capable of true greatness.

As a Christian, I see these things and wonder, "Where and how is God at work here?" God is at work in all our lives, in all our human endeavors, in a special way in our creative efforts, and even when we are unaware. So, when I see people rallying around something this enthusiastically, and when I find my own heart and mind fascinated and drawn into this wonderful, amazing universe of stories and characters, I simply must conclude that God is doing something, that this attraction we all have expresses a deep yearning of our hearts and a deep understanding that we have found something good, true, and beautiful. God does not *need* Star Trek. He is a part of it. It is he who put these desires into the human heart—the desire to search, to question, to seek understanding, to create, and to tell stories. When Gene Roddenberry calls God "that thing about humanity that makes them write poetry, paint pictures,"[1] and create Star Trek, he is absolutely right.

But if God does not need Star Trek, the fact remains that we need it. We need it for the same reason we need all art—as a way of understanding ourselves and of coming closer to God. As U2 lyricist and singer Bono explains, "Why do we need art? Why do we need the lyric poetry of the Psalms? Because the only way we can approach God is, if we're honest, through metaphor, through symbol. So art becomes essential, not decorative."[2] We as human beings deeply need this way of expressing and exploring ourselves and our world by creating and telling stories. It also seems, though, that the Church, the Body of Christ, the human community of those who follow Jesus, needs Star Trek as much as, if not more than anyone.

My greatest hope in all of this is that, through a thoughtful engagement with Star Trek, Christians can begin to explore that "undiscovered country" of our humanity as something good and beautiful and amazing, something God made, through which to express himself. We are God's art. If Star Trek can teach us anything, it is that our humanity is not something to hide, shun, ignore, or be ashamed of. It is not something to escape or overcome. It is who we are and who God made us to be—and we can become a better version of ourselves, not by putting aside our humanity, but

---

1. Fern, *Last Conversation*, 68.
2. Clarke, *Bono & Eugene Peterson on The Psalms*.

by exploring it, wrestling with it, seeking to understand it, and learning how to cultivate and encourage its best attributes.

In Star Trek, we consistently see remarkable parallels with Scripture. That is no accident. The fact of the matter is that Scripture, the gospel, the words of Christ, speak to our deepest human longings and needs and teach us a way to be better human beings that can be universally recognized as true. "Humanity needs God in order to be humanity," Roddenberry said. "It is part of them."[3] God and humanity are meant to work together, in concert, not separate from one another, battling with one another, or passing by one another on occasion. God works in and through our humanity, making understanding our human nature of essential importance. The story of Scripture is the story of God and humanity being split apart and coming back together again. It is a story of reconciliation and redemption, disunity that ends in unity, and a wholeness of self and purpose that comes from knowing and being known by God.

Star Trek is also about redemption, reconciliation, and unity. In all the very human ways through which its stories and characters seek these things, they create images both of how we can seek them in everyday life, and how we can pursue them on a broader scale. As we have followed the original crew of the starship *Enterprise,* from their quest for Eden, to their tearing down of false religions, to their reaffirmation of the essential importance of faith and love of our neighbors, we have seen a story that time and again teaches us to be better humans and, as though this were a separate thing, better Christians. As I explore the further adventures of the Star Trek universe and its many ships, space stations, captains, and crews in the forthcoming volumes of this series, I hope to see this conversation grow ever deeper and richer. I am honestly grateful to God for the work he has done in me through Star Trek. My hope is that in sharing it with you, you will find something of what God wants to say to you as well, that you may truly Live Long and Prosper.[4]

3. Fern, *Last Conversation,* 67.

4. John 10:10.

Bibliography

Abrams, J.J., dir. *Star Trek*. Paramount Pictures, 2009.

———. *Star Trek Into Darkness*. Paramount Pictures, 2013.

Abrams, J.J., et al. "Audio Commentary," *Star Trek*. The Compendium Blu-ray, Paramount Home Entertainment, 2014.

———. "Kirk and Spock," *Star Trek Into Darkness,* The Compendium Blu-ray special features disc. Paramount Home Entertainment, 2014.

Adelstein, Ellen. "Ellen Adelstein's Interview with Rod Roddenberry." *Gene Roddenberry: Up Close and Personal.* Adelstein-Beshert Productions, 2006.

———. *Gene Roddenberry: Up Close and Personal.* Adelstein-Beshert Productions, 2006.

Alexander, David. "Interview of Gene Roddenberry: Writer, Producer, Philosopher, Humanist." *The Humanist*, March–April 1991. Accessed August 3, 2016. http://web.archive.org/web/20060702000506/http://www.philosophysphere.com/humanist.html.

———. *Star Trek Creator: The Authorized Biography of Gene Roddenberry*. New York: Roc, 1994.

Alexander, David, dir. "The Way to Eden." *Star Trek*, CBS Television, 1969.

"Atheism." 1911 *Encyclopædia Britannica*, 1910. Hugh Chisholm, general editor. Accessed April 22, 2016. http://www.studylight.org/encyclopedias/bri/view.cgi?number=3047.

Augustine. *Confessions*. Translated by Henry Chadwick. Oxford: Oxford University Press, 2009.

Avery, Ben, and Evan David. "STAR TREK BEYOND review—SA195." *Strangers and Aliens*, July 25, 2016. Accessed August 7, 2016. http://strangersandaliens.com/2016/07/star-trek-beyond-review-sa195/.

Barrett, Francis. "VIII: The Annoyance of Evil Spirits, and the Preservation we have from Good Spirits." In *The Magus, a Complete System of Occult Philosophy*, Book II. New York: Cosimo Classics, 2008.

Beck, Donald R. *Star Trek 25th Anniversary Special*. Paramount Pictures, 1991.

Berger, Arthur Asa. *Media Research Techniques*. 2nd ed. Thousand Oaks, CA: SAGE, 1998.

Blake, Richard A. *Afterimage: The Indelible Catholic Imagination of Six American Filmmakers*. Chicago: Loyola, 2000.

Braga, Brannon. "Every Religion Has a Mythology." Speech transcript, International Atheist Conference in Reykjavik, Iceland, June 24 and 25, 2006. Accessed April 22, 2016. http://sidmennt.is/2006./08/16/every-religion-has-a-mythology/.

Brokhoff, John R. *Lectionary Preaching Workbook, Revised for Use With Revised Common, Episcopal, Lutheran, and Roman Catholic Lectionaries.* Lima, OH: CCS, 1993.

Butler, Robert, dir. "The Cage." *Star Trek*, CBS Television, 1964.

Caprio, Betsy. *Star Trek: Good News in Modern Images.* Kansas City, MO: Sheed Andrews and McMeel, 1978.

Clark, Mark. *Star Trek FAQ.* Kindle Edition. Milwaukee, WI: Applause, 2012.

Clarke, Nathan. *Bono & Eugene Peterson on The Psalms.* Fuller Studio, 2016. Accessed April 22, 2016. https://fullerstudio.fuller.edu/bono-eugene-peterson-psalms/.

Colthorp, Scott. *Trek Nation* two-disc Special Edition DVD supplemental disc. Film Buff/ MPI Media Group, 2013.

Corey, Barry H. "'I'd like to punch him in the face': The incredible shrill of this election season," *Washington Post*, February 2, 2016. Accessed April 22, 2016. Https://www.washingtonpost.com/news/acts-of-faith/wp/2016/02/24/id-like-to-punch-him-in-the-face-the-incredible-shrill-of-this-election-season/.

Cullmann, Oscar. *Christ and Time: The Primitive Christian Concept of Time.* Louisville, KY: Westminster John Knox, 1964.

Cushman, Marc, and John D.F. Black. *These Are The Voyages: TOS: Season Two.* Frazier Park, CA: Jacobs Brown, 2014.

Daniels, Mark. *Star Trek*, "Who Mourns for Adonais?" CBS Television, 1967.

Dickens, Charles. *A Tale of Two Cities.* New York: Penguin Classics, 2003.

Dubose, Todd. "Homo Religiosus." In *Encyclopedia of Psychology and Religion*, 2nd ed., edited by David A. Leeming, 827–30. New York: Springer, 2014.

Ecklar, Julia. *The Kobayashi Maru.* New York: Pocket, 2000.

Eisenberg, Eric. "The Star Trek Easter Egg That Helped Establish the Setting of Star Trek Beyond," *Cinemablend*, July 27, 2016. Accessed August 2, 2016. http://www.cinemablend.com/news/1539360/the-star-trek-easter-egg-that-helped-establish-the-setting-of-star-trek-beyond.

Engel, Joel. *Gene Roddenberry: The Myth and the Man Behind Star Trek.* New York: Hyperion, 1994.

"Enlarged Salem Covenant of 1636." In Paul Boyer and Steve Nissenbaum, *Salem Possessed: The Social Origins of Witchcraft.* Cambridge, MA: Harvard University Press, 1974.

Faulkner, Francis. "The Petition of Francis Faulkner, et al., (Mass, Archives Vol. 135 No, 110)." March 2, 1702/3, in Boyer, Paul and Steve Nissenbaum, *The Salem Witchcraft Papers: Verbatim Transcripts of the Legal Documents of the Salem Witchcraft Outbreak of 1692*, Cambridge, MA: Da Capo Press, 1977. Accessed April 22, 2016. http://salem.lib.virginia.edu/texts/tei/swp?div_id=n172#n172.5

Fern, Yvonne. *Gene Roddenberry: The Last Conversation.* Revised and expanded ed. New York: Pocket, 1996.

Fishkin, Shelley Fisher. *Lighting Out for the Territory: Reflections on Mark Twain and American Culture.* Oxford: Oxford University Press, 1996.

Flatley, Guy. "One Man's God, Another Man's Devil." *The New York Times*, April 20, 1969.

Fontana, Dorothy, et al. *Star Trek: The Animated Series* DVD special features. Paramount Home Entertainment, 2006.

Gerrold, David. Email message to author, April 22, 2016.

———. Email message to author, July 29, 2013.

———. "Audio Commentary," "Bem." *Star Trek: The Animated Series* DVD. Paramount Home Entertainment, 2006.

———. "Trials with Tribbles." *Starlog* Magazine # 234, January, 1997, 87.

Gershom, Yonassan. "The Jewish Origin of the Vulcan Salute." *Patheos*, January 1, 2000. Accessed April 22, 2016. http://www.patheos.com/Resources/Additional-Resources/ The-Jewish-Origin-of-the-Vulcan-Salute.

Goldstone, James, dir. "Where No Man Has Gone Before." *Star Trek*, CBS Television, 1966.

Harris, Laura. "Billy Crockett." Crosswalk.com, February 13, 1999. Accessed April 22, 2016. http://www.crosswalk.com/culture/music/billy-crockett-540226.html

Higa, Scott. "#669—The Return of the Archons." *The Christian Nerd*, August 29, 2013. Accessed April 22, 2016. http://www.thechristiannerd.com/2013/08/669-the-return -of-the-archons/.

———. "#1245—Star Wars vs. Star Trek." *The Christian Nerd*, December 11, 2015. Accessed April 22, 2016. http://www.thechristiannerd.com/2015/12/1245-star- wars-vs-star-trek/.

Kaiser, Walter, Jr. *The Christian and the Old Testament*. Pasadena, CA: William Carey Library, 2012.

Kelensa, T'Nara Valdrin. "How Leonard Nimoy Saved My Life." In *Spockology: Essays on Spock and Leonard Nimoy from the Undiscovered Country Project and Friends*, edited by Kevin C. Neece, 101–3. CreateSpace, 2015.

"Kirk n.1, v.1." *Dictionary of the Scots Language*. Scottish Language Dictionaries Ltd., 2004. http://www.dsl.ac.uk/entry/snd/kirk_n1_v1.

"Kirk Name Meaning." Ancestry.com. Accessed April 22, 2016. http://www.ancestry.com/ name-origin?surname=kirk.

"Kirk's Ripped or Removed Shirts," *Ex Astris Scientia*. Accessed August 2, 2016. http:// www.ex-astris-scientia.org/database/kirks_shirt.htm.

Kiselyak, Charles. "The Perils of Peacemaking." *Star Trek VI* Special Collector's Edition DVD, Paramount Home Entertainment, 2004.

Lin, Justin, dir. *Star Trek Beyond*. Paramount Pictures, 2016.

"Lucian." *Encyclopædia Britannica, Encyclopædia Britannica Online*. Encyclopædia Britannica Inc., 2016. Accessed April 22, 2016. http://www.britannica.com/ biography/Lucian.

"Lucien." *Memory Alpha*. Accessed April 22, 2016. http://memory-alpha,wikia.com/wiki/ Lucien.

Maslin, Janet. "New 'Star Trek' Full of Gadgets and Fun." *The New York Times*, June 4, 1982. Accessed April 22, 2016. http://www.nytimes.com/movie/review?res=9C0CE FDB103BF937A35755C0A964948260.

McEveety, Vincent, dir. "Balance of Terror." *Star Trek*, CBS Television, 1966.

McKim, Donald K. *Westminster Dictionary of Theological Terms*. 2nd ed. Louisville, KY: Westminster John Knox, 2014.

Melville, Herman. *Moby-Dick*. Ware, Hertfordshire, UK: Wordsworth Editions, 1999.

Meyer, Nicholas. "Audio Commentary," *Star Trek II: The Wrath of Khan* Director's Cut DVD. Paramount Pictures, 2002.

———. "Audio Commentary," *Star Trek VI: The Undiscovered Country* Special Collector's Edition DVD. Paramount Home Entertainment, 2004.

Meyer, Nicholas, dir. *Star Trek II: The Wrath of Khan*. Paramount Pictures, 1982.

———. *Star Trek VI: The Undiscovered Country*. Paramount Pictures, 1991.

Meyer, Nicolas, et al. "Captain's Log." *Star Trek II: The Wrath of Khan* Director's Edition DVD special features disc, Paramount Home Entertainment, 2002.

———. "Special Features." *Star Trek II: The Wrath of Khan* Director's Cut DVD supplemental disc. Paramount Pictures, 2002.

Mooney, Darren. "Star Trek—The Return of the Archons (Review)." *The movie blog*, May 23, 2013. Accessed April 22, 2016. http://themovieblog.com/2013/05/23/star-trek-return-of-the-archons-review/.

"Star Trek Filming Locations." MovieMaps. Accessed April 22, 2016. https://moviemaps. org/movies/2t;.

Muir, John Kenneth. *A History and Critical Analysis of Blake's 7*. Jefferson, NC: McFarland, 2006.

"Christian Humanism." *New World Encyclopedia*, September 23, 2008. Accessed April 22, 2016. http://www.newworldencyclopedia.org/entry/Christian_Humanism.

Nimoy, Leonard, dir. *Star Trek III: The Search for Spock*. Paramount Pictures, 1984.

———. *Star Trek IV: The Voyage Home*. Paramount Pictures, 1986.

Nimoy, Leonard, and William Shatner. "Audio Commentary," *Star Trek IV: The Voyage Home* Special Collector's Edition DVD. Paramount Home Entertainment, 2003.

Nimoy, Leonard, et al. "Future's Past: A Look Back." *Star Trek IV: The Voyage Home* Special Collector's Edition DVD. Paramount Home Entertainment, 2003.

Noll, Mark. *The Scandal of the Evangelical Mind*. Grand Rapids: Eerdmans, 1995.

Okuda, Michael. "Text Commentary," *Star Trek II: The Wrath of Khan* Director's Edition DVD. Paramount Home Entertainment, 2002.

———. "Text Commentary," *Star Trek III: The Search for Spock* Special Collector's Edition DVD. Paramount Home Entertainment, 2002.

———. "Text Commentary," *Star Trek IV: The Voyage Home* Special Collector's Edition DVD. Paramount Home Entertainment, 2003.

Okuda, Michael, and Denise Okuda. *Star Trek Chronology*. New York: Pocket, 1993.

Orci, Roberto, and Alex Kurtzman. Star Trek, draft dated November 2007, *The Internet Movie Script Database*. Accessed August 3, 2016. http://www.imsdb.com/scripts/Star-Trek.html.

Penn, Leo, dir. "The Enemy Within." *Star Trek*, CBS Television, 1966.

Pevney, Joseph, dir. "The Return of the Archons." *Star Trek*, CBS Television, 1967.

———. "The Apple." *Star Trek*, CBS Television, 1967.

Pierce, Richard, ed. *The Records of the First Church in Salem, Massachusetts, 1629-1736*. Salem: Essex Institute, 1974. Accesses April 22, 2016. http://firstchurchinsalem.org/documents/Original_Record_Book_3-83.pdf

"Positive Atheism's Big List of Quotations, Ro-Ros." Positive Atheism Website. Accessed April 22, 2016. http://www.positiveatheism.org/hist/quotes/quote-r1.htm.

Reed, Bill, dir. "Bem." *Star Trek: The Animated Series*. Filmation/Paramount Television, 1974.

———. "How Sharper Than a Serpent's Tooth." *Star Trek: The Animated Series*. Filmation/Paramount Television, 1974.

———. "The Practical Joker." *Star Trek: The Animated Series*. Filmation/Paramount Television, 1974.

Reiter, Geoffrey. "Star Trek Beyond Explores the Cosmography of Relationship." *Christ and Pop Culture*, July 29, 2016. Accessed August 2, 2016. http://christandpopculture.com/star-trek-beyond-explores-cosmography-relationship/.

"Religion in Star Trek." Ex Astris Scientia. Accessed April 22, 2016. http://www.ex-astris-scientia.org/inconsistencies/religion.htm.

Roddenberry, Gene. "Star Trek Creator Recalls 'My Favorite Voyages.'" *TV Guide*, August 31, 1991, 12.

Rogers, Carl. *On Becoming a Person: A Therapist's View of Psychotherapy*. 2nd ed. New York: Mariner, 1995.

Rowe, William L. "Atheism." In *The Shorter Routledge Encyclopedia of Philosophy*, edited by Edward Craig, 73. 2nd ed. Florence, KY: Routledge/Taylor & Francis, 2005.

Senensky, Ralph, dir. "Bread and Circuses." *Star Trek*, CBS Television, 1968.

———. "This Side of Paradise." *Star Trek*, CBS Television, 1967.

Shatner, William, dir. *Star Trek V: The Final Frontier*. Paramount Pictures, 1989.

Snyder, Tom. "Interview with Gene Roddenberry." *The Wednesday Radio Show*, January 18, 1989.

Spafford, Horatio G. "It Is Well With My Soul." Public domain, 1873.

"Spock Name Meaning." Ancestry.com. Accessed April 22, 2016. http://www.ancestry.com/name-origin?surname=spock.

Sutherland, Hal, dir. "The Eye of the Beholder." *Star Trek: The Animated Series*. Filmation/Paramount Television, 1974.

———. "The Magicks of Megas-Tu." *Star Trek: The Animated Series*. Filmation/Paramount Television, 1973.

Sweeney, Terrance. *God &*. Philadelphia: John C. Winston Company, 1985.

Taylor, Jud, dir. "Let That Be Your Last Battlefield." *Star Trek*, CBS Television, 1969.

Tescar, Kail. "The TAS David Gerrold Interview." StarTrekAnimated.com. Accessed April 22, 2016. http://www.startrekanimated.com/tas_david_gerrold.html.

U2. "Grace." *All That You Can't Leave Behind*, Interscope, 2000.

Vaidman, Lev. "Many Worlds Interpretation of Quantum Mechanics." *Stanford Encyclopedia of Philosophy*, Stanford University, 2014. Accessed April 22, 2016. http://plato.stanford.edu/entries/qm-manyworlds/.

Van Gent, R.H. "Distribution of Easter Sundays in the Gregorian Calendar." in "Frequency of Easter Sundays," Science Staff Website of Utrecht University. Accessed April 22, 2016. https://www.staff.science.uu.nl/~gent0113/easter/eastercalculator.htm.

Van Hise, James. *The Man Who Created Star Trek: Gene Roddenberry*. Pioneer, 1992.

Wise, David. "Audio Commentary," "How Sharper Than a Serpent's Tooth." *Star Trek: The Animated Series* DVD. Paramount Home Entertainment, 2006.

Wise, Robert, dir. *Star Trek: The Motion Picture*. Paramount Pictures, 1979.

Witherington, Ben. *Paul's Letter to the Romans: A Socio-Rhetorical Commentary*. Grand Rapids: Eerdmans, 2004.

Yiddish Book Center. "Live Long and Prosper: The Jewish Story Behind Spock, Leonard Nimoy's Star Trek Character." Wexler Oral History Project, February 6, 2014. Accessed April 22, 2016. https://www.youtube.com/watch?v=DyiWkWcR86I.

CPSIA information can be obtained
at www.ICGtesting.com
Printed in the USA
LVHW090441180519
618322LV00001BA/5/P